Praise for

CREATING A SEAT AT THE TABLE

"Brilliant. Brutally honest. Illuminating. Inspiring. A must-read for women at any stage of their legal career and for those who support them." —DELEE FROMM, author of *Advance Your Legal Career*

"This book weaves together humour, hard-wrought wisdom, and vulnerability with political insights from inside the practice of law. The authors range in years of experience and come from different starting places, including being Indigenous or LBGTQIA2S+, and all are courageous and generous in these revealing chapters: 'I am struck by my own lack of agency.' The imposter syndrome featured in many stories (but never forget that you are enough!) along with frustration at the deeply entrenched barriers, backlashes, racism, and sexist humour. There are powerful experiences of learning to recognize empathy as strength, of becoming visible, overcoming lateral violence, balancing family demands and loss, the gift of mentoring, and finally recognizing: 'You have everything to be a powerful advocate.' And of course, the practice of law itself has many hard edges—domestic violence, poverty, sexual harassment, and sexual crimes are often part of the work along with always having to be an advocate in one's own life. Read this book. It is an important view into the practice of law at every level, for every student, in every court, and in every place." —DR. VAL NAPOLEON, Cree legal scholar, Professor, and Law Foundation Chair of Indigenous Justice and Governance

"Read this book to know you're not alone. I believe this book shows that even if we feel 'imposter syndrome,' we've actually been part of the 'infiltrator syndrome.' Each woman in law school and the legal system has changed it—shaping it into a more equitable state. No snowflake in an avalanche feels how they've contributed, but these 18 different stories and lives are also 18 similar ones showing that we're all connected and contributing to an avalanche of inclusion, equity, and diversity, which will make the world a better place for all." —JAIME LAVALLEE, Assistant Professor, University of Saskatchewan College of Law

"This collection of intimately candid and vulnerable narratives by diverse women in the legal profession exemplifies the art of storytelling at its best, evoking a comforting sense of warmth akin to sitting around a cozy fire. It serves as a profound testament to our interconnectedness and beautifully portrays the timeless potential for personal growth and fulfillment that comes from embracing our true selves." —ANGELA OGANG, on behalf of the CBA Woman Lawyers Forum

"In this book are the warm words of friends and mentors—as if we were sitting together over a cup of coffee, sharing the real stories of our own lives, affirming each other's experiences, releasing it all. I had to keep reading until the conversation was finished (at least for now). What an inspiring book." —MICHAELA KEET, Professor, University of Saskatchewan College of Law

"*Creating a Seat at the Table* creates community through storytelling. A helpful text for new lawyers, law students, and senior lawyers alike, this book is part career masterclass and part intimate window into women's lives. Highly readable, the contributors model vulnerability, honesty, and nuance in narratives where practical career advice co-exists alongside personal tragedy, all told through feminist lenses that invite the personal into the professional.

This book reflects both the ugliness and beauty in a profession not always welcoming to women, especially LBGTQIA2S+, Indigenous, disabled, and racialized lawyers. In these pages, women will recognize themselves and engage with the experiences of other differently situated women. Ultimately a hopeful book, the authors indeed invite us into a narrative about how 'the power of individual and collective reflection [can] lead to action and change.'" —GEMMA SMYTH, Associate Professor at the Faculty of Law, University of Windsor

"Having taught and talked to many women in law, I found myself jotting down quotes on scrap paper, feeling my eyes well up at times, and wanting to photocopy entire letters to share with future students. These are stories of tenacity, failure, and resilience, of disappointment, disillusionment, and inspiration. They are also a chorus of resonant experiences of gender-based discrimination in a profession that is supposed to be the pathway through. The hope that transpires through these stories and reflections is not luminous and unburdened, it is gritty, honest, and unvarnished. A testament to those who have persisted against all odds, even more so it is a testament to all women who have charted new and needed legal paths, ultimately fashioning their own relationships with the law." —RACHEL LOEWEN WALKER, Assistant Professor in Political Studies, University of Saskatchewan

"A beautifully written reminder to take up space, ask for help, and honour yourself." —HANNAH JORGENSON, JD Candidate 2024, University of Saskatchewan College of Law

"The stories of experienced women lawyers provide an enlightening perspective that can save others from the school of hard knocks." —**BETTY-ANN HEGGIE**, a member of Canada's Top 100 Most Powerful Women Hall of Fame

"An inspiring collection of stories from remarkable women! Their candid reflections about their struggles and triumphs moved me deeply. I feel appreciative of how the power of presence and place created the space to reflect collectively, and how reflective writing became a catalyst for unearthing such heartfelt insights." —**MICHELE LEERING**, CM, lawyer, and Executive Director of the Community Advocacy and Legal Centre

CREATING
a SEAT *at*
the TABLE

Reflections from Women in Law

Edited by

BETH BILSON, LEAH HOWIE,
and BREA LOWENBERGER

University of Regina Press

Printed and bound in Canada at Imprimerie Gauvin. The text of this book is printed on 100% post-consumer recycled paper with earth-friendly vegetable-based inks.

Cover art: "Three women standing side by side" by Monica Jurczyk / Adobe Stock
Cover design: Duncan Campbell, University of Regina Press
Interior layout design: John van der Woude, JVDW Designs
Copyeditor: Kathryn Nogue
Proofreader: Rachel Taylor

Library and Archives Canada Cataloguing in Publication

Title: Creating a seat at the table : reflections from women in law / edited by Beth Bilson, Leah Howie, and Brea Lowenberger.
Names: Bilson, Beth, editor. | Howie, Leah, editor. | Lowenberger, Brea, editor.
Identifiers: Canadiana (print) 20230484913 | Canadiana (ebook) 2023048509X | ISBN 9780889779419 (softcover) | ISBN 9780889779440 (hardcover) | ISBN 9780889779426 (PDF) | ISBN 9780889779433 (EPUB)
Subjects: LCSH: Lawyers—Canada—Biography. | LCSH: Women lawyers—Canada—Biography.
Classification: LCC KE395.C74 2023 | LCC KF345.Z9 A1 C74 2023 kfmod | DDC 349.71092/2—dc23

10 9 8 7 6 5 4 3 2 1

University of Regina Press, University of Regina
Regina, Saskatchewan, Canada, S4S 0A2
TEL: (306) 585-4758 FAX: (306) 585-4699
U OF R PRESS   WEB: www.uofrpress.ca

We acknowledge the support of the Canada Council for the Arts for our publishing program. We acknowledge the financial support of the Government of Canada. / Nous reconnaissons l'appui financier du gouvernement du Canada. This publication was made possible with support from Creative Saskatchewan's Book Publishing Production Grant Program.

Dedicated to those who have mentored us,
those we have mentored, and the
women and girls who inspire us.

—Beth, Leah, and Brea

CONTENTS

CONTENTS

Stories...are a way that we can talk to each other without having barriers between us.

—MARIA CAMPBELL

FOREWORD

What is it like to be a woman in law? That is the question at the heart of this book, a collection of candid letters written by women who have walked the walk and talked the talk of a profession in the law.

And the answer is? The answer is that there is no answer. No single answer, at any rate. Each person who takes on the mantle of the law wears it in a different way. And each woman, depending on her personality and the particular challenges she faces, will experience the world she is entering in different ways.

Yet commonalities emerge.

Every woman who practices law will experience discrimination. It may be overt, although that is increasingly rare. It is more likely to be what sociologists call unconscious bias, born of unexamined assumptions about the way the legal profession and the world work.

Every woman who practices law will encounter fear of failure. From her first days in law school, a woman knows she is entering a man's world. She knows the legal world was set up by men, for men in the last century, and that while much has changed, its fundamental tenets remain. As she casts her eye about her on her first day of class, she knows that she has a greater chance of dropping out or earning less than the man beside her. She knows she will need to be better, smarter, and luckier to succeed.

Every woman who practices law has bad days. Sometimes really bad days. Days when she loses, when she feels she has let her client down. Days when a passing comment cuts her to the quick. Days when criticism—maybe from another woman—temporarily floors her.

Every woman who practices law and has children will simultaneously feel constrained and guilty. Constrained because she's having to leave meetings early or set aside her work before she's done. Guilty because there is never enough one-on-one time with her family. She will learn that the dream of being a perfect lawyer and a perfect mother is a chimera; she will never be perfect at either task, but she will muddle through and be all right. Just like the men, who worry about perfection a lot less than women.

Finally, to judge by these letters, a lot of women practicing law will, at some point in their careers, ask themselves the big question: Was I right to choose the law?

For most of these women, the answer to that question emerges as a resounding yes. The positive experiences associated with the practice of law more than offset the pain of discrimination, the loneliness of imposter syndrome, the fear of failure, and the existential stress of being a mother with a career in law.

The writers recount the intellectual joy of working with legal ideas; the opportunities that a career in law presents to help others and make the world a better place; and, over and over again, how the law has allowed them to get to know themselves better, to develop self-confidence and resilience, to meet interesting people, to travel—in a word, to find themselves. The law, one contributor writes, provides the tools with which to navigate the world.

Other themes come through. One is the importance of mentors, male and female, in the woman lawyer's life—people who look past gender and see ability and push the woman to new heights. Or the absence of mentors—people, sometimes other women, who criticize and tear down a young lawyer rather than building her up.

The courage and resilience that shines through these letters is perhaps best captured in the pithy words of "advice to self" the writers have formulated as they navigate the rough but exhilarating waters of a career in the law and now share on these pages:

"See something? Say something."

"Don't like it? Do something about it."

"Life isn't about waiting for the storm to pass; it's about learning to dance in the rain."

"Get job. Do job. Keep job."

And my favourite piece of advice:

"Learn to love yourself."

Cry with these writers; rejoice with these writers. Above all, enjoy.

—THE RIGHT HONOURABLE BEVERLEY McLACHLIN
The first female and longest-serving
Chief Justice of the Supreme Court of Canada

INTRODUCTION

When Clara Brett Martin decided in the late nineteenth century that she wished to become a lawyer, this aspiration was considered unusual enough that it required a statutory amendment by the Ontario legislature to allow her access to legal education and admission to the bar. In 1897, she became the first woman admitted to the bar in Canada, and her example was followed over the next decades by women in other provinces. The number of women in law schools and in the legal profession remained small, however. It was not until the 1970s that women began to make up a significant proportion of law students.

Since the 1980s, the numbers of male and female law students in Canadian law schools have been more or less equal.[1] As one might expect, this shift eventually affected the composition of the legal profession as well. According to statistics published by the non-profit organization Catalyst, based on 2018 data,

---

[1]   It is only in the last few years that there has been any consideration of gender identity in examining law school demographics, and there is little current information about how this might affect future discussion of this issue. We understand that gender identity is a spectrum, and that terms and pronouns used throughout the book may not resonate with everyone.

women lawyers made up 39 percent of the legal profession in Saskatchewan; women who had been called to the bar for under five years constituted 47.7 percent of the group with comparable experience.[2]

The expanded representation of women in the legal profession has certainly been a gain for young women who aspire to be lawyers. The presence of women in law classrooms, law firms, and courtrooms is no longer considered freakish or outrageous, and a great number of women have been able to pursue legal careers they find satisfying. On the other hand, studies of women in the legal profession have identified a number of barriers to full professional equality, and these barriers are even more evident for women of colour, Indigenous women, LGBTQIA2S+ women, and women with disabilities.

From the time of the first comprehensive study of the status of women in the Canadian legal profession,[3] conducted by a task force under the direction of the first woman justice of the Supreme Court of Canada, Madam Justice Bertha Wilson, through studies of the legal profession in the province of Saskatchewan,[4] and a

---

2   Catalyst, "Women in Law: Quick Take" (February 2023), online: *Catalyst: Workplaces that Work for Women* <https://www.catalyst.org/research/women-in-law>.

3   Task Force on Gender Equality in the Legal Profession, "Touchstones for Change: Equality, Diversity and Accountability" (Ottawa: Canadian Bar Association, 1993).

4   Susan Robertson, *A Study of Gender and the Legal Profession: A Report to the Law Society of Saskatchewan 1990-1991*, (Saskatoon, SK: The Canadian Bar Association Saskatchewan Branch, and the College of Law, University of Saskatchewan, 1992); Beth Bilson, Susan Robertson & Elizabeth Quinlan, *Women and the Legal Profession in Saskatchewan: National and Historical Comparisons: A Report to the Law Society of Saskatchewan, Canadian Bar Association, Saskatchewan Branch and The Law Foundation of Saskatchewan* (University of Saskatchewan, October 2013), available upon request from the Law Society of Saskatchewan Library; Zoe Johansen-Hill, Larissa Meredith-Flister & Coleman Owen, "Diversity and...

recent report from the International Association of Women Judges Canadian Chapter commissioned by the Canadian Bar Association Alberta Branch[5], among others, researchers examining how women experience their lives in the law have found that they face a list of challenges that is now becoming all too familiar. Indeed, studies done in other countries have found many of the same things.[6]

A number of common themes emerge from these examinations of the experience of women in their legal careers. Though women are represented in the legal profession in ever larger numbers, they still find themselves facing limitations on their opportunities and choices. In Ontario, for example, though women make up 43.5 percent of licensed lawyers, only 26.5 percent of the partners in law firms are women.[7] Surveys of women lawyers on which the reports cited earlier are based find that women state that they are still subject to stereotyping assumptions about the kind of work they

---

...Inclusion in the Legal Profession" (delivered at The Seventh Annual Dean's Forum on Access to Justice and Dispute Resolution, College of Law, University of Saskatchewan, 13 March 2019) [unpublished]; Zoe Johansen-Hill, Larissa Meredith-Flister & Coleman Owen, "Follow-Up Report & Summary Notes: Diversity and Inclusion in the Legal Profession" (delivered at The Seventh Annual Dean's Forum on Access to Justice and Dispute Resolution, College of Law, University of Saskatchewan, 13 March 2019) [unpublished]; "Saskatchewan Justicia Project" (13 March 2023), online: *Law Society of Saskatchewan* <https://www.lawsociety.sk.ca/initiatives/saskatchewan-justicia-project>.

5   Katrina Edgerton-McGhan et al, "Engagement of Women in the Legal Profession: Strategies for Retention" (International Association of Women Judges, Canadian Chapter, delivered at the Canadian Bar Association Alberta Branch, Calgary, 2021) [unpublished].

6   Law Society of England and Wales, "Advocating for Change: Transforming the Future of the Legal Profession Through Greater Equality" (London: Law Society of England and Wales, 2019). We are not including citations here to the extensive body of research that now exists concerning women in the legal profession; the studies we have listed will lead you to other references if you are interested.

7   Catalyst, *supra*.

would prefer to do or are competent to do; they may be directed to areas like family law or wills and estates law, rather than being assigned to prestige projects in commercial law or high-profile litigation. This makes it more difficult for them to establish the kind of reputation that will attract major clients, and has clear ramifications for their incomes and their chances for advancement within their firms or organizations.

Respondents to these surveys also talk about the "boys' club" culture in law firms and other legal organizations, a culture in which the opportunities for cementing relationships with clients are focused on "male" activities—playing golf, attending hockey or football games, drinking in bars, or even visiting strip clubs—that may still be less appealing to women or considered less appropriate for them.

There are still apparently concerns about the preferences, competence, or commitment of women lawyers centred around the assumption that they will decide to have intimate partners and children, and that this will distract them from their legal careers and make them unreliable contributors to the advancement of the goals of their legal employers.

Many women lawyers, of course, decide not to have children, perhaps because they feel forced to choose between having children and their career, or because they have other priorities. Those women who do have children, however, point to a number of difficulties they experience in finding satisfactory ways of balancing their family obligations against the demands of their legal careers, particularly in private practice. They point to the tyranny of the billable hour as the prevailing way to monitor the work done by lawyers. They observe that, notwithstanding changes in technology which allow some kinds of work to be done at a distance from the office, there is an expectation of physical presence to the extent that it may seem like a competition which distinguishes between those who are committed to their work and those who are not on the basis of how many hours they remain in the office. They describe a culture in many legal settings where women are criticized if they take time to be present at sports competitions, performances, or other important events in their children's lives, while men are seen as admirable fathers for doing the same thing; where men can justify recreational activities as opportunities for client development while women are seen as neglecting their responsibilities at work; and where men who have families are characterized as stable and dedicated, while women who have families are viewed as fulfilling expectations of their lack of commitment. In the reports we have mentioned, the top priority cited by women when asked what would improve their legal lives is greater flexibility in schedules and working arrangements so that they could better align their working and family lives.

One of the consequences of the barriers women face in legal careers is that they depart from the legal profession. People change their career paths for many reasons, but the departure of women lawyers, particularly from private practice, is disproportionate when compared to the exit of men, and the reasons they give for leaving often have to do with the gender discrimination they face and their difficulties in juggling their personal and professional lives.

In 2019, we decided to invite a group of women graduates of the College of Law at the University of Saskatchewan to share with us their reflections on their own careers as women in the legal profession—eighteen women accepted our invitation. We tried to include women from different generations, and from different kinds of legal careers—big law firms, small law firms, legal aid, government and politics, the judiciary, in-house positions, and administrative agencies. We also tried to include women who have dealt with the compound effects of discrimination based on race, sexual orientation or disability, and gender.

Primarily, however, we tried to invite women we anticipated would engage with our project, who would tell their stories fully and honestly. We invited them to write a letter to a younger self describing the unfolding of their careers, or, in the case of recent graduates, to try to predict what course their lives might take. Though some of them deviated from this specific assignment, we think you will find that they more than met our overall goal of having them examine their own experiences with law and the legal profession.

In June of 2022, after a number of COVID-related delays, we were able to bring these generous and accomplished women together in Saskatoon for a day of rich discussion of the interface between women lawyers and their profession. We were assisted by the wonderful Maria Campbell, who reminded us of the power of stories and storytelling. Following this workshop, the authors were given an opportunity to add any final thoughts to their contributions.

In many ways, the pieces in this collection mirror the themes identified in the research and studies we have alluded to earlier.

You will find that some of our authors entered the profession at a time when women were still rarities, and the appropriateness of their very presence in a law firm or a court was in question. Authors who came along when there were larger numbers of women lawyers still faced questions about their commitment to their careers and had to struggle to be taken seriously when it came to being assigned to pieces of work involving important clients or high-stakes litigation. Some of them speak of being mistaken for court personnel or administrative support staff and of dealing with clients who resisted being represented by women. They talk about being excluded from informal or social activities that might work to reinforce relationships with current or potential clients, and of the awkwardness for younger women lawyers of meeting male clients in traditional social gathering places like bars or clubs.

In a number of cases, the authors talk about feeling let down by other women lawyers or judges, from whom they had expected they would receive support. They observe that some women in the profession seem to feel that they need to follow a "male" model in order to be successful, and that this may lead them to adopt discriminatory practices and assumptions with respect to other women.

A number of the authors talk about the difficulties of balancing a demanding and time-consuming set of professional obligations and a personal life. Those who have had children talk about their efforts to find practical strategies for meeting their childcare responsibilities, and their sense of frustration or even guilt when the different facets of their lives do not line up smoothly. They also address the implications of the tensions in balancing work and personal life for their career aspirations, their incomes, and their relationships with their legal employers.

Some of these authors describe dark experiences, in law school or once they started their careers, with sexual harassment and even sexual assault, as well as with overt racism, ableism, or homophobia. The consequences of gender discrimination for women's income, their access to satisfying work, or the acceptance of their decision to have children seem serious enough, but these stories remind us that discrimination can cause even greater personal damage when it takes the form of direct attacks on one's identity.

Despite their descriptions of reversals and frustrations, of disappointments and even traumas, many of these authors also paint a somewhat more positive picture. A number of them speak with gratitude of significant mentors, many of them men, who supported them, advised them, or promoted them through their professional lives. They also allude to the importance of their personal support networks—friends, family members, partners, children—in reinforcing their decision to enter and pursue legal careers.

They speak of seizing interesting opportunities and provide fascinating accounts of where these new paths have taken them—to unusual administrative or advocacy work, to work or teaching in national or international organizations, or to partnerships with people in other parts of the country or the world. Though in some instances a well-developed case of "imposter syndrome" leads them to express some surprise that they were offered these opportunities, it is clear from their stories that they were well equipped to make significant contributions when they were invited to follow unexpected directions and to take up projects they had never foreseen.

Above all, these authors remain convinced of the importance of the law as a social institution and as a means of upholding the rights and interests of their fellow citizens. They are certainly aware that the legal system is flawed, that it operates to advantage some people more than others, and that many forms of legal practice can be a demanding and exhausting business. They do seem largely hopeful, however, that the law can serve positive social ends, and that it can be channelled in ways that would be more effective at serving the needs of their clients and the public at large. Whether they have chosen to work in the private or public sector, as politicians and judges or in administrative agencies, they can point to aspects of their careers that have been sources of satisfaction, and—though women are often reluctant to put it this way—of pride.

—Beth, Leah, and Brea

IT'S NEVER TOO LATE *to* BE WHO YOU MIGHT HAVE BEEN

ADRIENNE FORGERON
2007 JD

Dearest Adrienne (my younger self),

Here you are, on the precipice of deciding whether you should go into law school. With a couple years of undergrad under your belt, and at the tender age of twenty, you've decided to write the LSAT, submit your application, and see what happens.

We both know you know you're going to get in.

Of course you are! You are talented, and smart, and have the ambition of sixteen grown men thrown into one young and dedicated body.

But you wonder. Is the practice of law the right path for you? Do you have what it takes? What if you get it *all wrong*?

Luckily, as the older version of you, I know the answers to those questions. I'm you at thirty-six! I'm older and perhaps even a bit wiser!

Here's the deal. Law is both the right and wrong path for you. Law will make you crumble, but will not defeat you. And you will get it entirely wrong, while at the very same time getting it exactly right.

Confusing, isn't it?

It sure is, my dear.

But luckily for you (and me!), there's a truth you already know, deep down, and it will carry you through this chosen journey:

Listen to yourself, and you will never go astray. And when you forget to listen to yourself, you will eventually come back to yourself, stronger and more capable (of service and happiness) because of it.

As you stand on the verge of accepting your admissions offer, with a healthy dose of excitement and an equally healthy dose of fear, I can assure you that you will *always* figure it out.

You, my dear, were built for this.

Why this letter, and why now? I write you to point out some of the key lessons you're going to learn in your career as a lawyer, and to guide you when you feel full of doubt. Most of the following lessons might seem harsh and even unfair, but as we know, one little clue now can provide a lot of ah-ha moments down the road at *exactly the right time.*

Buckle up, my dear, and most importantly—enjoy the ride! I'm here every single step of the way.

With all of my love and unwavering support,

Adrienne

THE TIME YOU WILL FEEL VERY DUMB

You are currently used to being the top of the class. School, grades, and academic achievement—that's nothing. More, more, more—more learning, more knowledge, *more being the best*. The thrill of leading the pack! It's intoxicating, and one of the exact reasons you chose law.

But here's the deal. *Everyone in law school is smart.* For real! All the classmates you will meet are also used to being at the top of *their* class. You will now be surrounded by achievers, and competitors, and people just like you who always know what's going on.

This will be your first taste of not being the smartest kid in the class, and it will unsettle you. You will feel inadequate and very dumb.

It's going to be uncomfortable.

In the middle of your first year of law school, you are going to start to believe that you actually weren't that smart all along. As you get a C+ on your criminal law exam, you will feel a flush of heat rise up your body. You will feel ashamed.

It won't be until much later on that you realize that the belief that you aren't actually smart is an untrue story, and that your performance on an exam isn't an indication of your worth as a student, as a lawyer, or as a woman.

Luckily for you, on that day over ten years later and not a minute too late, you *will* realize you aren't dumb. In fact, you will realize that you actually usually *do* know what's going on. You will eventually learn to pay better attention to this knowing, and to always come back to this knowing. You will learn that you *always* knew.

But for now, look at your fellow classmates not with envy or competitiveness, but with recognition that the majority of them feel exactly the way you do.

Inadequate…and dumb.

THE TIME YOU FIND YOUR PASSION...
AND IT'S NOT LAW

Deciding that you aren't the pure academic type after all, you will turn your attention in law school not to burdening yourself with hours of reading, but to getting to know the *people*. You will learn the names of all your classmates, your profs, and the College of Law staff. You will breathe a sigh of relief, because even though all these classmates are just like you in their top-of-the-class ways, they are also just like you in their we-dig-the-same-nerdy-things kinds of ways.

To your greatest surprise, in the College of Law, you will finally find *your people*.

People here are smart, and funny, and generally in pursuit of something greater than themselves.

Growing up in a small town, where many of your friends would not pursue or consider the levels of professional achievement you were after, you were always a bit of an outlier. Wanting more— more than a good job and a family as soon as you secured said job—you always felt a bit *odd*.

But here, in law, you will find your people!

And in the finding of these aligned kin, you will beautifully find that you can *be yourself*.

As a result, you will take out your camera. You have always loved photography, but when you decided to become a lawyer, you put away your camera and got *serious*. Here among your people, where you can be *yourself*, you will take your little digital camera everywhere, and take pictures of all of your new friends. You will get so excited about these photos that you will start posting them on a PAWS group (which, you will soon find out, is a precursor to the social media options that will overwhelm the Internet in years to come!).

You will create captions for your photos, and you will become known as the law student who takes people's photos and then posts them. People will seem to like them, because they feel seen.

Then, somewhere along the way, your classmates will start asking when you're going to run for law students' association president. You're the natural choice, they will say—the way you connect people, and capture the fun, and bring all of us together.

You will become class president, and this is when you will first identify and realize one of your life's bigger themes at play: storytelling and capturing people's common humanity creates connectedness, trust, and leadership.

You will be surprised that you discovered this in law school. You expected law school to be about...the law. You didn't expect to learn other life lessons here.

But for now, enjoy the photo taking and the connections you are making. You will quite certainly practice traditional law, but the skills you are building now will serve you equally as well as any understanding of jurisprudence ever could.

THE TIME YOU BECOME A REAL-LIFE LAWYER

You will eventually graduate from law school, with very average grades and above-average social connections. Articling with a solid firm in Saskatoon, you will be, of course, the keenest of keen. Your ambition will never waver. Over time, it will change, and in ways that surprise you, but you were born to push ahead.

Here, in articling and in the next few years of practice, you will push.

However, pushing won't be easy. I'm sorry to tell you this next bit, but we ought to just cut to the chase: articling will be *brutal*.

You will be twenty-three years old when you start your articles, but you will feel thirty-six by the time you are done. As a farm kid who was blessed with a wholesome upbringing, you will be caught off guard by the real-life practice of law and its players. Grizzled partners, ruthless clients, time constraints, billing demands, foreign terminology, and astronomically high expectations of excellence (placed on you by you) mean you will come home to cry on more than a couple of days over the course of your articling year.

It will be during this time that you and one of your fellow young law school friends will moan and agree, "They shouldn't let anyone into law school until they are at least twenty-five years old. *We're so young and don't know anything about anything!*"

However, the kicker is this. It won't be the lack of maturity that's fundamentally unsettling; it will be the alignment, or lack thereof.

In the first few years of your practice, it will become increasingly apparent to you that "the practice of law" is a beast that cannot easily be commanded. Indeed, the practice of law you will be experiencing is so much more than applying rules and providing a well-crafted answer in exchange for reasonable pay. The practice of law is entirely gray and influenced by so many more variables than legislation or case law.

The practice of law is not the neat and tidy profession you were expecting.

The practice of law is a rollercoaster of emotion, changing minds, and unanticipated and uncontrollable factors that have little to do with legislation passed by a legislature or decisions issued by a judiciary.

The practice of law requires you to be savvy, and smart, of course, but the way you are practicing also requires you to be blunt, unkind, and often ruthless.

Oh dear.

At this stage, you are already going to feel the quiet undercurrent within you that whispers, "I don't know about this."

Over time, and with every new position you take as an associate or junior counsel hoping to find "the right fit," it will become increasingly evident that something is not quite lining up.

You will start to think, "I did something wrong." You will ask your family and friends, "Should I be a lawyer?" They will look at you and respond, "I *think* so."

But nobody—you *or* they—will really know the answer to that question.

For now, trust that at the right time, and in the right way, clarity will come.

THE TIME YOU STOP PRETENDING AND QUIT THE PRACTICE OF LAW

By the time you are thirty years old, you will have quit the practice of law. I kid you not. I realize this is probably very upsetting to you, because although you had heard of the trend of women lawyers leaving practice, you never thought you were going to be one of those women.

You will be one of those women.

But let me be clear. It takes a lot of courage to leave something that isn't working.

Leaving the practice of law isn't necessarily a sign of weakness; in fact, leaving the practice of law is the strongest thing you will have done to date.

Six years into it, having contorted yourself into multiple possible avenues of practice, yet never having found a good fit (or even a fit that "wouldn't be so bad"), you will toss in the towel.

It won't hurt that every other area of your life is also falling apart.

At this age, you will have checked off every item on the Success To-Do List. To your surprise and bitter anguish, you won't be happy. You will be miserable.

You will be miserable.

The day you hand in your resignation as an in-house lawyer for that big mining company, one of the senior lawyers will look at you, scoff, and say, "Being a lawyer, and having this job, is not *supposed* to be fun."

You will look at him, and even though you are deeply terrified of the head-first cliff dive you are about to take into the unknown, you will know, deep down, that he is entirely full of shit.

Full. Of. Shit.

You will think (but unfortunately not yet say), "Yes, maybe that is *your* story, buddy, but it sure as hell is not mine."

Even in the darkest moments, when your dreams did not come true, and practicing law crushed your soul, you *knew*. You *knew* there had to be more.

So you will quit your dream job, you will break up with your long-time boyfriend, and you will bid your joint-custody dog adieu.

You will look at your life as you know it, including all of the protective identities that you had carefully crafted over the previous ten years, and you will blow it up.

You will buy the dynamite, light the fuse, and run.

You will blow your life to smithereens.

I have no advice to give during this stage other than "Atta girl."

Atta girl.

THE TIME YOU LOOK WITHIN

After blowing up your life, you will feel both deeply lost and incredibly free.

You will pack your belongings and head to the cabin at Greenwater Lake to grieve, and breathe, and be entirely with yourself.

You will have no job, no partner, and no idea what you're going to do next.

"What went wrong?" you will ask yourself, the walls of the cabin, the silence, the universe.

But being the resilient woman you are, you will ask yourself that question for a mere two days. Then you will start to say this: "I have no idea what just happened, and I have no idea where I'm going next, but I know for sure this is what I had to do."

In the darkness of the cabin, you will realize that at some point a very long time ago, you decided you would settle.

You will now have the capacity to look into the mirror and acknowledge that in the practice of law and in the practice of life, you had settled.

You will realize it wasn't a conscious decision—the settling—but really a deeply rooted belief that somehow, someway, you didn't really deserve more.

You had bought into the lie that there was only one way to practice law.

You had believed that you had to practice law in a more masculine way—unemotional, savvy, and financially focused.

You didn't know any other way, and you never thought you could ask for more.

But here, in the dark, as you start to go inward and uncover what really happened, you will see so much more.

You will see that underneath it all is a woman who is kind, brilliant, and here to do work that is meaningful and true.

You're going to reactively wonder, "But what *is* the meaningful and true work??" You're going to want an answer to this question immediately, to ease your fear of the unknown.

But for now, know this.
There is nothing you need to do but breathe.
Let the fear and the failure and the grief wash over you.
It needs to be seen, and it needs to be *felt*.

THE TIME YOU DO EVERYTHING
BUT THE PRACTICE OF LAW

With shaky legs and a shaky heart, you will prop yourself up. No longer a lawyer, and with a bit of money to last you a little while, you will hope to find yourself.

Who are you, really?

You will *adventure*. You will travel solo to incredibly eye-opening places like Cambodia, Vietnam, Indonesia, Japan, Australia, Nicaragua, and Laos. Over the course of a few years, you will entirely *travel*. At first, you will be by yourself, but then, because you like to connect with people, you will soon make friends all over the world. You will visit those new friends. You will fill your passport, and you will fill your heart.

In the travelling, you will start to find yourself.

You will discover that you *crave* adventure. You *need* new experiences. You *have* to explore.

You will start to remember—and discover—who you really are.

When you come home, you will decide *not* to go back into the practice of law, although you know that it would be the financially prudent choice. You will recognize that if there were ever a time to take a leap into a different career, the time is now!

You will become a project manager for a video company, and you will learn how to shoot films, and light sets, and record in slow motion. You will then create your own photography and video company, and you will learn how to interview people, how to edit film and photo, and how to run a business.

You will also continue to do the deep work on yourself and focus on consciousness-based healing work. You will learn to pay attention, and you will remember that you (and everyone else!) can always see what's really going on, if they are willing to see the truth. You will become a practitioner who helps people remember who *they* really are.

You will become a teacher of a business law course. Initially, you will do it to bring in a bit more income, but you will soon realize how much you love to *teach*. Engaging with students, and encouraging their questions, and explaining *what really matters* when it comes to drafting a contract will be the most fruitful work you didn't expect to happen.

Over the course of five years, you will do everything that you've ever wanted to try.

You will gain a sense of self beyond what you ever knew possible.

You will learn to love yourself more deeply, with every passing day.

You will not settle.

And you will do it all by yourself.

Threaded throughout this journey will come an ancillary and strange path, which you will find at first uncomfortable, then somewhat reassuring.

You will become an active, practicing lawyer again, in the form of a part-time sole practitioner. You will do this because your family and friends will come to you for legal advice even when you are adamant that you are "no longer a lawyer." You will do this because *you know the answers* to their questions, and because you realize you actually did know how to practice law. You will do this because a part of you realizes that you still *like the law*.

You will be forced to admit to yourself that maybe, just maybe, being a lawyer isn't so bad after all. You will start to miss the spark you feel when you see a light of understanding come across a client's face after you have broken something complex down into something simple. You will find yourself researching areas of law *for fun*.

You will eventually realize that all the work you will do when you are not practicing law is actually a form of law itself.

Natural law.

Indeed, the greatest awareness you will gain during this time of not practicing law is that everything—*everything*—is deeply and intrinsically connected. And regardless of the existence of an English common law system, there are always much bigger and much more mysterious *natural laws* at work (and even at play!).

"Well, hot damn," you will say, "I couldn't get away from the law *if I tried.*"

You will have no idea how all of these skills and experiences are going to come together, but for now, know this.

Every step, every detour, every single exploration is an unfolding. You are constantly becoming yourself.

THE TIME YOU RESURFACE AND CHOOSE BOTH

After five years of self-employment and less-than-stellar income, you will eventually decide to return to the full-time practice of law.

You will be initially excited to earn an above-average income, but you will also be genuinely curious as to how you will practice law *now*.

What is possible this time around?

Throughout your entire journey, you will become a much more spiritual person. This won't look like the Catholic upbringing you had, but rather will be much…deeper, mystical, and *real*.

You will now know that there are things beyond your control (most everything, in fact!), and that your only job is to get out of the way so that your life can unfold.

While this will initially be deeply challenging to the part of you that is scared and programmed with attempts to control, you will practice letting go and surrendering on a daily basis.

As part of this, you will surrender to where you will next end up.

As you prepare your resumé and cover letter for that full-time legal practice, your mind will want you to move to British Columbia. You will crave the coast, but mostly because it seems beautiful and way more fun than Saskatchewan.

You wonder how the universe will lead you to your upcoming full-time legal job in a beautiful coastal city. How exciting, the potential!

The universe, in its knowing way, will lead you not to Vancouver, but to Moose Jaw, Saskatchewan.

Moose Jaw. Saskatchewan.

I know that this news will be strange, because you have dreamed of big cities since you were a young kid, but trust me on this one.

Go to Moose Jaw.

In Moose Jaw, you will work for the provincial Water Security Agency. You will learn about how the province protects and manages water. You will learn a bit about environmental law, a bit about Indigenous law, and a lot about procurement law (who knew!).

You will have no idea what is happening, but guess what?

Your journey has prepared you for this.

Here in Moose Jaw, you will get to hone in on what makes you a good lawyer—your ability to see *what's really going on* while helping people feel less anxious about their projects or decisions.

You will realize that in the here and now, you get to practice law on your terms.

The self-confidence and spirituality that you developed in your time away will serve you exponentially well. You will become a trusted confidante, a connecting leader, and a lawyer committed to serving at the highest levels of excellence.

You will get to be *more you*.

This does not mean that returning to full-time practice will be perfect. Not in the slightest. You will realize that just because you had the rare gift of taking time away to come back to yourself does not mean that others will now understand you. You will often feel alone, and unseen, and in the wrong place.

But ultimately, you are unshakeable. And for now, know this: even when it feels like you'll be in Moose Jaw forever, and when you doubt whether your work is actually meaningful and true, you are *exactly where you need to be.*

THE TIME YOU TRULY REALIZE
HOW SMALL YOU ARE

You will have been back to full-time practice for about a year and a half.

You may not understand this chapter, but you know you're in it, and it's going decently well. In ten months, life will surprise you with an incredible partner, a move back to Saskatoon, a beautiful marriage, and your first pregnancy. Whoa!! Life, you awesome thing!

It's true—life will be unfolding in ways that you had always hoped for but feared might never come true.

Then an unexpected shift within the world—the *entire* world— will happen. Here you will be, freshly married and expecting your first child, wondering how much time you should take for maternity leave and checking to see how your engineering colleagues are doing with their procurements, and the world will go on lockdown.

The COVID-19 pandemic will hit.

The resulting social isolation will take you by surprise, because you've come to value your freedom and your adventuring. You

14

will work from home for a long period, with no end in sight, and with only your weekly grocery run to entertain you. You will go for a daily walk, but you will be restless. As a healthcare worker, your husband will be on the front lines, and that will worry you. You will hug him as often as possible, and pray for his health when he leaves for his shifts. You will miss your visits with friends, your family, and your colleagues. As an extrovert who thrives on social interaction, you will feel deeply alone.

You will also be scared when the government that is your employer also *reacts and constricts* when it becomes apparent the pandemic is not ending after two weeks. Upper-level decisions *will* impact your ability to provide legal advice in an ethical manner. You will be confused when your general counsel and amazing mentor is asked to retire early. You will grip your desk chair tight in your increasingly pregnant state because you won't know what surprise tomorrow will bring.

You will be afraid, but you will be afraid mostly because you can't shake the fear. After all, life's lessons have already taught you *that everything is working out exactly as it should.* So why does it feel *so scary?*

For now, know this.

You've been through hell, you've been through heaven, and right now feels like a strange combination of both.

THE NEXT TIME

Whew. We've arrived.

Well kid, we are both now in the next time. I have no idea what's coming next, so I sadly can't give you more hot future tips. If there's a way you can teleport to the future and let me know what to do, that would be awesome.

Oh wait, there *is* a way.

We already both know, that we've always known.

:)

So what would we both say to ourselves, right here, right now, if we knew?

"It's never too late to be who you might have been," as the old line goes.

Huh. We always did love that quote, didn't we? I wonder how it applies to what's coming next.

Alas. Best we buckle up!

Let's do this.

Love,
Adrienne

JULY 15, 2022—ADDENDUM

P.S. Wow. April 2020 Adrienne! Look at *you*!

How I wish I could scoop you up in my arms at this moment, bring you to a bench by the river, give you a delicious iced coffee and a warmed chocolate croissant, hold your hand, and say this:

"Honey, you are nailing it."

As you gaze over the river, watching the wake boats and kayaks, and ducks and geese, you are scared. And that makes sense!

Feel scared.

It really *is* a strange time.

In a way, it's like you know there are some challenges ahead.

It's like you know the pandemic won't end soon and that the isolation will stretch you so thin you feel as though you might break at any moment. It's like you know that you will have the most beautiful and healthy baby (!!), but that severe postpartum depression and anxiety will unexpectedly creep up and hold you in its vise like grip. It's like you know you will come to realize the madness your mind is capable of, and that your only job is to *ask for help* so that you don't actually go and jump off of that train bridge.

"Ask for help," I say.

You look at me and you start to cry. I put my arms around you, hold you close while you sip your coffee and slowly eat your croissant, and we take big, deep breaths.

"You already know! It's going to be a hard couple of years ahead, and you know. So cry, and crumble, and go on maternity leave. Have the most wonderful little baby! Fight the depression. Breathe through the anxiety. Say *no*. Say *yes* to health. Know you will never harm your baby, or yourself, and that even though it's really hard to believe, *you truly are an amazingly wonderful mom.*"

You gulp, choke a bit on your croissant, take a big gulp of now watered-down iced coffee, and start to laugh.

"Are you for real right now?" You look at me with sadly hopeful eyes.

"I am for real right now," I reply in earnest, holding onto your hand.

We sit there awhile longer, watching the wake boats and kayaks, and ducks and geese.

"You also need to know that the government job is not going to get better," I eventually say.

"Oh noooooooooooo. What should I do?" you ask.

"Stay there until the moment of full clarity strikes and whispers in your ear, 'Leave. Leave now.' At that moment—and not a second before—take the opportunity to look in the mirror. Recognize the wounds of yours that are begging to be healed in that environment. Tend to yourself. Practice setting boundaries. Learn to say *no*. Watch the paternalistic patterns of the leadership. With curiosity, but not sympathy, recognize their behaviours. Like the most badass female spy you can think of, observe, learn, and file it all away."

You look at me with wide eyes and gulp.

"You already know it will all come in handy at a much later date," I smile.

"I do know," you smile back, and add, "Is there anything else I need to know right now?"

"One last thing! Make out with your husband even when you don't want to and get down on the floor to play with your son even if it will make you late for work."

"I'm going to have a *son*?" you ask.

I look at you and wink. "You already know that."

You smile.

Then you turn to me and say, "Hey, Adrienne. It's never too late to be who you might have been."

I smile and look out at the wake boats and kayaks, and ducks and geese.

Adrienne Forgeron graduated from the University of Saskatchewan with a Bachelor of Commerce in 2006 and a Juris Doctor in 2007. She currently lives in Saskatoon with her handsome husband, Gregor, their toddler son, Finn, and brand-new daughter, Francesca. Since the writing of her article's addendum in 2022, Adrienne's moment of full clarity struck, she left the government job, and she now finds great joy and satisfaction in building her own legal advising and coaching practice, known as The Gentle Lawyer.

TRYING *to* CHANGE *the* COURSE *of the* QUEEN MARY *with* OARS

ALMA WIEBE, KC

1978 LLB

BACKGROUND

Going to law school was not a dream for me, let alone a life-time ambition. In 1975, when I began law school, there were no lawyers in my family (there are half a dozen now). I come from a farm family and am third-generation Canadian. My grandparents, as young people, fled Russia with their parents in the latter part of the nineteenth century—all of them Mennonites and pacifists.

I went to law school because twelve of my older siblings (I am the youngest of fifteen children) are university educated, most in the "helping" professions—medicine, education, nursing, library science, politics, social work, and the like. I chose law because:

1. I had the necessary prerequisite classes.
2. I did not have the prerequisites for medicine.
3. I felt I had to choose a profession not already occupied by a sibling, and law was one that was "left over."
4. My parents really discouraged my choice, which added to the mystique. Rooted in a deeply anabaptist foundation, they were opposed to litigation as a form of dispute resolution.
5. I confess that, as a woman, choosing law also felt somewhat revolutionary. I had been schooled in feminism by my older sisters, and law seemed like a logical step along that path.

It is not my intention to sugar-coat my forty-three years of experience as a lawyer in this narrative. That said, I am, generally, an optimistic person and recognize fully that I am extremely privileged: white; healthy; bilingual; educated; the product of a loving, caring family; and well off by most standards. What follows is somewhat grim, but as honest as I am able to be from where I sit at present.

CLUELESS

I had no idea what I was getting into. Truly, not a clue. I hated law school and did not do very well at all. From being a "straight-A" student and top of my class, I plummeted to mediocrity (at best) in law school. Naturally, this was a major blow to my ego and self-confidence. I had been scared before, but it was in law school and later as a lawyer that I learned what fear really felt like. Coming as I had from a sheltered family environment where I was protected by everyone, cherished, encouraged and always met or exceeded expectations, I was shaken by law school.

There were, as I recall, twelve women in my section of sixty students in first year. We had, I believe, one or maybe two female professors. It was not unheard of for male professors to have affairs with female students. Even as late as the third year of law school, the only female practitioners I knew of in Saskatoon were Gwen Randall and Barb Foster. I recall them giving us a presentation, perhaps at the bar course, and admiring how poised, confident, and well dressed they were.

I clearly recall feeling overwhelmed by the volume and strangeness of the law class materials. Law school was, for me, a completely alien experience. I feel, in retrospect, like I did nothing but study for three years. Law was all-consuming. I distinctly recall a weekend night out at a local club with friends in other disciplines, listening to their conversation about psychology, political science, and other social science classes, and being struck by how little I knew, how uneducated I was. I had been buried in nothing but law and was totally out of touch with my contemporaries. It was isolating then and continued to be so in practice.

YEARS ONE THROUGH TEN

When I first began practicing law all of the judges I appeared before were older white men. Some of them were interested in what I naively thought was my progress. I recall being invited into a judge's chambers after a court appearance early on, and quaking, not sure what I had done wrong to warrant such attention. His office smelled of garlic sausage. As it turned out, he just wanted to check in with me. I was the only "girl" in court that morning and, as such, quite a novelty with my fresh young face, curly hair, skirted suit and high heels. I held such awe, respect, and fear for this man, to whom I had, as required, bowed as I entered and left his presence. I recall feeling so very relieved to learn that I had in fact not done anything embarrassing or inappropriate in court and that he just wanted to get a closer look at me.

Another old man (long since deceased) was assigned to me as a mentor early on to teach me how to properly run a Queen's Bench jury trial. We were in a hotel out of town for a week—working hard in the evenings and in court all day. I recall him chasing me, literally, around the room we worked in at night until he caught me, kissed me, and removed my clothing. I hated it, but would no sooner have complained than fly to the moon. It did not even occur to me. And, anyway, who would I have complained to? This was my career, my chance to learn how to be a trial lawyer from an expert. After that first night, I was submissive. He had me. During that long week, we were invited into the judge's suite at the hotel, where we drank and talked until the wee hours. Of course the judge was also an old man, and is now long deceased. I remember thinking at the time that it was highly inappropriate for one set of trial counsel to be socializing with the judge during the trial, but I was a junior and did as instructed. I do not think we talked about the trial. I know the judge drank a lot, because I recall being surprised at how sober and formal he seemed the following morning in court, after being seriously into his cups just hours before.

Notably, I am not alone in experiencing what I did. Every woman lawyer I know well enough to share these experiences with has walked this exact same path—some with much more strength than I had, but all dodging, placating, conforming to, accepting, and making the best of a deeply patriarchal profession. None overcoming it. None changing its essence.

I recall one dinner party with friends a number of decades ago— all female lawyers. As the wine flowed, the conversation became more personal, and we came to realize, to our surprise, that every single one of us was in therapy at the time.

I had one female mentor in my first years of practice, whom I respected enormously and from whom I learned a great deal. To this day, I recall her confidence, her fearlessness, and her work ethic with admiration.

In retrospect, the first ten years of practice are a bit of a blur for me. I vacillated between periods of intense fear of failure, almost paralysis, interspersed with euphoria and bravado after a win in court. Success and failure were measured solely by wins and losses. How head-down, frightened, and self-absorbed I was during that decade became really apparent to me only recently, when I read a chapter written by one of my sisters about her work in Vietnam during that time (the eighties). I had no idea that a sister I loved and had grown up with had been doing ground-breaking diplomatic work in a country closed to North Americans at the time. I was both proud and ashamed when I read her piece. (Another sister was building university libraries in the Middle East, and yet another was a force in agriculture and food security around the world.) Mostly, in retrospect, I am shocked at what a stern, strict, relentless taskmaster law was for me. It narrowed my learning, my perspective, my horizons, my ambition.

It also contributed, over the years, to my loathing of patriarchy. As a woman, I knew from the get-go that I had to work harder, be smarter and quicker, and dress better than my male counterparts to make it in this profession. No one told me that. It was just obvious, and I felt helpless to do anything but ride along. For the most part, my male counterparts had wives who tended to all of their needs apart from work. Their social lives, families, physical needs, and even the purchase, care, and cleaning of their clothing were looked after. It was a 1950s suburban household model. Law was not meant for women, and did not accommodate us well or at all.

So why did I stay? Most of my female classmates left the practice of law within the first ten years after graduation. The answer is no more sophisticated or interesting than lack of imagination. I was on a hamster wheel and didn't even think of climbing off.

IMPOSTER SYNDROME

I know I am not alone in having experienced (still experiencing) imposter syndrome. Law school taught me how to think like a lawyer, not how to be one. Adults with serious legal problems placed them in my hands when I was still in my mid-twenties. I felt like a total fraud, and I was one. What I learned quickly was how to be a good imposter—listen, ask questions, nod wisely, feel and show empathy, dodge questions, and then head to the library to try to figure out what the hell to do. That feeling of being not quite as advertised has abated, but still remains. I learned (harshly) to restrict my practice to areas I could learn and, mostly, not to take on work I could not do. This has apparently been a hard lesson, because even within the past five years I have had files I did not know how to handle.

So what is that about? Ego? A desire to please? Probably both. I think also that one of the mixed blessings we experience as lawyers is the general community's perception of who we are—smart, crafty, articulate, strategic problem-solvers who are strong, persuasive, and right. Those expectations are impossible to meet, so we fake it until we make it.

AGENCY/CHANGE

As I review what I have written, I am struck by my own lack of agency. I have no good excuse for this. I look at the women who have broken ground in our profession (the first female judges, the first women appointed to the Court of Appeal and to the Supreme Court of Canada, the first woman president of the Law Society of Saskatchewan, the first female dean of the College of Law, etc.), all within the span of my career as a lawyer, and I am filled with gratitude and admiration. I look also at the brave women of the Me Too movement with awe, respect and wonder. That strength of character, resolve, and mission eluded me. Ironically, during the past two decades of my career, and particularly in the last fifteen years, most of my work has been in the area of harassment!

During the first twenty-five or so years of my career, I, along with other women, made efforts to raise the profile of women in law, highlight the inequities, encourage, mentor, and effect change. Sadly, while the enrolment of women in law school increased enormously, those who survived in private practice beyond seven or ten years did not rise proportionately. It felt at times like we were trying to change the course of the *Queen Mary* with oars.

Establishing a new firm with a new model in 2004 was, for me, like dropping the oars, jumping into a small boat, and veering off. My dearest friend, Karen Prisciak, a fellow feminist, and I spent years planning our "escape." We thought about and documented what we abhorred about private practice and mapped out what we wanted for ourselves. Not as a model for others to follow—just as a way for us to step off the treadmill, do the work we enjoyed, do it well, and, mostly, allow ourselves to be women and lawyers at the same time. The firm we dreamt of would be female only. We would not "grow" like traditional firms—there would be no associates, no students, limited staff, no chasing of big money. We would earn a decent living, no more. We would take time off generously. We would support and care for those around us—clients, staff, each other. We would share the burdens and rewards equally and resolve disputes without rancour.

We opened A.S.K. Law on July 4, 2004, and closed it on August 31, 2021. We brought with us the smartest, most efficient, and most competent legal assistant, Brenda Enden (who has now worked tirelessly with me for over twenty-nine years). For the most part, our plan worked, and for me, those seventeen A.S.K. years were, without a doubt, by far the best of my career. With unfailing compassion and encouragement, Karen saw me through the death of a parent and the loss of a marriage. Despite a personal collapse at about the midpoint, the decision to hive off on our own and establish an environment and a practice outside of the mainstream was the best professional one I could have made. It was by no means revolutionary. Just made to order, tailored to fit women. Sadly, I hasten to add we could not have done this until we had built individually solid reputations as respected, seasoned lawyers in the male world.

CONCLUSION

So what has my career as a lawyer given me? A tidy living (which is not to be underestimated) on the plus side; social status which, though largely unearned, is satisfying and sometimes handy; and a body of knowledge, including methodology, which is a useful lens through which to view the world. Oddly, what it did not give me was resilience. Not because I had a silver spoon in my mouth—I did not. How do we learn to solve other people's problems but not our own? Is the answer in the question?

About twelve years ago, after three decades of successful private practice, I ran into a personal crisis. I crashed. When the dust settled, I had lost a marriage and was in recovery from an addiction.

My work, however, went on almost without a hitch. It was not the lessons I took from years of practice that got me through. It was family, friends, rehab, and lots of therapy, which, if truth be told, counteracted those lessons. I learned I did not have to be tough, strong, and without emotion. In fact, to recover, I could not be. I had a lot of unlearning to do; a lot of guard to let down; a lot of "it's okay to be vulnerable" to absorb. In short, a long career in law did not prepare me for life.

Alma Wiebe practiced law for forty-three glorious years before quitting. Now she travels and reads, sleeps and serves.

INSTEAD, I JUST KEPT DRIVING

AMELIA LOWE-MULLER
2015 JD

Dear future apprehensive female law student,

In order to understand my experience as a lawyer, I think it's important to provide context...so let's start from the beginning. I did not grow up wanting to be a lawyer. I did not know anything about the legal system. What I did know was that I was not keen on injustice and I did not appreciate being told I should be barefoot and pregnant.

I was born in 1980. I arrived home from the hospital to a dusty farmhouse with no running water. My dad was a third-generation farmer, and my mom had moved to rural Saskatchewan from Saskatoon in the seventies because she was in love with my dad. They were married at nineteen. My mom did not attend university. Nor did my grandmother on either side of my family. Many hands make light work, I suppose, and I grew up around many women who stayed home to raise children while husbands went to work in the fields or the potash mines.

My childhood was interesting. I was surrounded by a community of artists and farmers, forward-thinking liberal folks, and a contingent of conservative people whom I considered homophobic, racist, and narrow-minded. As a kid, I was lulled to sleep by heated debates about politics and the comforting smell of cigarettes. I knew I didn't fit neatly into either camp. I was not interested in the often narrow-minded, conservative plight of the farmer, nor was I keen to make a living crafting pottery or putting my mark on a blank canvas.

I certainly had a sense of what I thought was "justice" from a young age. On a particularly stifling day in kindergarten, all the boys were allowed to take their shirts off. As far as I was concerned, that was unfair, and I swiftly took off mine too, creating a bit of a concern for my teacher. I suppose I had a bit of a flair for the dramatic.

While I loved the food that came from the giant garden, I hated weeding that garden. Although the endless skies gave me comfort, I felt suffocated by small-town living.

At nineteen, I started university with the intention of becoming a drama major. I took a smattering of liberal arts classes and learned that sociology was my favourite. At twenty-two, before I could finish my degree and as I held a steady job as a waitress in a pub, I found myself pregnant. Although I had never considered myself to have a firm life plan, if ever I had mapped out my life's trajectory, this particular destination was not on the map.

So what was a gal to do? Like many women who found themselves in this position, I pulled up my boot straps, moved in with my boyfriend, and started a family. Much to my chagrin, I had fulfilled the prophecy of many an outspoken farm boy. Here I was, barefoot and pregnant.

I became a mom, went to university part time, continued working in a pub, finished my sociology degree at twenty-seven, and gave birth to my second child. At twenty-nine, I married the father of my children (the love of my life) and I settled into a career as a university administrator. I loved my kids. I loved my husband. I did not love being a university administrator. I did not love being in a room where people talked over me. I wanted to be seen. I wanted to be heard, and I wanted to do more in the world.

Enter my father-in-law. He came from a family of eighteen. He grew up in South Africa and immigrated to Canada with his children during apartheid. He saw the way the world was opened up to those who had a university education. He inherently understood the life that could be made when one obtained an education, and he had spent his whole life learning.

I mentioned to him that I might be interested in law school. He was so excited. He told me he had every confidence in me. We stayed up late drinking whisky and he waxed philosophical about how he had always wanted to go to law school. I regaled him with my thoughts on injustice and my hopes of being an agent of change. We laughed and debated. He told me if I was accepted, he would pay my tuition. That was not inconsequential, and to this day I do not think I would have gone to law school had he not been so supportive.

While my interest in law was certainly driven by a desire to change, to learn and grow as an individual, it was also motivated by a sincere desire to do good—to positively influence people, places, and ideas.

Before starting law school, I was told that when it comes down to it, the legal system is really only about money. The only way that one can compensate people for wrongs being done to them is financially. The system cannot reverse a surgery that may have gone wrong. There is no opportunity to go back and undo actions that cause harm. The only way to remedy negligent behaviour is through monetary compensation. I vehemently disagreed with this viewpoint. I intended to go to law school to help people. I saw it as a way to use my privilege to assist those less privileged.

I started law school at the age of thirty-two. I had a lot to learn.

First, I knew nothing about the Canadian legal system. I had been able to obtain a grade twelve education and post-secondary degree with nary a thought about the Constitution, about the fundamental differences between different levels of court, about crown prosecutors and defence lawyers. It was astounding how little I could string together when it came to the procedural order of laws and systems in Canada. My first year of law school was like an all-out, drag-'em-down, knock-'em-out disaster.

Second, I learned how important my familial and friend relationships were. In a year full of falling down and self-reflection, it was not lost on me that at the end of the day I had two little kids who thought I was amazing and who had no interest in my LSAT score or my final marks. Those two kept me grounded. My husband gave me constant words of encouragement and support and spent many nights with the kids after long days at work so that I could sit in the library. It was wonderful and it was impossible, and I wouldn't have had it any other way.

Finally, I learned just how much agency I felt after learning—or, more accurately, meandering my way through understanding—the legal system.

I possess a number of characteristics that had led me to believe I would struggle as a lawyer. While I am competitive, I am largely non-adversarial. Ironically, I do not like conflict and rarely do I engage in a heated discussion. Then there are the more stereotypically female traits. I am sensitive, I am empathetic, I am crushed by seeing others suffer. The LSAT surely convinced me I wasn't smart enough for law school, and I felt like I got through it on a wing and a prayer.

Before law school, I was not burdened with the knowledge of what was really going on in our criminal justice system. I hadn't read detailed Supreme Court cases about rape and murder, or discovered just how unjust our criminal justice is. I felt wholly unprepared for this knowledge, and first-year law school created a crisis of confidence.

Despite this crisis of confidence, in my first and second years of law school I secured a summer job with an excellent law firm, and I then managed to secure an excellent articling position with the same firm. I was not convinced that private practice was the right fit for me, but I had ideas about how I could create my own work-life balance and how I could supplement my work in the firm with pro bono files that would be meaningful. I knew that to be a good lawyer, I had a lot to learn, and this seemed like a great place to start. From the very beginning I had a keen interest in labour and employment law, which I was able to cultivate, but the truth is that private practice was a struggle.

Perhaps it was my past and the fact that I had had no experience with lawyers or the legal system prior to law school. I couldn't shake the feeling that I was an imposter. I do believe it is common in many professions to suffer from "imposter syndrome," but my lack of confidence in my work was disconcerting. My peers did their level best to encourage me, but I spent most of the time feeling inadequate. I was not confident in my decisions, and I felt like there was always something that I was missing.

Anecdotally, I can say with relative certainty that my male peers did not suffer from the lack of confidence that I did. I have not been able to put my finger on why. It could be that when young men look at people in positions of power and in government, they see themselves. Maybe my male peers inherently knew that they were entering a realm where they were accepted. Men have occupied the legal sphere for decades and they have a level of comfort with it. I did not have that level of comfort in the law firm.

I had felt for some time that my lack of confidence was going to be detrimental, if not fatal, to a legal career. What I came to realize was that confidence in decision-making can lead to mistakes, and while it is easy to write off a lack of confidence as meaning you are not cut out for legal work, this is not true. It is possible to lean in to feelings of trepidation. A lack of confidence can prompt you to prepare, which is arguably one of the most important things you can do, both in legal arenas and in life itself.

I really enjoyed files where I was working with other partners or associates. I liked the feeling of working as a team, and there were clients that I also really enjoyed working with. The unfortunate reality was that a lot of the legal work I was doing was isolating. It was hours of writing and researching on my own. When I had a couple of years under my belt, I started to take files on my own, which meant it was just the client and me. Many of the clients were only notionally involved in the work. This was especially true of insurance files where the large majority of interaction on the files was done via written correspondence with an individual working for an insurance company. This was hardly the pursuit of justice that I had hoped to seek.

There were lots of social opportunities for lawyers, but when the newfound sheen wore off, the experience became dull. There are fascinating lawyers doing important work, but when you get them all together in a room, there is nary a conversation about anything other than either the business of law (the money, the billable hours, the time), procedural gaffes made by opposing counsel, or war stories about past legal encounters. Some people seem thrilled by this and can engage in these conversations over and over. I started to avoid socializing because I was fatigued by this constant self-important chatter.

I really started to struggle with my motivation to do the work in an environment constructed to reward those who work the most and who, at the end of the day, make the business the most money. I wanted to be motivated to do my job because of the intrinsic value I felt that it held for me. I wanted to feel like I was part of something greater than lining the pockets of business owners. It was becoming increasingly clear to me that my career goals were not going to be achieved in private practice.

On top of this, I really struggled with billable hours. The constant pursuit of the billable hour was very difficult for me. I resented having to keep track of every single email and every phone call, and it constantly interrupted my workflow. I started to obsess about how many hours I had worked, where I was deficient, and how much money I was collecting. Instead of being motivated to work, I had days when the bean counting was paralytic. It seemed like an enormous task just to start my timer when I sat down to start my day. Admittedly, I could chalk this up to personal failure. Maybe I just didn't want to work as hard as I needed to; maybe I just didn't have the professional drive for success that I saw in other lawyers. But this didn't make sense. When I was working on files I was interested in, when I had deadlines, I could always work as hard and as much as I needed to. Something was not adding up for me.

For example, there was a substantial contingent of lawyers who saw mediation as a waste of time. What I came to learn is that mediation is not for the lawyers. It is an opportunity for those who have been involved in a dispute to sit in the same room and listen to each other. Once mediation is complete, the remainder of the litigation process is highly controlled by legal counsel, and there may actually be no other opportunity for the parties to speak freely. From where I sat, lawyers were failing to reflect on the old adage that the legal issues belong to the client, not to the lawyer, and the mediation process should serve the client's needs, regardless of how the lawyer feels about the process.

What I came to understand through my experience is that the only way mediation can work is if all parties are invested. It is fine for one party to arrive at a mediation and expect that an outcome will be achieved, but if opposing legal counsel thinks it is a waste of time, any expectations cannot be met. I struggled to identify with my peers in private practice, and the differences in approach to mediation solidified for me that it was likely time to change course.

One day, I had dropped the kids off and was driving to work. As I approached the firm, I knew I had to turn in and park. Instead, I just kept driving. I physically could not go into the office that day. I can pinpoint that moment as the moment I really felt a shift.

I now work in the public sector, and reflecting on six years of practicing law has taught me this: in law school, you will focus on "legal issues." You will be asked over and over to read a scenario and identify the facts and the issues, do the analysis, and find the applicable rule of law. Undoubtedly, this is important. What you don't learn in law school is that behind every legal issue is a person, and people are complex. Very rarely will somebody's legal issue fit neatly into a box or be solved by a legal test. Very often, people just want a lawyer to listen to their story. Sometimes people just want an apology. It is amazing what a sincere apology can do.

The characteristics that led me to believe I would struggle as a lawyer have turned out to be my most valuable secret weapons. I enjoy interactions with opposing counsel, and I have developed great relationships with lawyers who are in opposition to me. I seek to find results that account for the needs of all parties; I do not attempt to win at all costs. My sensitivity and empathy allow me to not only understand my client's needs, but to also understand how the opposition feels, and I can use that to come to a resolution.

Chances are that the qualities that you believe will be detrimental in your career will turn out to be your greatest assets.

So I guess the question is, should you go to law school? I truly believe that a legal education gives you tools and the foundation to fundamentally change how you engage with the world. Lawyers are in an extraordinary position—they are both revered and despised, but powerful nonetheless. If you are considering law school, you should go. It will give you the tools needed to navigate the world with a newfound confidence and a baseline understanding of the legal framework that you exist in. When I reflect on my career so far, I can say without a doubt that going to law school was the best career decision I could have made.

Amelia Lowe-Muller works as legal counsel for the Saskatchewan Health Authority in the area of labour and employee relations. She enjoys her dynamic work environment and supporting healthcare across the province. Amelia continues to seek balance between spending time at work and enjoying all aspects of her life, including spending time with her family, enjoying time outdoors, and engaging with her community in Saskatoon.

SEE SOMETHING?
SAY SOMETHING

BREANNA NEEDHAM
2015 JD

Dear Beth, Brea, and Leah,

Thank you for inviting me to participate in the CREATE Justice project focusing on the experiences of women lawyers.

Women in law have a vast array of interesting stories and experiences from their careers in law; these stories have traditionally gone untold. I am pleased to see the law school that I attended taking active and dedicated steps to rectify the long-standing equality imbalance in the profession through this endeavour.

Despite the increased number of women who began entering the legal profession in the 1970s, and the fact that approximately 50 percent of law school students across Canada in the 1990s were women,[1] it is both perplexing and regrettable that women

---

1   Linda Robertson, "What Law Firms Can Do to Stop the Exodus of Women"…

in law are still largely underrepresented in the profession. For example, while women lawyers accounted for nearly half of all practicing lawyers in Canada in 2016, significantly fewer women attained recognized leadership or senior positions, such as law firm partner.[2]

One question that really brings this issue to the forefront for colleagues is when I ask, "When you think of a successful lawyer, what does that image look like?" More often than not, the response is an older, distinguished-looking (likely white) man, with gray hair and a dark suit.

Having grown up in the age of Reese Witherspoon's *Legally Blonde* with the mantra of "What, like it's hard?" and having been in the midst of law school at the time of Sheryl Sandberg's "Lean In" campaign, the message has always continued to be clear: women can succeed in anything, including law, as long as they work hard enough.

Despite what media and myth may tell us, this is not necessarily the whole truth and nothing but the truth. For women in law to succeed, hard work is only half of the story. My hope for future law graduates (and for the future of my career path) is that the status quo in the profession and society more broadly will no longer continue, and that the talk and discussions on the advancement of women in law and diverse lawyers that are so popular today will turn into true action that creates real change.

...(2023), online: *The Canadian Bar Association* <https://www.cba.org/Publications-Resources/cba-Practice-Link/Work-Life-Balance/Women-and-Law/What-Law-Firms-Can-Do-to-Stop-the-Exodus-of-Women>.

2   Catalyst, "Women in Law: Quick Take" (February 2023), online: *Catalyst: Workplaces that Work for Women* <https://www.catalyst.org/research/women-in-law/>. The report identifies 43,595 practicing women lawyers in Canada, with even distribution across all provinces except Quebec, and the percentage of women law firm partners vs. men in Ontario as 9.3 percent vs. 22.3 percent.

EXPERIENCE IN LEGAL EDUCATION
(AS A FIRST-GENERATION LAW STUDENT)

While I had an excellent experience during law school, attending university for undergrad and then law school was certainly interesting. Neither of my parents hold degrees, nor do they work as professionals in traditional white collar jobs. Attending university for the first time was an eye-opening experience, and returning to university for law school after time working in the agriculture industry following my graduation from the College of Agriculture & Bioresources was a bit like déjà vu.

While many people who attend university also have parents, friends, siblings, or family members who attended university before them to learn from, this is not the case for so-called first-generation university students. While I discovered the difficulties that go along with a university experience without precedent in undergrad, I was surprised to discover that law school presented its own unique set of experiences in this regard. In 2012, when I began law school at the University of Saskatchewan, many (although not all) of my fellow law students were from families with at least one parent who was trained as a lawyer, if not two; those without lawyers as parents tended to have other professionals in their families (doctors, accountants, dentists, etc.). One thing I have learned since joining the legal profession is that becoming a lawyer is a family legacy for many, and my first exposure to this phenomenon was during law school.

While this seems like it might be a rather small consideration, learning how to "think like a lawyer" is a large part of first-year law school—a unique challenge that those with parents in the profession certainly have assistance with. Law school (and later, the practice of law) has a unique ability to make even the most confident and intelligent people feel as if they don't know what's going on and as if they don't belong. Fellow students in first year had sitting judges and experienced advocates at home helping them learn to read case law, write briefs, and critically analyze legal questions outside of class. I was fortunate in that I had a very successful academic experience, despite my lack of a learned legal family legacy, thanks in part to the support of generous upper-year students who served as both friends and guides in navigating everything from legal writing to the expectations for law firm interviews and firm politics. It was through this process in law school that I first began to see the ways women law students would band together to support each other to achieve success through sharing outlines, supporting moot team try-outs, interview prep, and more.

My law school experience was one that had it all, despite my maintaining a full-time job through my first year of law school and continuing to work part-time for the remainder of the program. I was fortunate enough to not only attain academic success, but also to enjoy participating in the Jessup Moot with my teammates, act as an editor of the *Saskatchewan Law Review*, join the Dean's Forum on Access to Justice, and to do a term abroad in Australia as part of my law school experience. I also believe that, as a result of the scope and breadth of my experience during law school, I was able to have choices with respect to where I articled and chose to practice, and to this day, I remain grateful for the nature of my law school experience in this regard.

While I managed to find success in law school, not everyone in my position is so fortunate. Now, as a lawyer several years into my career, I actively make an effort to mentor law students who might need the support I found among my peers at the time, with a particular focus on women students, racialized students, first-generation students, and LGBTQIA2S+ students.

EXPERIENCE IN THE LEGAL PROFESSION

I currently practice commercial litigation in Toronto. If I had been told seven years ago when I entered law school as a first year that this was where I would be, I would have been very skeptical. At the time, I was grateful just to have the chance to join the profession, and I looked forward to being able to advocate for others for a living.

Now, in my fourth year of practice (at the time of writing this letter), I have a sense of confidence in, and enthusiasm for, my work that I could not have anticipated having while I was in law school. I currently enjoy a commercial litigation practice that includes everything from fraud matters in far-flung locations to emergency injunctive relief and contract disputes, with a bit of professional liability litigation and class actions work thrown in. Some of my time is spent with files on the Toronto Region's specialized commercial list, where a subset of civil matters is heard by a team of judges who have experience in managing complex commercial litigation. While this particular area of law has a long-standing reputation as being one of the more notable "old boys' clubs," I am fortunate to work with other lawyers in my current practice who not only encourage my contributions and participation, but also collaborate on files.

I have had the opportunity to work at several firms, both large and small, which has provided me with a broader perspective on the profession, including its highlights and challenges. In addition to focusing on advocacy formally on behalf of my files and clients, I also engage in advocacy in the profession more broadly, with a focus on advancing equality, diversity, and inclusion initiatives, and particularly on issues that involve women in law.

Unsurprisingly, much like in law school, "legacy lawyers" remain a constant in the profession, and there are many practicing lawyers from the same families (which tend to be both racially homogenous and financially well off) who support and promote family members in job applications, client pitches, new endeavours, and more. While I do not have the benefits that come from being from a family with a legacy of bringing lawyers to the profession, I do have the advantage of bringing fresh perspective. I do not believe in doing things the same way because they have always been done that way. While I don't have the built-in "what to do" support system that others may have, I am also not beholden to the traditionally acceptable ideas of what not to do, either. This has been a strong foundation for advocacy in a sphere that many are hesitant to engage in.

Notably, there seems to be a large number of lawyers who are comfortable with a sustained status quo in the profession, particularly in respect to equality, diversity, and inclusion initiatives. Recent events in Ontario, including the election of the slate of Benchers known as StopSOP which ran on an alleged "free speech" platform that has since been described as devolving further into an anti-diversity mandate, are just one example of the resistance that exists in the legal profession when it comes to change.

Equality, diversity, and inclusion problems can be hard to see for those who have never experienced the unfortunate side effects of such bias, and even more difficult for those who experience such bias to raise. Seemingly small issues are often representative of systemic problems that are inherently difficult to address. Focusing on the system as a whole can make the task of effecting change seem overwhelming. The barriers that women in law and other equity-seeking groups face in both society and the legal profession frequently can and do fall into this category. Questions and issues including how to ensure more diverse lawyers are represented in equity partnership, acceptance of LGBTQIA2S+ individuals, and the dearth of racialized lawyers in the legal profession are all issues that still exist in 2020 and must be addressed.

My approach to advocating for change is "See something? Say something" and "Don't like it? Do something about it." I believe that when a clear, unequivocal example of inequality arises, however small it may appear, it can often be the opportunity to start long-overdue discussions and catalyze change. As advocates, we must speak out and step up for ourselves and others when these examples of inequality present themselves. Sometimes it can be hard, and often there is inherent personal and professional risk in doing so. While equality, diversity, and inclusion have become the latest hot issues in law firms and the profession, many engaged in the discourse are only comfortable with talk, not action. However, only talking about a problem without taking any concrete steps to solve it imbues the profession with a false sense of progress, without actually advancing the issues.

Last year, I engaged in an initiative that brought awareness to the lack of equality in the profession through a local representative example. At Osgoode Hall, where the Ontario Court of Appeal sits, there were two robing rooms—one for the men to gown in, which was large, spacious, well-appointed, and contained approximately seventy lockers; and one for the women to gown in, which was small, appeared to be an afterthought, and contained approximately twelve lockers. Osgoode Hall is a historical building that was designed and developed in the late 1820s and early 1830s, at a time when women lawyers weren't even being contemplated.[3] Decades later, in the 1960s, a women's robing room was added at Osgoode

---

3   The first woman called to the bar in Ontario, Canada, and the British Empire was
    Clara Brett Martin, in 1897. See Mary Stokes, "Who Was the First Woman Called
    to the Bar in Ontario, and Canada, and the British Empire?" (9 July 2015), online:
    Osgoode Society for Canadian Legal History <https://www.osgoodesociety.ca/
    encyclopedia/clara-brett-martin-first-woman-called-to-the-bar-in-ontario-and-
    canada-and-the-british-empire/>.

Hall when Judy LaMarsh challenged the lack of facilities for women at the courthouse by storming into the men's robing room to use it.[4]

Most women who have been to Osgoode Hall have had the unenviable experience of waiting outside of the men's robing room while most or many of their colleagues (who still tend to be men for many matters) discuss and debate the case without them due to the gender segregation of the rooms. This was a well-known and common complaint, as I discovered after raising it with colleagues and mentors after it happened to me the first time during my first few months of practice. At the time, I was the junior lawyer on a team of four attending a multi-day, determinative, pre-certification summary judgment motion in a class action. I spent countless hours waiting outside the men's robing room for the remaining three (male) lawyers on the team, who would emerge together with the discussions done and the day planned.

In June of 2018, *Canadian Lawyer* published an article on women in criminal law with commentary on the discrepancies between the robing rooms, including the following:

> On the ground floor of historic Osgoode Hall in downtown Toronto, there is a hallway linking the Court of Appeal and the Divisional Court with the section occupied by the Law Society of Ontario.
>
> This is also an area of the building where there are change rooms for female and male lawyers who are there to appear in court on any given day. The male change rooms are opulent and spacious with nearly 70 full-length lockers, benches, several

---

4   Mary Jane Mossman, "Gender and Professionalization Projects: Rethinking Stories of Early Women Lawyers" (presentation delivered at the Berkshire Women's History Conference, Toronto, 10 June 2014) [unpublished].

mirrors and a spacious bathroom area. There is also a comfortable lounge section with a sofa and a large wooden table and chairs for writing any last-minute notes before appearing in court. The feel inside is that of a male locker room in an old-money golf and country club. Not many steps away is the change room for their female counterparts. The sign on an entrance door says "Lady Barristers." Inside, there are 12 lockers. There is mismatched furniture and an old desk in the room. The décor is best described as "chintz," says Toronto criminal defence lawyer Apple Newton-Smith. The disparity in size and comfort level sends a message, even if inadvertently, says fellow defence lawyer Lori Anne Thomas. "It is like there is a sign there saying we don't think you are staying long."[5]

The backlash at the time was instant and fiery. Complaints and debates, in real life and online, began as to why this discrepancy continued to exist and what could be done. Shortly after the release of the article, the commentary died away as the next debate of the day arose.

In early February of 2019, Fay Faraday appeared at Osgoode Hall with an all-women litigation team on a pay equity case. There were so many women on the team that the women's robing room was too small to accommodate all of them, and she took to Twitter to voice her complaints about the then named "Lady Barristers" robing room, sharing a photo of the small number of women it took to fill it.[6] Fiery commentary again arose online, less than a

5   Shannon Kari, "A Woman's Place" (25 June 2018), online: *Canadian Lawyer* <https://www.canadianlawyermag.com/practice-areas/criminal/a-womans-place/275239>.

6   Fay Faraday, "First thing every woman litigator who came in this week said was 'are all the lockers full again?'. Answer: eye roll, sigh...yes. The lawyers for just 3 of 6 parties on ONE case fill more than half the robing room. I hear the men...

year after the previous round in the summer of 2018. I found this redundant and wondered why nothing had been done after all of these years. The disparity—not only in space, but in terms of professional access—was so obvious, so physical, and so clear to me. So I started a petition to have the men's robing room turned into a space that would accommodate all lawyers, regardless of gender, gender identity, religion, or any other factors.

The response (both good and bad) was immediate. Widespread support for the petition arose online, and many members of the bar reached out to express their enthusiasm for the initiative. Unfortunately, however, there was some dissent, primarily from well-established and very senior male lawyers, including some at the firm I was practicing with at the time. The continued external support from key mentors, whom I am so fortunate to have in my life, allowed me to persist despite the resistance I faced (and pressure from some to cease, desist, and tone it down). Less than two weeks later, on February 20, 2019, the Law Society of Ontario announced that the men's robing room would be converted into an all-gender space. The new robing room opened in September of 2019.

The robing room experience taught me a lot about what goes unsaid in this profession. While I was generally more supported than not, those who were opposed were not publicly vocal given the widespread support for the initiative, but rather were aggressively critical behind closed doors. Unfortunately, several senior

---

...have 75+. #RoomOfOurOwn" (7 February 2019 at 14:38), online: *Twitter* <https://twitter.com/FayFaraday/status/1093610017377398784?s=20>; Fay Faraday, "But after 25+ years doing this, I still need to walk past the so-2-centuries-ago #LadyBarristers sign & there are still only 12 lockers for women litigators at 130 Queen St. in T.O. where the Court of Appeal, Divisional Court and Superior Court all sit." (7 February 2019 at 14:38), online: *Twitter* <https://twitter.com/FayFaraday/status/1093610001044815873?s=20>.

male lawyers who had publicly professed their enthusiasm for diversity and inclusion in the legal profession were among this group, despite the fact that they could articulate no reasonable basis for opposing the change other than that they thought it was "inappropriate." Overall, while I did learn who was only willing to talk the talk (but not walk the walk) on diversity issues, I also had the opportunity to connect with so many lawyers and colleagues at the bar who were truly allies. I am also very grateful for my mentors who supported me, and who continue to do so to this day.

ANTICIPATIONS FOR THE FUTURE

Women in law face many challenges that their male counterparts do not. This is particularly true for racialized women lawyers, as well as women and women-identifying members who are part of the LGBTQIA2S+ community. Despite the increased presence of women in law in the profession, the same issues that have plagued the profession for decades continue to persist.

For example:

- Nearly half of women executives believe their careers would have been more successful if they were men;[7]
- Women lawyers are assumed to be non-lawyer staff 50 percent more often than their male counterparts;[8]
- Women lawyers of colour are eight times more likely than white men to be mistaken for non-lawyers;[9] and

---

7   "Time to Put Certain Beliefs in the Past" (2023), online: *Ontario Bar Association* <https://www.oba.org/Momentum/Awareness/Beliefs>.
8   *Ibid.*
9   *Ibid.*

- Women represent 30 percent or less of partners (income and equity) at the majority of Canada's largest law firms with offices in Ontario.[10]

I hope to see real change on these issues, among others, during the course of my professional career. Women represent over 50 percent of the Canadian population; we are not a minority.[11] When diversity initiatives are being addressed, the question that needs to be asked is not "What do we do about the women?" but rather "Why are we failing half of the population?"

There is no reason for old stereotypes to continue to persist. There is no reason to see women as less than capable. There is no reason for the continued bias against racialized and LGBTQIA2S+ lawyers. The amount of biased behaviour that continues to be accepted (and, to a certain extent, promulgated) in a profession that inherently relies on standards of reasonableness and objective critique is both hypocritical and unacceptable. There is still a gender pay gap, both broadly in society and in law specifically. Notably, there is also some evidence that this pay gap exists beginning in the second year of practice due to the discretionary nature of the pay grids and bonuses at many firms.[12] This is well before many of the traditional reasons (read: excuses) why women

10 Jacques Gallant, "The Biggest Law Firms Employ Plenty of Women – But There Aren't Many at Senior Levels" (27 September 2019), online: *Toronto Star* <https://www.thestar.com/news/gta/2019/09/22/analysis-finds-biggest-law-firms-employ-plenty-of-women-but-there-arent-many-of-them-at-senior-levels.html>.

11 Statistics Canada, *Female Population*, by Covadonga Robles Urquijo & Anne Milan, in Women in Canada: A Gender-based Statistical Report, Catalogue No 89-503-x (Ottawa: Statistics Canada, 2011).

12 Daniel Fish, "Even Among Second-Year Lawyers, Women Earn Less Than Men" (9 September 2015), online: *Precedent Magazine* <https://lawandstyle.ca/news/on-the-record-even-among-second-year-lawyers-women-earn-less-than-men/>.

lawyers are paid less, such as parental leaves and transfers to counsel-track positions, come into play, and is indicative of a pervasive inherent bias in the profession when it comes to women in law, regardless of their age, status, position, or family status.

This is not to say that there are not women who do succeed in law. However, women in law in senior positions are much rarer than their male counterparts. At some (not all) firms, there is also often only one archetype of how to be a woman lawyer that is seen as acceptable. Even those who do make it to the top still struggle with bias, including age bias, in a way men do not as they advance through their careers.

In Toronto, a number of women have recently left larger firms to start their own firms, with the general reason for these departures being that they felt underappreciated—and underpaid. A national survey of law firm partners in the US found that male partners earn 44 percent more than their female counterparts.[13] While such detailed data is not available in Canada, it would be illogical to assume there is a stark difference in Canadian numbers on the pay gap when numbers on partnership, presence, inequality, and lack of advancement of women in law and diverse lawyers mirror US statistics so closely. While exiting large firms (and private practice) is one option, I hope that in the future, this will not be the primary way women can truly succeed. I hope to see firms that recognize the value that their female lawyers bring, not only in terms of billable hours, but with a true view to their contribution as a whole (particularly given that women still do double to triple the amount of non-billable work, including more "office housework,"

13   Jeffrey Lowe, "Compensation Survey 2016" (13 October 2016), online: *Major, Lindsey & Africa* <https://www.mlaglobal.com/knowledge-library/research/compensation-survey-2016>.

recruitment, mentoring, and other administrative and core firm functioning tasks than men do).[14]

I hope that one day (and preferably sooner rather than later), a figure of 30 percent representation of women equity partners and an even lower figure for representation of racial and ethnic minority partners in the legal profession is no longer considered progress, but rather horribly insufficient.

While I, of course, hope for my own professional success, including a long and enjoyable career that I will continue to be enthusiastic about for years to come, I know from my experience in legal education and in the legal profession to date that no one can truly make a go of it alone. We are what we give back; we are stronger together. By supporting other women in law and diverse lawyers, I believe we can create a profession that is not only better for ourselves and our colleagues, but for future lawyers who will practice for many years after I am done—a future where "What, like it's hard?" is no longer a testament to being truly underestimated.

JULY 17, 2022—ADDENDUM

P.S. It has been over two years since I first wrote my contribution for this book. Much has changed in the world and the legal profession since March of 2020. Unfortunately, the many great and sweeping changes have not included as much advancement for equity-seeking groups in the legal profession as many (myself

---

14   Diversity Lab & ChIPs, "2019 Inclusion Blueprint Report" (2019), online (pdf): <https://diversitylab.app.box.com/s/pon6fvko717f1vcfwlhlyt3wlkzhc6c8>. See summary by Dylan Jackson, "Women, Minority and LGBTQ+ Attorneys Still Struggle to Rise Within Law Firms" (28 January 2020), online: *The American Lawyer* <https://www.law.com/americanlawyer/2020/01/28/women-minority-and-lgbtq-attorneys-still-struggle-to-rise-within-law-firms/>.

included) may have hoped. The available information indicates that little has changed in terms of representation, retention, advancement, and attrition when it comes to women, BIPOC, and LGBTQIA2S+ lawyers.

What has changed? There is now more of an emphasis on authenticity in the workplace. A great deal more flexibility is now available as to when, where, and how lawyers can work and engage with their work and colleagues. Attracting, retaining, and championing diverse advocates continues to grow as a focus in the profession. This all bodes well for the future.

Why is that?

Authenticity Does Not Negate Advancement

We are better when we can bring our whole selves to the job. Working somewhere you feel like you have to pretend to be someone else from the moment you arrive until the moment you depart is exhausting. Not only that, the time it takes to "look like a lawyer," "think like a lawyer," "dress like a lawyer," and "act like a lawyer" takes away from the fact that you *are* a lawyer.

So many people who enter the legal profession are told, in one way or another, to engage in this kind of playacting, despite the fact that attempting to align with a (white, cisgender, heterosexual, male) stereotype robs young lawyers of some of their greatest assets: their identity and their time. While traditionally viewed as a barrier, authenticity is something that lawyering needs more of.

Professional success and authenticity are not mutually exclusive; they should go hand in hand.

Mentoring Matters

We are better together. A post-pandemic world with a wide availability of remote work has opened up so many new possibilities for reaching out to and connecting with mentors. We all benefit when we take advantage of the expertise of others, as long as mentees remember to use their mentors' knowledge as more of a set of guidelines for success, rather than a strict rulebook.

Mentoring is a foundational part of my approach to practice, whether in a mentor or mentee role. I encourage my mentees to be themselves and to take advantage of being underestimated when it happens (and it does). Everyone should find a mentor they trust, who will guide them and provide great opportunities. The best mentors help bring you to the forefront and keep you top of mind.

Practicing law can be a tough profession, but you don't have to go it alone.

P.P.S. When imposter syndrome strikes, never forget that you are enough.

Breanna Needham is a lawyer who practices commercial litigation with a focus on civil fraud matters in Toronto, Ontario. A few of her favourite things include her cats, naps, books, and snacks.

NEVER USE OTHER WOMEN *for* KINDLING

BROOKE JOHNSON

2016 JD

Dear fellow female-identifying justice sector colleagues,

A disturbing and recurring theme I have recognized in my career thus far has been the many ways in which women's voices, value, and aptitude are hushed and the tenacity with which that work is sometimes undertaken. The lack of acceptance into the professional sphere of women in our complete form ranges from an unwillingness to fully acknowledge us in the workplace and not hearing what we have to say at all to concerted efforts to thwart attention away from what we are saying after hearing it and simply not liking it.

It occurred to me that this is a symptom of a much larger and more sinister issue; "professionalism" vehemently excludes almost everything that is typically associated with women and girls. The accepted definition of professionalism is tremendously narrow, and has failed to expand as the demographic of those who comprise the professional world has expanded beyond men, specifically white men.

Although I, along with all other women in the professional sphere, have been expected to quietly conform to the expectation that I soften my femininity, as I have been told that it has no place in the workplace, that is something I have not been able or willing to do.

This letter is a glimpse into my discovery of the covert forms of silencing used against women in law, my efforts to display gender biases in the workplace for all to see, and my dismay to learn that overt efforts to silence women are often undertaken by other women. It also provides a starting point for recognizing how incivility toward female-identifying colleagues not only causes harm to the receiving individual but to the profession as a whole. Lastly, this letter outlines ways in which we can work toward the betterment of our profession by valuing and respecting the women within it.

Women have been taught that silence would save us, but it won't. As the brilliant and brave Audre Lorde wrote, "I have come to believe over and over again that what is most important to me must be spoken, made verbal and shared, even at the risk of having it bruised or misunderstood."[1]

ASCRIBING INVISIBILITY TO WOMEN

The meeting started as I expected it to. I and two male partners met in the more senior partner's corner office to discuss the pre-trial

---

1   Audre Lorde, "The Transformation of Silence into Language and Action" in *Sinister Wisdom*, 6 (1978) 13.

brief we were working on together. Because I was the most junior on the file, it was my job to capture their stream of consciousness on paper. I tried to record every nuance that was mentioned by the two men, who had a far greater understanding than I did of the civil litigation process; the file itself, which pre-dated my existence at the firm; and the area of the law, to which I'd had no previous exposure.

I was given the opportunity to recover from the cramp in my hand when I realized that the focus of the conversation surrounding one of the plaintiffs, a wife and mother, had shifted to the male partners' own wives and women in general. They began conjuring up a long list of mindless and purely recreational activities that they believed women must fill their days with. Inherent in the premise of their exercise was the notion that women don't work, experience no valid stressors, and spend their valueless time skipping from one fun and purely self-serving activity to the next. Their laughter that followed each addition to the "day in the life of a wife" story they were creating indicated to me that this was supposed to be funny.

I didn't find the humour in the misogynistic exchange that was unfolding before me as if I wasn't even there. They exhibited a seemingly shared understanding that women had minimal responsibilities and a corresponding abundance of stress-free time. Their entire conversation was built on a disgusting lack of awareness of the crippling amount of invisible work that falls almost entirely on the shoulders of women as well as on the sexist misconception that professions that are comprised mostly of women are inconsequential, require minimal skill, and have a low degree of difficulty, if any at all.

"No man ever got married to be rich!" was sputtered out through laughter as they joked about how women, as the naturally avid shoppers they are, somehow manage to spend even more money per day than their hard-working husbands can earn.

My brain registered a taste of blood, which awoke me from my state of utter shock. My teeth had put my tongue through a fraction of the amount of trauma my ears had been subjected to for the preceding ten minutes of this conversation. I didn't know what to say—where would I start with the mess their words had created as they carelessly threw them across the room, flying right past me like I was invisible? To add a layer of difficulty, I felt pressure to fashion a statement that was poignant, insightful, and inoffensive, given that I was an articling student and these two men had a direct say in my continued employment. As they continued to thoughtlessly exchange harmful jokes about married women, my brain decided to shortcut my regular decision-making process and words suddenly came out of my mouth.

"I'm a wife."

Silence.

"Well, back to work," the senior partner grumbled. The meeting was over. What in the old boys' club had I just experienced?

Beyond the obvious inappropriateness of the entirety of the conversation, what I am unable to reconcile to this day is why they felt so comfortable saying those things in my presence. My status as a woman and a wife made me the furthest thing from the target audience. I, and women like me, were simply the target.

The next occurrence of invisibility felt far less accidental.

I was solely responsible for conducting the preliminary inquiry on a sexual assault file that I was working on alongside a male partner. Although he was present with me at counsel table throughout the proceeding, I exclusively addressed the judge, cross-examined all witnesses, made and responded to all objections, and argued committal. Aside from the complainant, I was the only woman in the courtroom during the six-ish hours we all spent together that day.

Once court had concluded and we were able to converse directly with one another instead of through the judge, I turned to opposing counsel as we were packing our days' work back into our bags and shared that it was nice to meet him in person and that he had done a good job. He turned away from his bag and toward me just before bending an uncomfortable forty-five degrees at the waist to look around me and say "great job" to my male co-counsel. Without even an ounce of acknowledgment for my role in the matter, he put the last binder into his bag and left the courtroom.

Due, at least in part, to the adversarial nature of trial work, counsel are hyper-aware of one another and become fiercely familiar with each other over the course of lengthy proceedings. They learn the small shifts of weight and breathing patterns that precipitate each other's objections, their facial expressions when they try to conceal their surprise at unexpected testimony, and the slight changes in their voice when they are annoyed, confident, or running out of steam. The fact that they come to know these small nuances of one another during the time they spend together leads me to believe that obvious aspects, such as gender, do not go unnoticed.

I didn't need praise or a pat on the head from the opposing counsel. I wasn't seeking reciprocation of my extension of kudos, just a simple and friendly acknowledgment of the person he had spent the day working with. What was unsettling was that commendation for my work, my preparation, and my acumen was given to the man who stood silently behind me.

These instances stuck with me, and I became exceedingly aware that I was not seen as a lawyer; I was seen as a female lawyer. This qualifier led to the unfortunate outcome of being overlooked in harmful ways.

MAKING THE INVISIBLE VISIBLE

These experiences are not unique to me, as many female-identifying law students, lawyers, and judges can attest. Women in law have long commiserated with one another about how they have been (mis) treated, how they have been overlooked, how they have been over-burdened with non-promotable and non-billable work, how they have been spoken down to and treated as objects, how for significant portions of their careers they have not been considered or respected in the same light as their male counterparts, and the list goes on. These discussions are almost always had in hushed tones behind closed doors or in women-only conferences and CPD sessions.

Perhaps this was why in the first year of law school I, along with my female classmates, were encouraged to downplay our feminin-ity, specifically with regard to our appearance. "Wear a pantsuit. It can't be colourful. Pull your hair back. Wear minimal and natural-looking makeup. Heels are distracting—wear flats. No red nail pol-ish." We were advised to blend in. But what were we, the female students, blending in to? It sounded like advice to someone who was trying to go undetected in a place they weren't supposed to be.

Women in the workplace are consistently told that stereotyp-ically feminine appearances and traits are unprofessional. To be taken seriously, we are encouraged to abandon our femininity in both big and small ways. The number of articles that have been written declaring that the use of exclamation marks is unprofes-sional!! is one small example.[2]

---

2   Research has concluded that 73 percent of exclamation use is by women. See Carol Waseleski, "Gender and the Use of Exclamation Points in Computer-Mediated Communication: An Analysis of Exclamations Posted to Two Electronic Discussion Lists" (2006) 11:4 CM Cmns 1012 at 1020 (Wiley Online Library).

The message seemed to be that exhibiting traits often associated with women and girls is unprofessional. I disagreed. I had no interest in blending in—especially when that meant masking my feminine traits to fall within the professional norm that was established when only men, specifically white heterosexual men, were granted access to the corporate realm.

Had "blending in" led to the unsettling instances of invisibility I experienced as a female lawyer? Maybe. Maybe not.

What I was certain of was that I had no interest in either. And I wanted no part in perpetuating an archaic and sexist definition of "professionalism." I was a lawyer who was also a woman. I didn't have to sacrifice one of these identities for the other, and they were not mutually exclusive.

I decided to discard the narrow and exclusionary workwear norms of dark pantsuits and replace it with colour, voluminous skirts, and the like. I decided to dress in an explicitly feminine way in an effort to make it impossible to ignore that a woman was in the room and had a seat at the same conference table as the men who had dominated the space for so long. I also did this to expand the primitive definition of professionalism ever so slightly to include something beyond the wardrobe expectations that were made for and by men decades ago.

In male-dominated industries such as law, especially in powerful positions such as partner or judge, we need more examples of what a lawyer "looks like" for more women to be comfortable going into law and feeling like they belong in positions of power within the industry. When there aren't multiple examples of what it looks like to be a female lawyer, the idea that there is limited room for women at the top or that there is only room for one is perpetuated. For the sake of clarity, this is a terrible message to uphold.

I also began facilitating a public conversation via a blog about the everyday sexism that women in law navigate, so as to pull the words that had been shared behind closed doors for decades out of the shadows for everyone to hear. If we never bring issues to the surface, how will solutions and positive change ever come to fruition? We need to unabashedly name and discuss problems in order to solve them. Conversation is a catalyst for change. Pretending that gender inequality doesn't exist and is completely absent within the corporate world (yikes) is certainly not going to produce a more positive experience for future female professionals.

Although I, as one person, could not alone move the needle on what was considered "professional," my hope was to shine light on the very basic idea that accepting and portraying qualities typically linked to women and girls was not unprofessional. Wearing a pink dress didn't reduce my understanding of the law of evidence or inhibit my ability to follow criminal procedure in the courtroom. My use of exclamation marks in an email didn't interfere with my communication surrounding a plea deal for a client.

BETRAYAL RARELY COMES FROM YOUR ENEMIES

Given that lawyers are quite literally in the business of problem solving and fixing, I thought our profession would be up to the challenge of correcting a problem that was being identified. I expected some degree of backlash for openly discussing the gendered barriers women experience at work, and for stepping outside of the long established norms of what it meant to look like a lawyer, but thought it would be minimal. How mad could an A-line skirt make someone? What I never expected was where that backlash would come from: women. Specifically, older women in positions of power.

The first time I became aware that some women were committed to shutting down the conversation I was attempting to openly facilitate was during a panel presentation to a group of female law students. I was very excited to have been asked to be part of the panel, as one of the other panelists was somewhat of a career hero of mine. She had attended law school at a time when women typically did not advance positionally beyond the front desk. She had practiced criminal defence prior to being appointed one of the first female judges to her court. I not only wanted to emulate the strength and tenacity that I had assigned to her in my mind but I wanted to follow in her career footsteps.

I had appeared before her in court on a few occasions, but I was over the moon to be able to work alongside her, even if it was only for the two hours scheduled for the panel discussion. As a precursor to the panel, I had been asked to write an article for the publication of the organization that was hosting the panel discussion. I was specifically asked to write about women's workwear and the prospect of bucking traditional workwear to embrace a more personal and less masculine corporate uniform. As someone who has always aimed to please (thank you, female socialization), I gladly wrote the article—which apparently went over like a lead balloon with my hero herself.

I was seated directly beside her at the panel discussion. She was set to speak to the not-insignificant number of female law students and a sprinkling of practicing lawyers first. I was scheduled to speak second. Each panelist was assigned a speaking topic, hers being her journey and experience as a lawyer and a judge, which in her time was an act of bravery and defiance of norms and expectations in and of itself. I had been assigned to touch on and expand upon the article I had written, which had been published about one week before. Excited to learn more about the first-hand experiences of the woman I admired so much, I brought a note-pad and pen to the event to absorb as much information as I could from her.

She only spoke for about five of her allotted twenty minutes on the topic she had been assigned. This did her story and the audience a large disservice, as I have no doubt she could have spoken for hours about her experiences as a female criminal defence lawyer at a time when women were expected to be nothing other than obedient housewives, and about her experience of being invited to the ultimate boys' club of that time, being a judge. Her experiences, if shared, would have provided immeasurable value to everyone in that lecture theatre. But she shifted gears. And it wasn't smooth—at least not for me. She abruptly centred her attention on my article, of which she largely disapproved. With me sitting right next to her, she generously misconstrued the thrust of my article, overlooked the statistics and realities that supported the points made within, and strongly impressed upon the room that if they were to accept the contents of the article, they were doomed to failure as a lawyer.

I was completely caught off guard, confused, and immensely disappointed. A part of me left my body, hovered above, and wondered "What kind of status-quo-perpetuating monster occupied the body of my fierce hero?" She wielded her positional power and consequent influence to speak about how women should not step out of the current narrow parameters of the profession—many of which are sexist.

I shuffled through my papers to locate the email that had invited me to be part of the event, to be sure I had not unknowingly agreed to participate in a debate. It became clear that the woman whom I held in such high regard as a champion for progress and women within the legal profession had decided that her time was better spent warning the room that they would never be taken seriously or succeed professionally if they were to consider entertaining the ideas I was presenting.

In that moment, the "never meet your heroes" cliché became a devastating realization.

As deflated as I was, what was far more concerning to me was the room full of future female lawyers who had just been told by a judge to conform or else. It is impossible to quantify what the future has lost due to up-and-coming women being told that progress, even with regard to something so simple and personal as how we get dressed for the day, is not welcome.

A less public silencing attempt came from a female partner who was, not coincidentally, my assigned mentor. She was well aware of the blog I had started and monitored it closely. At various events the firm hosted to woo law students, she would stand idly by and silently smile or nod in agreement as female students expressed their gratitude for the messaging of the blog. However, one afternoon she and I had a meeting in a large board room in which she explained that while she understood why I was discussing women's equality in the workplace, it would be best for me to stop. Although her request was at first presented gently and as though it was for my benefit, she became increasingly hostile and rudely disapproving when it became clear that I was not going to end the forum I had created for discussing gender inequality, and that thousands of women were part of at this point. Following that meeting, she stopped providing me work that she had previously made me the lead on, and her "hellos" in the hallway, or any positive acknowledgement of my presence, stopped.

While I experienced far more support from women in law than the opposition outlined above, the incivility of these two powerful women deeply affected and confounded me. Why were these women, who themselves had undoubtedly experienced unfair treatment simply on the basis of their gender, so against this topic being discussed openly? Their passionate resistance to me reminded me of the "working woman" trope played out in so many Hollywood depictions of the workplace.

In the 1970s and '80s, the increasing number of women in the workplace was paralleled in movies and television shows. These pieces gave us the working woman, whose ambition made her difficult because she was constantly aware that she had to play a man's game. Her devotion to succeeding in a world dominated by men led to her full embrace of harsh traits, iciness, and the absurd notion that any display of stereotypically feminine traits equated to not having what it took to be successful and destroyed any chance of being taken seriously. Think Katherine Parker in *Working Girl* and more recently, Miranda Priestly from *The Devil Wears Prada*.

The working woman trope suggested that although the presence of women in the workplace was becoming more commonplace, there was only room for so many, creating a climate of female competition. Women were pitted against women and, commonly, the female boss and her younger female mentee became adversaries. Just beyond the woman-on-woman sabotage that took centre stage in these films was the more important story that women were held to a much higher standard than their male colleagues, and had many more hurdles to overcome in the workplace simply to get the job done—hurdles that were nowhere in sight for their male counterparts. In the working woman films, the anger that these women directed at one another was entirely misplaced and reinforced the idea that there is only room for one woman at the top.

I think it's likely that woman-on-woman incivility was and is also fuelled by the workplace itself. Workplace culture as we know it doesn't offer a level playing field for women with regard to pay or opportunity to reach leadership positions. This in and of itself breeds competition among women, who are taught that there is severely limited room in the upper echelons for them. When there appear to be few opportunities for women, research shows women begin to view their gender as an impediment; they avoid joining forces, and sometimes turn on one another.

Studies have demonstrated time and time again that women experience more incivility from their female colleagues than they do from their male colleagues. What is important to recognize is that studies have also concluded that in response to being mistreated by their female counterparts, women report lower job satisfaction, lower levels of vitality, and increased intentions to quit their job. Incivility from men does not garner these same results.[3] How we as women treat our female colleagues has grave implications. A scarcity of sisterhood could very well result in a scarcity of women in the profession and of women reaching the highest ranks of the profession.

WHERE DO WE GO FROM HERE?

Given that women who feel optimistic about their career prospects are less likely to tear one another down, it is imperative that employers, or partners in the context of the legal profession, make more of an effort to show talented women that they're valued. Although there is little doubt that employers benefit, at least for a period, from an aggressively competitive work environment, what

---

3   Allison Gabriel et al, "Further Understanding Incivility in the Workplace: The Effects of Gender, Agency, and Communion" (2018) 103:4 Journal of Applied Psychology 362.

would be of greater benefit to the profession as a whole in the long term would be the retention of women and more women rising to the highest positions of power.

As a collective, we need to accept a broader definition of "professionalism" that doesn't conflate femininity with incompetence, distractedness, or unfitness for the workplace. We must allow room for women to embrace any archetypal feminine characteristics that they wish to instead of being pressured into hiding those parts of themselves to be taken seriously. Permitting people to show up as their whole selves will not destroy professionalism but will enrich the profession.

While we need to avoid placing the onus of fixing an issue on the group it afflicts, it is necessary to issue a plea to the women who tear down other women in law. If you can't help but become angry with a female colleague, for the sake of the rest of us, keep it to yourself. Your incivility will always cause more harm than good for that individual and will work to maintain the status quo of devastating unequal representation of women at the top. Instead, foster alliances with one another, support each other, and watch all of us rise.

I'm still working on forgiving these women—I haven't quite gotten there yet. Although they too have been limited by the patriarchal systemic issues within the legal profession, they have taken the sword and harmed their own. They haven't yet learned that "the first rule of burning down the patriarchy is to never use other women for kindling."[4] I choose to continue on this path to eventual forgiveness because I understand that they have chosen to attempt

---

4   Libby Bakalar, "The first rule of burning down the patriarchy is to never use other women for kindling." (17 January 2022 at 12:12), online: *Twitter* <https://twitter.com/libbybakalar/status/1483140227568844800>.

to silence me because they were afraid of what men taught them they would be if they didn't. While I await a sense of forgiveness, I am committed to continuing to do my part to normalize femininity in the workplace and demonstrate its harmonious coexistence with professionalism—and I hope that you, as current or upcoming members of the bar and judiciary, will join me.

Brooke Johnson is a mom, practices criminal law, and teaches criminal jury trial advocacy. She unashamedly loves fashion as much as she loves the practice of law and has advocated for the norms of the profession to be more representative of the diversity within it.

THE YIN *and* YANG *of* LEGAL PRACTICE

CHRISTINE J. GLAZER, KC
1980 LLB

Wow, you have successfully completed law school. Now you aspire to become a respected litigator in Saskatchewan. With hindsight, what can I offer to my younger self, having survived forty years of private practice in litigation?

Let me start by making a few observations. Although it may seem counterintuitive, you are only now starting the learning process of how to practice law. This process will involve numerous challenges throughout your entire professional career; they can eat you up or make you stronger. Your experience thus far as a woman in the legal profession is in a graduating class with a relatively equal gender split and participation level. This is about to change as you enter a male-dominated profession. Your professional pursuits will conflict with your personal and family obligations and goals. The road ahead will require careful and assertive planning and triaging of your professional and personal interests.

What I would say, first and foremost, is that you are unreservedly fully equipped to achieve your goal of becoming a respected litigator. Do not doubt your ability; let your passion, hard work, and perseverance drive you through your day-to-day practice.

You perceive yourself to be an inarticulate bag of nerves when speaking in public. You question how you could possibly appear in a court of law and impress your peers, your opponents, and the sitting judges, all of whom you consider to be ten times more intelligent and gifted than you. You are fearful of failure, and intimidated by other lawyers, most of whom are men. You question whether you can fit into the profession. You grew up in a rural community distant from the firm that hired you. You have no business or community connections to offer the recruiters.

Regardless of gender, the really good and even great litigators start out with these or similar insecurities and self-perceived weaknesses. The source of these insecurities is fear—fear of failure and of the unknown. Left unchecked, these powerful emotions can evolve into anxiety, procrastination, excuses, and anger directed at yourself and your opponents, and sometimes even hatred for the process that dictates and governs a lawyer's practice. Fear is destructive to one's soul, one's progress as a lawyer, and enjoyment of life in general. It is mostly generated by deep-seated false perceptions and beliefs about oneself and must be confronted and harnessed.

The most powerful antidote to fear, anger, and hate is love—loving yourself first, and then others. Let me explain. This statement will be misunderstood by most professionals and thought to have no place in the business world or practice of law. I believe it is a fundamental truth that can guide one through life.

Consider the power of love in the lives of Mahatma Gandhi, Martin Luther King, and Nelson Mandela. These great leaders never succumbed to fear, anger, or hatred of their foes. Instead, they advocated in favour of truth, justice, and the power of love of others. They confronted their adversaries' violence with respect, grace, and honour. Their advocacy eventually influenced the world. They were courageous men, but there are also many examples of courageous women who have spoken their truths and risen to great heights. Take, for example, Emily Murphy, who was the first female magistrate in Canada and the British Empire; Ruby Bridges, who, at the age of six, was selected as the youngest and among the first Black students to test desegregation in American schools; and Malala Yousafzai, a female Pakistani education and human rights activist whose advocacy grew into an international movement. They too were driven by their conviction to truth, justice, and love for humanity. The power and simplicity of their leadership in combatting hatred, fear, and violence in their lives was exponential in its influence.

How does the power of love apply to a young lawyer entering the practice of law? On a very basic note, the tone and words chosen to address or respond to your adversaries matter. Hostility, threats, or name-calling are clearly not productive in resolving legal disputes. Your words will often attract a reply similar in kind, thereby escalating or de-escalating a dispute. You will hear your valued mentors recommend you take the high road, but that is often very difficult to put into action. Hostile interaction is seen in everyday life, but has no place in the world of litigation. There are many subtle and not-so-subtle forces that will challenge your values and ideals as you enter the practice of law.

As a young student, you entered law school with aspirations of helping others and doing something of value for the planet. Like many others, you chose the legal profession and advocacy as an avenue to achieve lofty ideals. While this logic is evident and well grounded historically in the many great achievements of jurists and lawyers, the business of law can impact or even erode these ideals. There is a challenging dichotomy: is the practice of law primarily a business or a profession?

In private practice, you will be required to record and track your time. You will soon realize the "timesheet" is primarily used to gauge your value to the firm. You may question your worth as you ponder how your clients will afford to pay your hourly rate. This is a difficult feature of legal practice for most lawyers. The timesheet, electronic or otherwise, remains the dominant tool in the business of law for valuing the work product, determining lawyers' compensation from the firm, and deciding upon partnerships. Higher-billing lawyers tend to have more influence on decisions made by the firm.

You may find it challenging and stressful to meet the firm's time and billing targets. It is difficult to guard against objectification of oneself when one is viewed as a number. Focusing on the well-being of one's clients must remain a priority. It was of utmost importance to inject my personal values into daily routines to stay grounded. Having patience and taking the time necessary to understand my clients' personal values and financial and practical issues was part of the process of developing trust and respect in the solicitor-client relationship. Clients responded much better to good and bad news if they knew I cared. This process takes additional time with the client, but is fundamentally important to the service you will provide and how that service is delivered. You will also stay grounded if you maintain an unyielding commitment to your core values in your dealings with clients.

Additionally, it is important to not simply accept everything your client says or demands. It takes experience and confidence to provide leadership to your clients to do what is right or best for them and credible to present to your opponent or as an officer of the court. This requires a deep understanding of the facts and your client. The business side of law may appear to create roadblocks in your serving clients to the best of your ability. This is the challenging life you have chosen. At times, it will be exhilarating, and at other times, defeating. If you are true to your values, you will not just survive, but thrive. You will learn to manage your client's expectations while garnering respect from your opponents and the court.

The business of law demands respect for numbers, sometimes seemingly at the expense of people. Associates and partners in a law firm must pay attention to the threshold requirements for billable hours, non-billable work, firm administration, and marketing. Finding the appropriate balance in triaging your energy requires recognition of your strengths and weaknesses in your skill set. Finding this balance was critical to my contributing to the overall success of the firm while staying true to my personal values. You do not have to do it all, but you must pull your weight in a partnership. This was very challenging for me.

I recall continually assessing if the values and expectations of the firm aligned with my values. If not, the plan was to exit once I exhausted the opportunities to expand upon my skill set and knowledge. My approach as a lawyer commencing practice in a large firm was to set a five-year plan, with no expectation at the end of that five years. My objective was to work as hard as I could to maximize my learning and experience from the gifted people who surrounded me. When I started practice in the firm, a female partnership had never occurred, and in my mind, was improbable. Unlike my male contemporaries, who all set goals of partnerships, I went with a five-year plan to extract what I could for my career.

While this may sound mercenary, by working hard and learning as much as I could from the exceptional lawyers in the firm, I contributed to the work product on each file. At the same time, I benefitted personally and prepared myself for a possible exit strategy. I did not invest my heart in a relationship that was highly unlikely to elevate me to a partnership. I nevertheless had to "love" the firm in order to love the work.

Integral to my achievements in the firm was my fortunate early alignment with one of the senior partners, who would become a mentor, confidant, and advisor over the next twenty-three years. He provided work opportunities and explained the dynamics of the personalities within the profession to aid in my management of files. I learned how to rise above the conflict and to put the inevitable missteps behind me. I always tended to dwell on my not-so-great performances. The mentorship got me through the first five years and helped build other strong relationships with partners with whom I was privileged to work. My mentors tended to view the practice of law as a profession first and foremost, while providing leadership within the firm. They also consistently met the financial expectation of the firm.

The contributions of trusted advisors and colleagues to my professional development were immeasurable. Eventually I would have the benefit of input from other women in addressing challenging professional issues.

Not only did the number of women grow in the firm, but it grew professionally in the bar, as did my connections through such organizations as the CBA. I was eventually able to move the dial on gender-related concerns in small ways. It was not sufficient to tolerate passive aggressive behaviour on the basis that "boys will be boys." There were times when intervention was required and a bright line was drawn.

I did not realize that when my second five-year plan commenced, I would be married and pregnant with my first child. This complicated my professional commitment. For reasons I later discovered, my decision to stay in the firm and private practice paid off. It is now hard to speculate where my life would have led with a different decision.

Learning to manage the expectations and requirements of the workplace became part of the yin and yang of legal practice. Establishing good work habits during early years went a long way to reduce stress as the workload increased and other factors were added to the mix. I succeeded in some, but not all, areas of practice management. The timesheet remains a source of anxiety, but only if ignored. Something as simple as keeping close track and documenting my time each day reduced my stress.

It was and remains common to invest ten hours in the office to achieve five hours on the timesheet. This created more pressure on life outside of the firm and drained personal energy. One approach I found helpful to achieve balance was to establish a daily goal for billable time. I resisted leaving the firm until the goal was met. This had a beneficial impact on efficiency, as I was always highly motivated to go home at the end of each day and needed to ensure the billable work threshold was met.

Like many of my contemporaries, I also had a tendency to judge my efficiency in terms of value to the file, and would undercut time recorded to compensate for my perceived inadequacies. Write-offs on the timesheet are never advisable. Time can always be written off when the bill is prepared if the account does not seem fair. When one is a young lawyer, the hourly rate is intended to reflect the inefficiencies of inexperience. Most importantly, the firm needed to see my actual work effort and time invested.

Another lesson I learned was to prepare a very rough draft for the work product in process, even when it was only half-baked. Leaving a file temporarily will often hamper continuity of thoughts if the thoughts are not recorded. A visible work product is also much easier to value retrospectively and provides a more efficient starting point when you return to the work. The road to valuing and documenting work and time is difficult for most lawyers, but is an important element of achieving success in private practice.

After many years of practice, I eventually realized that time recorded at work was much less valuable than time available in my private life. As a person who always felt compelled to respond to any and all calls for help, without considering the time commitment or energy requirements, I was prone to over-commit. Having done so, I did not want to under-deliver. As a young, energetic, healthy lawyer, over-committing can actually be very fulfilling and manageable. This, however, changes with time, as the work of a litigator knows no boundaries. Time flies when you're having fun, and when you're working on files.

Over-commitment has been a problem throughout my professional career. Knowing when to say "no" is crucial to setting boundaries necessary to your personal well-being. The time commitments you make may be rewarding, but may also escalate your stress and anxiety. The biggest window of opportunity to learn time management is during your first five years of practice, when expectations are measured at a junior level. As your years of practice advance, so do the expectations regarding the quality of work, the hourly rate billed, and client oversight. This adds to your responsibility to manage time.

Practically speaking, the more file work I did during the early years, the greater the confidence I developed as the degree of file complexity increased. Confidence is a huge part of managing time and achieving success as a litigator. Appearing confident when you are not is also a skill to be carefully honed. This is part of the art of advocacy.

For women, appearing confident can be difficult to achieve. This is because confidence not only comes from within, but is empowered by the positive reinforcement of those around us. The legal profession remains male dominated, and so do the business and social structures created for team-building and networking. These structures often did not align with my interests or available time for networking.

In private practice, opportunities for men to network and socialize far outweigh those available to women. Women are much more likely to be isolated in the workplace. Isolation leads in turn to negativity and self-doubt. This cycle is damaging to the development of both external and internal confidence, which is an essential ingredient of advocacy.

While unintentional, the isolation factor puts women at greater risk than men of being excluded from challenging work and advancement in the courtroom. The availability of social and net-working opportunities within and outside the firm is also a relevant factor affecting work distribution in firms. I found that socializing in a male-dominated profession was not only difficult due to different skills and interests, but also due to personal, gender-related obligations in the home and family. This was further complicated by perceptions surrounding social interaction between men and women. As a young single woman starting practice, I had greater opportunities for socializing and networking, but even then, gender-related interests and activities often diverged, affecting these opportunities. I would say that as a new or even an older member of the firm, it remains important to stay true to who you are, but efforts must still be made to fit in. You may ask what is meant by this esoteric statement.

Productive social and networking interaction should feed, not use up, your energy. Attempting to portray yourself as someone you are not will suck massive amounts of energy away from your limited resources. This, however, does not mean that you should stop working at your lawyerly image. For most, this is a learned behaviour and is particularly important in the early stages of your career. The lawyerly image avoids behaviour that may be interpreted as immature, irresponsible, or uncontrolled. Women's behaviour, emotions, and engagement are too frequently misinterpreted and judged inappropriately. What seemed to work best for me was to save the fun for the safe zone, at least until the professional zone had been carefully gauged and tested. The safe zone is an environment of people who know you well, who are your promoters and true friends. They may be lawyers and friends of the firm. They may not be lawyers at all.

The first or even subsequent impressions created in the "unsafe zone" can be long lasting. You are wise to exercise caution in social environments where colleagues or clients are present. I found the management of my behaviour and communications to be stressful, particularly as a newly minted lawyer. Today, you have the added complexity of social media. Limiting your audience on social media to your safe zone participants would be wise. With time, you will develop greater comfort in social and business networking environments, and your safe zone will expand.

The most powerful tools in your advocate's box consist of self-confidence, caring for yourself, and conquering fears that detract from your ability to progress in your pursuit of professional and personal goals. My confidence as a young lawyer was strengthened by extensive preparation. This involved searching for the truth through fact-finding and establishing an understanding of my opponents, the clients on both sides of the problem, and researching the relevant law.

This has become the underpinning of my work as a trial lawyer. In law school, students are taught to research the law and analyze cases for application to factual scenarios. Law school does not train you in fact-finding and investigation, one of the core, and perhaps most important, skills of a successful litigator. You will wonder how deeply you must dive to know your client, the witnesses, and the case you must meet. To what extent must you yourself review the primary evidence? The answers to these questions are based on your instincts, which are constantly evolving with experience.

At the beginning of my career, I felt I must always dive deep, or I would miss an important fact. One of my mentors tended to look under every rock. While it seemed unproductive at first glance, it was a key to success in many cases. This did occasionally require writing off some time and working very long hours. Unfortunately, there are no shortcuts. The thorough investigation of your case will provide strength and credibility as you speak your truth with conviction as an officer of the court. You will always find the relevant legal principles to weave into your argument. The facts, however, are frequently hidden from sight and mind unless rigorously pursued and carefully presented.

A caring and comprehensive approach to preparation of your cases will always be respected by the client. Involving the client in the preparatory process will also enhance the client's insight into the strengths and weaknesses of the case, which will empower the client to make informed decisions.

It is trite to say that any case should be judged on the facts and the law, not smoke and mirrors. As a young woman, you are well equipped to handle this mission. When facts are well supported by the evidence in a coherent and compelling presentation, whether through the mouths of witnesses or through documents, the smoke and mirrors will dissipate.

While I started my career as a single person without children and invested most of my energy during the first five or more years in the hardcore practice of law, this is not the only approach to take as a newly minted lawyer. For me, it provided a strong springboard for my decision to start my family and my decision to stay in private practice.

I married in 1983 and had my first child at the age of thirty-two. By this time, I had accumulated a number of years in private practice and litigation, sufficient to give me confidence that a partnership was a reasonable possibility. I had hoped the firm would support me during my first pregnancy but it was unknown as there had been no precedent. On my return from a three-month, part-time departure from practice, I could see myself progressing in the profession. This made it easier to decide to have further children. I was motivated to find solutions for the many challenges I would face in combining a demanding career with the role of wife and mother of three children. The confidence I built, which was supported by others around me during my early years of practice, helped carve a path that could merge with family obligations.

My decision to combine practice with childbearing likely delayed partnership. Being invited to the partnership with colleagues who graduated after me was not a big concern then, or even now. My second child was born in 1989, my partnership commenced in January 1990, and my third child was born in October 1991. Despite a three-month statutory maternity leave, I experienced self-imposed guilt, which, in retrospect, should not have entered my mind and should not enter yours. Your decision to have children should be unreservedly supported by your firm.

The decision whether to have children or to delay the start of a family is a very personal one. There are many more options available to women today, in contrast to the eighties or nineties, due to established and longer maternity leaves and services within the community. That said, it is never an easy decision to make.

There will also be times when you make mistakes that could affect your family. For instance, being in a hurry to get to work after attending to child-related obligations and shoving the kids through the door of my home, believing my husband was there to provide childcare, did backfire. When it turned out that he had previously left without me knowing, my resourceful children knew to knock on our neighbour's door to ask for babysitting services. While I am not proud of this, children can be taught to respond to unforeseen mistakes and events of life.

I also missed the odd Christmas concert, school event, and dance recital, but my children were not emotionally damaged by this. When the children were younger, my pattern was not to take work home. This worked for me, but often meant late arrivals home and a pattern of late dinners, as I chose to home-cook meals based on my farm background. The balanced home-cooked meal at 7:00 p.m. or later may well be a healthy alternative to McDonalds, but is not necessary. In today's environment, there are more alternatives to achieve a healthy diet and wise choices, but you must search for what works for you if this is a priority.

In making a choice to continue the tradition of my farm background with late home-cooked dinners, I compromised on time with the kids—personal time, as well as professional time. It can easily be argued that my kids were the "losers" in this choice. My visits with the children were often in the kitchen. I still sometimes question whether the children benefitted from this stubborn pattern.

Now I have three children, four grandchildren, and likely more to come. My children have no memory of missing me at school activities or at extracurricular events. They have good work ethics and are independent. My husband, Del, deserves huge kudos for this; he supported their independence and confidence daily as he ran his home-based business while keeping an eye on them.

We also hired an in-home care provider for the girls during the early years.

Some of my conviction about the power of love in defeating fear and anxiety arises from the recent illness and eventual death of my husband, Del, who suffered stage IV brain cancer. How is this relevant to the practice of law? It often takes a severe tragedy for us to search our inner selves and realize we are heading down a dangerous course. In my case, my hours of work were increasing with age, while my energy and my time with family were decreasing. Del's illness and eventual death in our home shattered our family's world and tested our resilience, but also strengthened us.

I continued to practice law but at a reduced level for the year and a half of Del's illness as we had no idea how things would turn out. We opted for normality to the extent possible. As a family, we chose to believe Del might be in that very small percentage of people who would defeat his illness with good care, love, and attention. While he did not survive, I was able to care for him and support the family. I could have never contemplated this happening to me. The experience of being with Del in our home to his death was very special. One of many symbolic events happened around the time of Del's passing. When he was taken from our home, a great horned owl was seen perched high on the giant spruce tree located in front of the room where he had spent his last days. It remained perched throughout the day, while smaller nesting birds chirped in desperation to scare it away. We had never before spotted this species in our neighbourhood.

Through these experiences, my children and I witnessed the power of love in conquering fear and empowering ourselves to accept the outcome after a battle well fought. I used daily meditation to combat negative emotions and rejuvenate energy during

Del's illness, a technique I also used to address the stress of practice. I continue to find amazing benefits from meditation, like many other lawyers who apply similar techniques to combat the stress of life and work.

It is important to consider how the workplace will address issues that can challenge your personal life, whether these relate to happy events involving pregnancy and family or to caring for loved ones who are ill or dying. Everyone's circumstances are different; no one has a crystal ball. All roads will not lead to a successful co-mingling of the professional and family life, but many will.

I must diverge again to share one of my darker and more challenging times in the profession, following the release in 1990 of the report by Madam Justice Bertha Wilson, *Touchstones for Change: Equality, Diversity and Accountability*. The report addressed gender equality in the legal profession. The CBA, as the national voice for the profession, initiated this important project.

There has always been a degree of hostility toward women in the profession. Often, the hostility manifests itself as passive aggressive behaviour. This was not the case in years past, when men felt free to be "openly" hostile. For example, when women entered the RCMP, the list of applicants grew beyond the demand for positions. When sons of male colleagues were occasionally passed over in favour of female applicants, the men commonly expressed a sense of betrayal toward female candidates, who they believed were not as qualified or fit for police work, and openly berated them.

This attitude followed female appointments to public positions, whether in government or to the Bench. The often-heard comment was "What did she do to get that position?" What a contradiction it was to live and work during this era. "Political correctness" grew, in part, out of this and other forms of disrespectful and aggressive commentary. In my view, political correctness is another term for being respectful to one another. It is mind-boggling how so many bright people could attack a concept built on the development of mutual respect.

Madam Justice Wilson, together with her committee, interviewed many firms and individuals to determine why women were not advancing in the legal profession and to gather information about impending issues. A number of controversial recommendations were made and debated extensively at the annual mid-winter meetings of the CBA in 1993 and 1994.

Of importance is the fact Madam Justice Wilson and her committee chose to push the issues beyond what could be considered "motherhood and apple pie." Had only the obvious been recommended, there would have been no debate and no education on the issues challenging women.

Through these often-hostile debates, a number of recommendations were adopted by the CBA. The controversial topics covered included maternity leave policies and benefits, as well as family and child accommodation to recognize the difficulty of combining a professional career with childrearing. The speeches were passionate and spoke to the economic value of keeping women in the practice.

These debates generated so much hostility in the profession that some members of the bar, and even entire firms, left the CBA. To this day, some of those lawyers and firms remain distant from the CBA, viewing it as a political organization for women's issues and so-called political correctness. The debates also occurred in law firms across the country and lingered on throughout the 1990s. This was likely the most hurtful part of practicing law for me. These discussions often caused anxiety and stress for women, but were necessary to advance the profession. I believe the progress that has been made to improve gender equality and diversity within the profession in Canada was sped up significantly because of the thoughtful and courageous work of then Madam Justice Bertha Wilson and others on her committee.

Today, there is a general acceptance of what were previously considered controversial recommendations, including those related to the value of diversity within the profession. Unfortunately, many challenges still remain.

I repeat, the most powerful antidote for the destructive emotions of fear, anger, and hate is love—love for oneself and for humanity. While your clients may choose a path of escalating conflict, you have a choice in how you conduct your litigation practice. The key to staying grounded, in my view, is to have an unyielding commitment to your core values.

As a young woman practicing law, you are a minority voice in a world governed and managed by a majority that does not always reflect your values. Through careful and detailed investigation of each case undertaken, you will build a strong factual foundation to buttress your advocacy and legal analysis. How you present your case and facts will reflect your core values. The respect for you as a litigator is sure to grow. You are not a shrinking violet, a weak link in the chain, or a distant voice that no one can hear. You have everything you need to be a powerful advocate for change.

Christine Glazer is a senior litigation lawyer in the Saskatoon office of McKercher LLP, whose practice focuses on medical malpractice, personal injury, and disability claims, as well as on administrative law including professional licensing, discipline, and labour law.

THE OTHER SIDE

COURTENAY PHILLIPS
2008 LLB

This all feels so wildly personal, but here we go.

I remember wanting to be a lawyer since I was young. When I told people about my dream, they would tell me I was too nice, too happy, too whatever to be a lawyer. That the hours were tough, that it was a racist and sexist profession, and that I would be miserable if I chose that path. For a lot of years, I listened to what they said. They were people who I respected, who had watched me grow up, and I trusted their opinions.

Then, one day, I realized that I needed to try it out and see how it fit. Honestly, I was pursuing another path, and I had this moment when I saw my future and I just saw myself being really, really unhappy but also being stuck in my unhappiness. I wanted more for myself.

So I went for it and got in. I had only applied to the University of Manitoba, as I am a Winnipegger through and through, and I could not imagine going anywhere else. In a follow-up letter, the university mentioned the Native Law Program at the University of

Saskatchewan, but noted that I would not get credit for the course. I remember going back and forth about how I should spend my summer, because I would be giving up a job that paid well for a course that would not allow me to work, and for which I saw no real advantage.

Eventually, I decided to take the Native Law Program because there was something in my gut that was telling me it was the right decision. It was the right decision. I spent the summer getting to know fellow Indigenous law students from all over Canada. What struck me was how we all worked together and supported one another. How we always included everyone when we hung out, to make sure that no one felt left out and alone. It was a really supportive summer.

The night before the final exam, a friend who was in the program wrote me one of the best emails I have ever received. He told me that out of everyone in our class, he believed that I had the best chance of excelling the next day in our exams. It was an act that still blows me away. We were friends, but we were not that close. We were in competition, but it was the type of competition that defined my life. It was a competition to be the best versions of ourselves, which meant that you challenged those around you to do the same.

This guy, this guy was next level. Because that night was full of doubt and fear, and when I read the email, I was touched that someone believed in me that much and took the time to tell me. It was such a simple act of kindness. Back then, I did not think that I would ever have the kind of character required to send that kind of email to someone who I was in competition with. To this day, it is still something I aspire to be, and its memory still warms my heart.

Because I did so well in the program, I was offered a spot at the University of Saskatchewan's law school. I remember sitting with it for almost a day before calling my parents and letting them know that I had decided to move to Saskatoon in a number of weeks. They were happy for me and supported my decision, as they usually do. I was so happy and full of hope and excited to start the next three years of my life.

Law school would prove to be one of the hardest experiences in my life. I felt so alone and out of place. It was not because I was too nice or too happy. The people that discouraged this path that would test me, maybe in the end they were not wrong to voice their concerns. Maybe I should have seen their warnings in a different light: that the characteristics they did not think fit a lawyer were actually the characteristics that I should have fought for, because they were the parts that would see me through. Either way, there were parts of me that I shut off during law school, and this decision would amplify my experience in law school.

All my life, I have never had problems making friends. Normally, I am a happy, smiling, energetic little spirit who tries to make those around me feel comfortable and at ease. This is not how I was in law school. In law school, I struggled. I struggled to make friends. I spent my long weekends and trips home soaking up all the love and laughter shared with friends who had known me my whole life. These trips fed my soul during the weeks in between, when I found myself alone and unsure of my place in the world.

I grew up in Winnipeg, which has got to be one of the most racist cities in Canada, especially against First Nations people. However, my life in Winnipeg did not prepare me for the racism I experienced in law school. I was surrounded by it in a way that I never had been, and it hurt. I had no way to escape it. Reflecting back, I think I had been protected from the racism in Winnipeg, in part, by being surrounded by people who loved and encouraged me to be the best version of myself. The words and actions I encountered in law school fuelled doubt in myself, doubt that I would be able to survive my profession, and thoughts about whether the family who had listed their concerns about me entering the legal profession were right. It caused me to withdraw and isolate myself more and not shine a light on the happy, shiny parts of my Indigenous self.

I think one of the reasons the racism in law school, especially in the University of Saskatchewan, is so prevalent is because of the advantage Indigenous students receive by taking the Native Law Program. We take one less course if we successfully complete the program. I felt that jealousy and this feeling of misdirected privilege, and I could not understand it. Because there is a curve and the valued articling positions are few, this messed-up competitive environment fuelled racism and a lot of Indigenous students were on the receiving end.

I do not know what caused me to talk about it, maybe it was the simple act of someone asking but I discussed my experiences in law school once. Once to someone I had just met. I made one of those prestigious interviews that my classmates coveted. During the interview, when I was asked what my least favourite thing about law school was, I answered him honestly. I told him my least favourite part was the racism of my fellow law students. The interviewer quickly dismissed my statement and told me that the University of Saskatchewan did not have racist law students. He boasted about the students he had met and worked with and listed their credentials—credentials and accolades that held no weight for me. After dismissing my response, he asked the question a second time. I provided the same answer, but this time I went into detail explaining the racism I had experienced, and how problematic it was, and how I was struggling to understand it. At this point, he started to get mad, and he asked me the question a third time.

Here is where I wish I had ended the interview and left. But I did not leave. I stayed and I provided a rote answer, and I continued on with the interview, faking the answers and feeling like a part of me was dying. I made him and the other people in the room feel more comfortable with my safe answer, and we continued on as if my first two responses had the weight of smoke. I hated myself for it. I hated myself a long time for it.

Afterwards, fellow students asked me how the interview went and I confidently told them I did not get the articling spot. They kindly said that I was mistaken and that they were sure I did not do as bad as I thought. The other students did not dig any deeper, and even if they had, I do not think I would have provided any more detail about why I was so sure I would not be receiving an offer. I was too ashamed of how I had acted to be honest with them, and the confidence I once had to stand my ground if they disagreed with my experience had taken a serious hit. I replayed that moment in the interview and many others in my head so many times, wishing I had acted different, better, and feeling like I had failed in some quiet but major way.

I believed I came away from the experience unscathed, but I did not. I mistakenly believed that that moment taught me how I needed to act, and I quietly silenced my voice in an effort to conform. It will be this moment I will turn over and over in my mind trying to make sense of it. The reason I hope I kept returning to it and others is not because I should have acted differently but because I learnt the wrong lesson. Sometimes when I am in an unfamiliar situation, it is okay not to know how to act; I cannot always be prepared. Sometimes my voice will not be heard but in those moments I still have a choice of how to act and sometimes the right choice is to walk away.

When I applied for law school, I had a fellow classmate who had similar aspirations. He proudly boasted who his references were, people of high social status. When he asked about my references, I simply told him they were written by people who knew me my whole life. He was not prepared for this response and acted embarrassed for me. I was so confused. It reminded me of when I asked one of my references to be my reference, and he actually got embarrassed, like he and his achievements were not enough to get me to where I wanted to go. When he reacted in this manner, I felt a great sadness because my intent had never been to make him feel less than, he was the kind of person I aspired and still aspire to be.

After finishing the Native Law Program and advising the professor that I would happily accept the University of Saskatchewan's offer, I asked the professor about the purpose of the references. According to him, their purpose was simply to make sure a prospective student had three people in their lives who would vouch for them. I left the office confident I had asked the right three people.

I think law school is full of people who are not sure of themselves so in an effort to find grounding they relied on putting others down, and this showed itself in so many ways. I just wished I had held onto that person I was on the day my fellow classmate asked about my references. I was never embarrassed about my response; I was proud that I was surrounded by such inspiring, good people. Later though, later I began to doubt myself and feel embarrassed in an effort to fit.

I feel like that was so much of law school. People putting on an appearance that would have the effect of making me feel less than for lacking knowledge, seeing things differently, or lacking people in my life with a high social status or connections. There was so much hype that there was a right path and that you needed to figure out this path in order to succeed. I wish I had made more time to reflect on my experiences. I wish I had relied on the teachings that had always informed my life, instead of quietly silencing them. The way that things were framed in law school would never work for me; the frame through which we view our world is what nourishes our souls, and I was starving myself.

Honestly, I have to guess what got me through some moments. While throughout my life, I have never had problems making friends, I also was routinely bullied. I think it is those experiences that later gave me the strength to keep plodding through law school. Those experiences taught me strength when I felt alone and persecuted for traits that I loved about myself, in those moments when I did not fit.

I am Cree. The way I learn is by watching. This is why I may have noticed the void. There was no one to watch, to show me the way or at least ways that were possible, who looked or acted like me. I did not see myself in those that were succeeding in this profession. When you do not have anyone to model, you can risk losing yourself. I know I struggled with this in law school, which is one of the reasons it was so hard. I have always had moments in my life where I felt this way. The reason it was more pronounced in law school is that I started to believe that I needed to fit in order to succeed. It led to this weird dichotomy where in law school I tried to enjoy all those pieces of myself that I celebrated and loved because of my mistaken belief that these pieces had to be silenced if I was to succeed as a lawyer. Law school was full of so many sad little celebrations of all those pieces that I loved before I eventually killed them off one by one.

In those dark moments, those moments where I thought I would never fit, I remembered my mom reflecting on her hard times during dental school. She told me that she just needed to pass the courses and try her best and that she had a deep-seated belief that she would be a good dentist. She is an amazing dentist. In those dark moments, I remembered her words and truly believed that I would enjoy being a lawyer and it was okay that I hated law school. I just needed to get through it and get to the other side.

I found my way back to the person I used to be, but it took time. About a year into my law career, the monotony of a simple task drove me to take the first step. Instead of completing a rote task that so many lawyers had done before me, I wrote a poem and I showed up every day for four days. After a week full of poems, a fresh week saw me return to the monotony that had bored me before. Then the best thing happened. The person on the receiving end of my poems demanded their return. For the next two and a half years, I wrote a poem almost every day and received a few in return. He and others encouraged me to play, to be myself; they encouraged me to be myself in a profession where I doubted I could be and still succeed.

I played and was engaged and this trickled into other areas of my career. I enjoyed and was excited by the creativity and the freedom and the encouragement from my colleagues. I let people see me and I got a glimpse that I could be myself and excel at my job. It was such a wonderful feeling and it all started with a simple poem.

During law school, one of my good friends died. It was sudden, and after her funeral, I continued on with my life as if it did not happen. I did not make time to reflect on the impact her death had on me or celebrate what her life meant to me. I think I numbed that pain, like I was numbing a lot of other parts of myself. Once I started waking up, I heard the echo of the other parts of myself that had been silenced. Every now and then, I would test those parts by throwing a stone into the darkness, and I would hear the familiar echo of their ghosts. I started to crave their return. After enough stones, I knew I needed to seek help. I missed those parts, but I could not bring them back with my own efforts. I could not talk about my friend without succumbing to grief. All of the encouragement from my colleagues steadied me to seek help and learn how to grieve. I learned how to sit with my sadness.

The grief therapist encouraged me to find a way to celebrate her life and what she meant to me. Around this time, a friend asked if I could fill in as a boxer for a charity boxing match. The fundraiser was for palliative care, which is where Anna spent some of her last days. I had a month to train and raise as much money as I could so I decided to join and I set to work. Anna brought me back to working out and trying things that scare the shit out of me; there is a willingness to be vulnerable that you cannot escape when you are dealing with grief. I often think back to how much that experience brought me back to life and how grateful I am to Anna for this gift.

There is a closeness in boxing that was both new and old to me. One of the things that motivates me is working with people in whatever context who believe in me, who are in my corner. The boxing coaches worked with me through my thoughts, my fears and my weaknesses as a boxer. They allowed me to be vulnerable and reminded me to keep trying when I was so sore and tired that I did not care if I took the hit and I loved them for it. My coaches were a reminder that I needed to seek out people in my life who inspired me, who made me laugh and who would work with me to become the best version of myself. The boxing ring brought me back to all the lessons I learned while I trained for various sports in my youth. Those lessons and the traits they bring out in me will be ones that I will lean on throughout my career.

During first year, they talked about a fit—that we would find a law firm or articling position that fit. During second year, I finally understood what they meant, because it was so painfully obvious that I was not fitting. I interviewed a lot in many provinces, but there was no fit. During this time, there was a feeling of relief.

Maybe because there was a hope that I could return to the person I once was. There was also a part of me that knew I would be okay and that I would find my way whatever that path looked like.

Finally, in third year, I applied for articles with the Ministry of Justice in Regina, a job I thought held no interest in a city that had no appeal. On the day of the interview, I almost didn't show up. I hate wearing a suit and the thought of suiting up was almost enough to send me back to bed. Then I thought of the four people who had spent their morning driving and who had made time out of their day for me. I thought of how I would explain my decision not to show up to my parents. I had been raised to treat people and the time they give you with respect and I quickly put on a suit and raced off to the interview.

During the interview, there was a moment where something clicked and I wanted the articles. This must have been the moment where I could sense I was fitting in, where I could sense I was being myself and I went for it.

After more than a decade, I have found myself on the other side. I have found and brought life back to those pieces that I silenced in an effort to fit in. I am not sure I will ever fully understand why I spent my life confidently being my own person and why law school and being a lawyer had such an effect on me but the truth of it is that it did.

Ultimately I think it comes down to trusting in myself. There were moments when I completely doubted myself because I did not see myself reflected in the people around me. I still have those moments. In those moments, I have found that I need to dig deep. I need to trust in myself and the gifts and teachings that have helped me become the person I am today. I also have to trust that I will find my place in this world. I need to surround myself with people who lift me up and have faith in me, especially in those moments where I feel lost and alone. I made the mistake in law school and early in my career of believing that those people needed to be law students and lawyers. When I was finding my way back, some of those people were lawyers but really they were people who drew me to them because they had characteristics I wanted to emulate or they gave me the freedom to be myself. What a gift it is to be seen and heard.

Hy hy.

Courtenay Phillips is a Cree woman and a member of Barren Lands First Nation. She is a Crown Counsel with the Ministry of Justice and Attorney General in Saskatchewan. Courtenay is also a member of the appeal body for Nekaneet First Nation.

YOU HAVE *to* STAND
for SOMETHING

THE HONOURABLE
GEORGINA JACKSON
1976 LLB

Dear Jeannie (as your law school friends call you),

On this the eve of your graduation, I want to tell you about the journey you are about to take. 2020 is the best year to do this. This is, after all, a letter of reflection, which is best written in a year that is synonymous with lessons learned from hindsight.

It's pretty weird to be writing to you, my younger self, as though we were two separate persons. But, weirdness aside, it is an oddly satisfying experience to reach back to you and reflect on the forty-four years that lie between us. To continue the mirror metaphor, if I say the *one* right thing as if to you, it may be the same right thing that gives someone in the graduating class of 2020 perspective on an issue important to them. It is also an opportunity to express my gratitude to all the people who have helped me along the way. Through this letter, I hope you will learn how important others will be to you in your life.

It would be remiss of me not to begin by saying you are going to have so much fun. Law was a good choice for you. You will see why.

Before I delve too deeply into your career, I must congratulate you on one decision you are about to make. You are about to marry your classmate Gerald Garnet Tegart, BSc (Civil Engineering) '73, LLB '76, and you will stay married.

Beyond the joy of having a life partner, marrying a law school classmate will be a good thing for the two of you. Insofar as the bounds of the duty of confidentiality permit, you will be able to share in each other's professional lives and participate together in the profession and in the institutions of the profession. It will be personally and professionally rewarding to live your life and your career alongside and with Gerry.

You will, of course, discover three things you need to achieve success in your chosen career: a curiosity about the world, a deep interest in the law or some aspect of it, and mentors. The first will take you to the second and the second will reveal you to the third. You will never have a formal mentor but, as your career progresses, mentors will enter and leave your life, always having an influence. Usually, a mentor will come in the form of someone who is prepared to take a chance on you based on an interest you have displayed or a task you have completed.

Your first mentor will be Dr. Richard Fraser Gosse, who will become the deputy attorney general for Saskatchewan. You and your future husband will be articled to him for part of your articling year. In the summer of 1977, Dr. Gosse will invite you to take on the role of Saskatchewan's Local Secretary to the Uniform Law

Conference of Canada (ULC) and to be part of the Saskatchewan delegation to the ULC that year. In the fulness of time, your involvement with the ULC will lead you to become its president in 1988. During the intervening years, you will participate as part of working groups in the development of legislation for the ULC. You will visit every capital city in Canada, and you will come to know many colleagues from every government in Canada. You will participate in a major reform of the ULC. You will represent the ULC at a UNIDROIT conference in Rome and at the annual conferences of the National Conference of Commissioners on Uniform State Laws in Hawaii and in Washington.

Also in 1977, the Law Reform Commission of Saskatchewan (LRC) will release its report recommending the adoption of a new Personal Property Security Act (PPSA). Hugh Ketcheson, the executive director of the Civil Law Division, with whom you will work, will ask you to "just do something with it." Because you were interested in secured transactions and debtor-creditor law in law school, you will naively say yes. Here will enter someone who will become a second mentor to you: Professor Ron Cuming, who will be, at the time, the chair of the LRC.

Between 1977 and 1981, you will work closely with Prof. Cuming on the PPSA project. In addition to developing the PPSA and related legislation, you will work along with Deanna Koskie on the creation of the new computerized personal property registry. As well, over this time period, many provinces and the federal government will become increasingly interested in developing uniform secured transactions legislation. This will dovetail with your work with the ULC and allow you to participate in various working groups that will ultimately lead to the preparation of the Model Personal Property Security Act. The Lieutenant Governor in Council will proclaim the PPSA into force in 1981.

In 1981, Dr. Gosse will invite you to take on a new role as the master of titles and the executive director of the Property Registration Division for the province, with responsibility for the land titles system, the personal property registry and the Chief Surveyor's Office—a legal and management position. Do not be daunted by the demands of this task—200 employees; a major budget; and a significant source of revenue for the provincial government, a completely manual system, which will often be behind. The legal aspects of the job too will be challenging, but you will be up to it. At the time, the master of titles position will still have the status of a s. 96 judge, and your decisions will be appealable to the Court of Appeal. You will work with many dedicated men and women across the province, and again you will be invited to be part of a national working group focusing on how to improve land and personal property registration systems. You will write several manuals explaining the workings of the land titles system.

While you are serving as master of titles, Dr. Gosse will ask you to assume a leadership role in studying the province's construction liens law, which will allow you to deepen your interest in the connection between law and business. It will lead to the preparation of a major report; a new Builders' Lien Act; and the opportunity to work with an architect in Regina, Kirk Banadyga, and leaders of the bar like Gary Semenchuk and Ted Zarzeczny. The latter will go on to be a judge of the Court of Queen's Bench.

As an aside, it is important to mention that almost immediately after being called to the Saskatchewan Bar, you will take an interest in continuing legal education. Your first foray into the world of lawyers' education will be setting and marking the bar admission course statutes examination. As you assume your work on the PPSA, you will begin teaching about the new system. Such work will continue when you become the master of titles and expand to include land law. Then, a senior member of the bar, Jack Safian, will ask you to become involved with the Saskatchewan branch of the Canadian Bar Association (CBA) to help organize the first mid-winter meeting for the branch. This will be the beginning of your lifelong interest in organizing legal seminars and teaching about the law. Your interest in continuing legal education will pair up with your interest in law reform at several points in your career, most notably through the ULC and, later, when you become a member of the LRC. You will become the president of the Saskatchewan branch of the CBA in 1987, again having the opportunity to represent the province at national and international events.

In 1988, Carl Wagner, a lawyer from MacPherson Leslie & Tyerman (MLT), will ask if you would like to continue your interest in property systems but do so from a solicitor's position in that firm. While you will only spend a few years at MLT, it will be an important and enjoyable part of your career.

1991 will be a significant year. You will receive a phone call from the Hon. J. Gary Lane, then minister of justice and attorney general for Saskatchewan, advising that you have been appointed Queen's Counsel. You will chair a committee organizing a national mid-winter meeting of the CBA, which will take place in Regina. In the spring, you will become a partner at MLT. In the fall, you will receive a phone call from the minister of justice for Canada, the Hon. Kim Campbell, asking if you would accept an appointment to the Court of Appeal for Saskatchewan. Minister Campbell will call you on September 9, 1991, which (as you know) is your birthday. It also happens to be the birthday of the Hon. Ed Bayda, who in 1991 will be chief justice of Saskatchewan, and with whom you and your friends will celebrate on the day of your appointment and almost every September 9 thereafter (along with his wife Lorraine Bethel) until his untimely passing in 2010.

With the phone call from Minister Campbell begins your long career as a judge of the Court of Appeal for Saskatchewan. It is a cloistered life, but your interest in continuing legal, and then judicial, education will continue. A colleague, the Hon. William Vancise, will encourage you to become bilingual, which will allow you to teach in both official languages. French language study will also lead to an immersion stage at the Quebec Court of Appeal and the University of Montréal in 1998, and again at McGill University in 2006–2007, where you will be able to teach a course on International Comparative Perspectives on Judicial Ethics. It will also lead to an involvement with L'Association des juristes d'expression française de la Saskatchewan.

Recommended by the Hon. Lynn Smith of the British Columbia Supreme Court, you will supplement your judicial life with an associate judicial director position with the National Judicial Institute (NJI), organizing and teaching national conferences for federally appointed judges for over six years along with the Hon. Dolores Hansen, then the executive director of the NJI. This will lead you to the first international conference organized by the International Conference of Judicial Training in Israel and to the task of organizing the second such conference in 2004 in Ottawa, alongside George Thomson, the executive director at the time. Over 80 countries will be represented at the conference.

In 1998, the Canadian Judicial Council and the Canadian Superior Court Judges Association will jointly issue the *Ethical Principles for Judges* (the *Ethical Principles*), which will call for the establishment of a national advisory committee on judicial ethics. Once established, this committee will be responsible for giving informal, confidential advice to judges contemplating what to do with a problem of an ethical nature. The Hon. Ron Barclay, then of the Court of Queen's Bench, will invite you to represent

Saskatchewan on the committee. You will be a member of that committee for a number of years, ultimately becoming the co-chair.

Your work with the National Advisory Committee will lead to invitations to teach in many places in Canada and around the world: Italy, Germany, France, the Philippines, Japan, Turkey, and the United States. Often, one invitation will lead to the next.

To show you how interconnected the world is, and how the most unexpected invitations can lead to adventures, I will tell you about your first professional trip to Italy. You will be in Montréal in 1998 when the Federal Commissioner for Judicial Affairs will need someone on short notice to represent the Canadian judiciary at the European Judicial School's Spring Conference, taking place in Rimini, Italy. That first invitation will lead to a second invitation to the same organization's 1999 conference in Bertinoro, Italy. This second invitation will come just after you become a member of the National Advisory Committee on Judicial Ethics, and your talk this time will be about the work of that committee. A delegate to the conference, Judge Barbara Krix, a district court judge in Itzehoe, Germany, will become interested in the topic. This will lead to the opportunity for you to work with her on a seminar for German judges at the Deutsche Richterakademie in Trier, Germany, which you will visit many times.

One of Judge Krix's faculty at the Deutsche Richterakademie, Professor Yasutomo Morigiwa, will invite you to give two lectures in Japan—also on the *Ethical Principles*—and to join him on a panel at Stanford University in California.

The second trip to Italy will also introduce you to Judge Antoine Garapov, a member of the French judiciary, and at the time, the head of L'institut des hautes études sur la justice (IHEJ). As a result of that encounter, a doctoral student from the University of Paris II who will be working at IHEJ then, Harold Epineuse, will be encouraged by Judge Garapov to come to Canada to meet with you to discuss judicial ethics. This encounter will lead to many speaking engagements in France, including an appearance before the Cabannes Committee studying the utility of written ethical principles to France's judiciary in the context of the aftermath of the Outreau affair. In 2020, Louis Epineuse, a law student in France and the son of M. Epineuse, will come to Regina to spend a few weeks with you at the Court of Appeal to learn about common law appellate courts.[1] Louis will not have been born yet when his father comes to Canada to visit you and talk about judicial ethics. You may be thinking that, if you were writing to me, you would say it truly is time to retire.

One day in 2010, you will receive a phone call from the Hon. Adèle Kent, judge of the Court of Queen's Bench for Alberta and then the executive director of NJI, asking if you could come to Ottawa on short notice and give a presentation about the *Ethical Principles* to a large group of Moroccan judges and judicial school administrators. The group will be visiting Washington at the request of the American Bar Association Rule of Law Initiative when they will express an interest in learning about Canada's system so as to compare it to the American system. This invitation will lead to a further invitation to help develop a judicial ethics training program for new Moroccan judges. You will visit Rabat on two occasions, when you will work with the administrators of the judges' school. All of you will work primarily in your second language of French.

Your connection with NJI will be a rich and fruitful one. Asked to become NJI's liaison with a sister organization, the Canadian Institute for the Administration of Justice (CIAJ), you will become deeply involved with it, first serving on its board of directors,

---

1   Due to the COVID-19 pandemic, Louis was not able to come to Canada in 2020. We are still hoping he will make it sometime in his career.

leaving for a while, and then coming back to join its executive, where you will serve for eight years, becoming its president in 2016.

Another connection you will make while working with NJI will be with Dr. Janis Sarra, a thinker and writer about all matters pertaining to the financial health of commercial entities. In 2003, Dr. Sarra will establish the *Annual Review of Insolvency Law* (ARIL). She will invite you to join the first board of directors, allowing you to maintain an interest in the intersection of business and commercial law and insolvency. Dr. Sarra will involve you in the ARIL seminars, expanding your interest in the fascinating world of corporate insolvency.

One of the tasks of a table officer with the CIAJ is to organize national annual conferences on significant issues facing the administration of justice. Working with Mme Michèle Moreau, the executive director of the CIAJ, the then president, Beth Symes, Professor Marilyn Poitras, and Dr. Maria Campbell, you will have the privilege of organizing Canada's first national education program for judges and lawyers on "Aboriginal Peoples and the Law." Over a two-year period, you will be able to work with a large planning committee with an equal number of Indigenous and non-Indigenous leaders. The program will have many spin-offs, including the expansion of the CIAJ's mandate to include Indigenous issues and perspectives as part of its regular programming.

A deep and abiding connection with Québec, which you will begin to develop in 1998, will give you many close friends. One of them, the Hon. Louise Otis of the Court of Appeal of Québec, will also establish a professional connection. Madame Otis has an extraordinary gift with respect to mediation. She will ask you to spend time thinking and writing about the intersection of judicial ethics and judicial mediation. This too will lead to more opportunities to teach.

Now, it is the time for us to talk about gender and success in the law. As you will see from the above, your gender will not be an impediment to a full and happy career. But you will know now—now as of 1976—that you have already begun to think about the intersection of law and gender.

I know you have participated in some of the first meetings of the Women in Law group. You have seen how few women participated. Some are too busy, some do not think it necessary, and some are afraid of being labelled feminists (seen to be a negative) and activists (also seen to be a negative) and being ostracized as a result (clearly a negative!). At the meetings you attended, the issues were about getting jobs and how to manage a career and a family. Over the years, little will change in that regard except that, as time goes on, more and more young men will also become concerned about the latter issue.

Issues around gender will be important to you throughout your career. The primary issues will be about sharing of power. You will speak about these issues—a lot. Like many others, you will be labelled a feminist—sometimes as a negative and sometimes not. Even as a negative, it will be worth it. After all, you have to stand for something. You will be part of the CBA President's Committee on Gender Equity. You will participate in the work of the CBA that will lead to the Bertha Wilson report *Touchstones of Change*. You will be part of the Law Society's Committee on Gender and Diversity. As a judge, you will be part of a similar committee for the Canadian Superior Court Judges Association, and you will have the opportunity to serve as a board member of the International Association of Women Judges. You will play a role in developing judges' courses pertaining to gender and diversity. As a judge, you will see a great deal of change. Even when you look back at the previous paragraphs, you will see that in the beginning all of your mentors were men because there were few women in positions of authority. Then, slowly, women will come to wield greater influence.

Over the course of your career, so many men and women will work to improve the equality of women. There will be a number of milestones: the enactment of the *Charter of Rights and Freedoms*, the release of Bertha Wilson's report, and the addition of "equality" as a judicial ethical principle, to mention only a few. Organizations like the Canadian Bar Association and the Law Society of Saskatchewan will be committed to working on questions of diversity and equality.

But in 2020, there is still more to be done, and it is important to be vigilant. Only a small number of women occupy positions of real political power, civically, provincially, nationally, or internationally. Often women who try for the brass ring are haunted and trolled by those who make their very gender the issue, in pointed and degrading ways. Domestic violence, sexual harassment, and sexual crimes against women continue to be significant issues in 2020. Many women live in poverty. For women in vulnerable minority groups, these issues are considerably magnified. At this moment in history, there is also the very real fear that, without male and female leaders committed to gender equality, women will lose what ground they have gained.

What can be done? As with every complex challenge, there is no one solution. It is important to be an advocate for systemic change. Supporting the efforts of the organizations and others working toward greater equality is important. However, you will see from your own career how important individual leadership can be. You will try to live your life walking both of these lines—acting as an advocate for change within the equality agenda when it is appropriate in your career to do so, but also trying to make an individual difference and opening doors as others did for you.

As you will come to see, you will be given the opportunity to work for over forty years with many articling students, and serve as a principal to many of them. Working with these young people will leave an indelible imprint on your life. Many of them will become lifelong friends. You will write many letters of reference. Some of your former articling students will become law professors and one, Lauren Wihak, will begin organizing seminars for the CIAJ.

Enough about you. It is time for me to say how grateful I am to all my teachers, of whom only some have been mentioned in this letter.

I'm going to sign off now. Lord willing, I will write to you in twenty years and let you know how we're doing.

Maybe someday, you could write me a letter.

Sincerely,
Your much older, but only marginally wiser, self.

Georgina Jackson is a judge of the Court of Appeal for Saskatchewan, where she has served for over 30 years. She still believes in teaching, mentoring, and giving back.

A HUMANIST VIEW

GWEN J. GRAY, KC

BA(USask), LLB (USask), LLM (Cornell)

Letter to Younger Self,

From my current vantage point at the end of my seventh decade, I am amazed I decided to become a labour lawyer even before attending law school. I am even more impressed that I was able to achieve this goal.

My determination to specialize in labour law arose mainly from my involvement in the women's movement of the 1970s. However, before attending university, I possessed a feminist bent, having been a keen observer of women in my family and community. My mother was an intelligent woman with unfulfilled ambitions rather typical of the post-war lives of many women.

I started university in 1970. As part of the Baby Boomer generation, I benefitted greatly from the expansion of universities, student loans, and programs like Opportunities for Youth (OFY), which made university education possible for many working- and middle-class kids. University education was becoming a right, not a privilege. At the same time, society was undergoing a great deal of social unrest. Many progressive movements emerged in the 1960s and 1970s, including the civil rights movement, women's movement, anti-war movement, New Left movements, and environmental movement. It was an exciting time to be a university student.

In my undergraduate years, I participated in the Women's Centre, part of the Students' Union at the University of Saskatchewan, and the women's liberation movement, a group of students, professors, artists, and workers who met regularly for supper at one member's home. She was a fine host and cook, and we all benefitted from her kindness and intellect. Robin Morgan, famous for her 1970 anthology, *Sisterhood Is Powerful*, graced us with her presence at one of our regular gatherings. Through participation in both groups, I became immersed in feminist politics, a somewhat natural extension of my childhood observations concerning the general position of women in the family and society.

From there, I participated in the formation of the Canadian Women's Calendar Collective (CWCC) in 1972. One of my sociology professors returned from a trip to the United States with an American "Herstory" calendar. I was impressed by the calendar and its method of conveying historical information about women. A group of five women, mostly sociology students, formed the CWCC and, with OFY grants in hand, began to chronicle women's history in Canada in a similar manner. The Women's Press in Toronto, another women's collective, published the first edition of the Canadian version of "Herstory" in 1974. The CWCC continued to publish an annual calendar until 2015. I participated in the first two volumes.

I had the pleasure of meeting and working with the Women's Press in Toronto. It was quite a transformative experience. Of course, there was a lot to learn about book publishing. In addition, the women at the Women's Press had lots to say about the content of the calendar. They were concerned it failed to focus on working-class women, marginalized women, Indigenous women, and other racialized women, and brought forward many examples of women who should be included in the calendar. I must admit I did not expect this reaction at such a critical time in the calendar's production. But it was an honest and important critique that needed to be addressed.

During my time in Toronto in the summer of 1973, I also was exposed from the sidelines to international solidarity work following the CIA-supported coup ousting Salvador Allende in Chile. Various international solidarity groups in Toronto rallied in support of Chileans and began organizing government and other support to help Chileans escape the viciousness of the Pinochet junta. I was totally ignorant of the events in Chile and had to ask my friends if the coup was a good or bad thing! Thank goodness, they recognized my naïveté and patiently educated me about the coup and the significance of the efforts Canada needed to make to save the lives of many Chileans.

While in Toronto, I also attended my first picket line. The Canadian Textile and Chemical Workers' Union (CTCU), a Canadian union headed by Madeleine Parent and Kent Rowley, successfully organized employees at Artistic Woodwork. They faced a hostile employer in bargaining a first collective agreement, mainly over issues related to management rights. The picket line was marred by police violence on a daily basis, resulting in the arrest of many strikers and their supporters. The strike was held for four months, from August 21 to December 5, 1973. A description of the strike can be found in Ian Milligan's paper "'The Force of All Our Numbers': New Leftists, Labour, and the 1973 Artistic Woodwork Strike."[1]

---

1   Ian Milligan, "'The Force of All Our Numbers': New Leftists, Labour, and the 1973 Artistic Woodwork Strike" (2010) 66 Labour/Le Travail 37 (JSTOR).

I found the experience frightening and eye-opening. Having grown up in rural Saskatchewan, I had no contact with and limited knowledge of trade unions, even though we lived close to Bienfait, where, in 1931, striking coal miners led a march in Estevan that resulted in a confrontation between the strikers and RCMP. The event is known (inappropriately) as the Estevan Riot. Armed RCMP officers killed three of the striking miners. Annie Buller, a political activist and member of the Workers' Party of Canada, and one of the women featured in "Herstory," organized support for coal miners and was jailed after the confrontation.

After this crash course in progressive politics and working-class issues, I returned from Toronto with an understanding of the need to merge working-class issues with feminism, although much debate ensued within the CWCC, the broader women's movement, and the New Left on how that would be achieved. I was struggling with the question of how to move the feminist agenda forward. What would make the biggest difference to the lives of women, particularly working women? This issue continues to be debated among progressive people, but is now addressed in a broader sense, incorporating LBGTQ2S+ issues, and includes much more informed discussions of the impacts of race, Indigenous rights, and environmental rights on equality.

In the fall of 1974, I participated in a strike support group, comprised largely of faculty and students at the university, for members of the University Employees' Union, a direct affiliate of the Canadian Labour Congress (Local 54), who were on strike against the University of Saskatchewan over pay issues for clerical, cleaning, and food service workers. Inflation at the time was running around 18 percent, and some of the largely female staff's wages were less than the minimum wage required by law. Elaine van Oder, the union's first female president, led the strike. I admired the way in which the union put forward its collective bargaining agenda to improve the wages and working conditions for women (across-the-board wage increases, demands for child care, fairer promotion processes, etc.). Glen Makahonuk wrote an excellent paper on the strike, entitled "In Union Is Strength: The University of Saskatchewan Employees' Union Strike."[2]

As a result of this experience, I learned about the roles of lawyers and courts in supporting or hindering trade union struggles. Shortly afterward, I became involved in the National Association of Women and the Law (NAWL), which formed in March 1974. At the end of the 1974–75 term, largely as a result of these experiences and after meeting a group of progressive law students, I enrolled in law school for the upcoming term with the goal of becoming a labour lawyer. I don't think many people took my ambition seriously. My then partner's mother thought I would be better off to stay home and take in boarders!

Academic mentors also played a significant role in my university education. A female sociology professor took me under her wing and provided me with work as a research assistant in her field of sociology of education. She encouraged thoughtful debate, and was part of a group of women students and professors who met informally to discuss gender and other political issues of the day, including the touchy subject of the Americanization of Canadian university faculty. She was one of the transplanted American academics and pushed back against my nationalistic tendencies. Two other faculty members were also pivotal mentors. They imparted a humanist view of the world both in academics and in their daily lives.

---

2   Glen Makahonuk, "In Union Is Strength: The University of Saskatchewan Employees' Union Strike" in *Saskatchewan History*, 48(1) (Saskatoon: Saskatchewan Archives Board, 1996) 30.

In law school, professors encouraged me to stretch myself academically, and provided practical experiences and exposure to trade unions.

Later, when I attended Cornell University for my graduate degree, I was lucky to study under many excellent professors, all of whom provided useful feedback and encouragement.

Looking back, I feel very fortunate to have had such strong mentors who supported me and helped direct my education. I have tried to "pay it back" by mentoring young lawyers and doing what I can to help their careers advance.

So, the question at this stage of my life is whether I succeeded in advancing the feminist/progressive cause through the practice of labour law. This is a complicated question. Certainly, I think I brought a feminist/progressive approach to analyzing issues and benefitted greatly from working with wonderful lawyers and trade union representatives who were keenly aware of feminist and working-class issues.

With hindsight, though, I make a number of observations. First, in a private litigation practice, you rarely choose the files you will litigate. While you can explain the significance of a feminist, human rights, or trade union issue to your clients, it is up to them to decide if they will pursue the case. This is why organizations such as the Legal Education and Action Fund (LEAF) are so important. LEAF can harness the financial and intellectual resources necessary to pursue litigation advancing feminist and progressive causes. There are other examples of collective approaches to litigation. For instance, in the *Vriend* case, which established human rights protection for the LGBTQIA2S+ community, my former colleagues at Chivers Greckol & Kanee in Edmonton worked with a group of like-minded lawyers and academics to pursue the case up to the

Supreme Court[3]. Organizations such as the Canadian Association of Labour Lawyers (CALL), a national union-side labour law organization, provide a forum for developing strategic approaches to litigation, particularly Charter cases affecting trade unions. In Canada, although we lack a strong tradition of public interest law such as exists in the United States through various organizations like the ACLU, we are evolving a more collaborative approach to litigation concerning important legal issues on behalf of women, workers, and all vulnerable groups. In this context, it is important for law schools to provide students opportunities to interact with and assist vulnerable and underrepresented communities.

The second insight arising from my experience is that in order to advance feminist, human rights, and working-class issues, support for the cause needs to come from the affected community. While you may be the spokesperson, the cause belongs to the community. This lesson was brought home to me during UFCW's strike at Lakeland Feeders in Brooks. The strength and determination of the union representatives and the workers, which included refugee workers from Sudan and Somalia, was key to any litigation success. The union took a long-term view of its organizing efforts in the community. It opened an office and provided broad supports to the workers over a long period. The office provided a community centre workers could rely on for help with work and day-to-day issues. Once organized, the union aggressively pursued litigation before the Labour Relations Board to establish representation rights for the workers during the negotiation of the first collective agreement, a crucial period in maintaining employee support. As expected, it took a lengthy strike in order for the workers to obtain a first agreement. During the strike, I and other members

---

3   *Vriend v Alberta*, [1998] 1 SCR 493, 1998 CanLII 816.

of my firm worked 17 days straight, driving between Brooks and Calgary to deal with constant Labour Relations Board and court applications. An agreement was eventually reached. This achievement was remarkable both for the workers and the union, and only came about through their ability to build solidarity among various groups and the community.

The third insight is personal. Work of this nature takes a toll on you and your family. It is intense, stressful, and unpredictable, sometimes in the extreme. During the Lakeside strike, I would frequently wake up to phantom rings on my cellphone. I neglected my parental responsibilities, leaving my teenage daughter to fend for herself in Edmonton while I worked on the strike. It took some time to come down from the intensity of the workload.

Would I choose the same career if I was starting out today? I always tell young people that a law degree will always stand you in good stead no matter what career path you choose. There are many opportunities in the private and public sectors for lawyers. Even if you decide not to practice law, you have training and knowledge that will help you in any career. Knowing what I know now, I probably would choose to work in labour policy, similar to the work I did in the Policy and Planning Branch of the Department of Labour under the NDP in the late 1990s. Policy work within government provides opportunities to contribute to long-lasting changes in labour and employment laws. I had the pleasure of witnessing such changes first with the NDP government in Saskatchewan from 1994 to 2003 and again with NDP government in Alberta from 2016 to 2019. Both governments made significant changes to labour, employment, occupational health and safety, and workers' compensation laws. Measures were taken to reduce poverty, especially childhood poverty. The quality and accessibility of childcare was improved. Human rights laws were expanded and enforcement of human rights was improved. While litigation can shine a light on important social issues, overall, it is not as effective a tool for achieving social and economic justice as political and governmental action.

Could a different career have led me to greater successes in forwarding a feminist, human rights, and working-class agenda? I think it is quite probable. However, I had an interesting and engaging career. I met many fine people, worked with wonderful lawyers and legal assistants, and have lifelong friends resulting from my work. And retirement is not the end of the story—there is the time and many opportunities to contribute to important progressive issues.

Gwen Gray, KC, BA, LLB, LLM, is retired from law practice. She lives in Edmonton and enjoys visiting her two grandchildren in the Yukon. She consults on labour relations matters and is active in the Alberta NDP.

I DID *a* LOT *of* READING *at the* HOCKEY RINK

JESSIE BUYDENS

2006 LLB, 2008 LLM

When I was approached to be involved in this project, I wasn't sure how qualified I was to give advice, to myself or anyone else. As you'll see from the sections below, a lot of my career has happened by coincidence. I've been very "go with the flow" about the whole process. I didn't have a lifelong plan to be a lawyer. I didn't tailor my education to achieve an end goal of being a lawyer. So, with that reservation out in the open, I hope that you find the "wisdom" below to be at least somewhat useful.

My most important pieces of advice to my former self or young women entering a profession are:

HAVE FAITH IT WILL ALL WORK OUT

When I was a kid, I never had any expectation that I would be a lawyer. I didn't aspire to be a lawyer; no one in my family was a lawyer. I don't think I even knew a lawyer.

I got pregnant when I was fifteen years old. My son was born when I was sixteen. I know that a lot of people didn't think I would even graduate high school, let alone go on to a professional career one day. They were wrong. I graduated on time, at seventeen years old. I went straight into the College of Arts and Science at the University of Saskatchewan. After a few undergraduate degrees, I decided I wanted to do my master's. I applied to the master's program in the Department of Sociology. When I went in to drop off my application the secretary asked me what other schools I was applying to. The answer was none; it hadn't occurred to me to apply anywhere else. I knew I wanted to do my master's at the University of Saskatchewan. Despite that, she had got me thinking: What was my backup plan?

I didn't have one.

As I was leaving the school, I walked past a poster advertising the LSAT. I had never before contemplated going to law school, but it seemed like as good a backup plan as any. So I signed up last minute and wrote the LSAT. Turned out I was good at standardized testing, and I scored really well. At that point I hadn't heard back from the sociology department about my master's application. I decided to apply to the College of Law at the University of Saskatchewan.

Eventually, I received an acceptance letter from the College of Law. I had five days to put down a $100 deposit to secure my spot. I waited until the fifth day. I still hadn't heard back from the Department of Sociology so I put down my deposit for law school. I'm super cheap, so once I put down that deposit there was no turning back. I completed my law degree (LLB 2006) and went on to do my master's in law (LLM 2008). So everything worked out in the end.

During law school, I had some challenges being a single mom. It limited my study time and the time that I could spend hanging out in the library between classes with the other students. I would pick my son up from school and we would do homework together until he was done his work. Then we'd spend the evening at his sports or just hanging out, and I would finish my work after he went to bed. This is a work pattern that carried over into my life after law school until he was old enough to take care of himself.

It was also hard financially being a single mom going to law school. I worked two or three part-time jobs while I was in school. I tried to only work when my son was at his dad's. As much as possible, I structured my schedule so that work and school work would get done when he was at his dad's, sleeping, or otherwise occupied. I did a lot of reading at the hockey rink during his practices.

During the second year of law school, everyone started the hunt for articles. I didn't get any. The weekend before the interviews with the big firms in Saskatchewan, my dad was in a motorcycle accident and broke his neck. I dropped everything to go to the hospital. I spent time tracking down my siblings to let them know what had happened, as they were both out of town with sports. I didn't go to any interviews that week as I was too preoccupied with my dad's injury. He ended up making a full recovery and life went back to normal.

After all the big firms had hired, I kept looking at smaller firms, putting out resumés, getting rejection letters. I also applied for my master's in law. I was accepted into the program, during which I had the opportunity to teach a few lectures for my supervisor. I loved teaching. I loved the atmosphere in the graduate students' office. I ultimately completed my thesis in the area of sexual exploitation of children and youth through the sex trade. While I was working on my thesis, a posting was released for a clerkship with the provincial court, with a start date only a few months away. I applied, got the job and started clerking within a few months. Again, everything worked out.

Had I been accepted into my master's in sociology, I never would have gone to law school. Had I gotten an articling position during second year, I never would have done my master's in law, and I never would have clerked with the provincial court. All of which were amazing experiences.

My time with the provincial court was some of the most memorable work I did in my early career. I worked with exceptional judges and learned more than I could have imagined. This opportunity provided me with a huge head start on my career, as I wanted to practice in criminal law. The clerkship allowed me to see the inner workings of the court. I was able to observe many different lawyers and the styles and strategies they employed to represent their clients. While it was extremely stressful when I didn't get articles in second year, I wouldn't change anything about the trajectory I took.

After my time with the court, I started work at my current firm, Scott Phelps & Mason. As a single mom I was worried about how I would fare at a law firm, trying to balance my career and parenting my son. During my interview, I asked about work expectations. One of the partners told me that he pencilled all his kid's sports into his planner at the start of every season so that he didn't miss them for work. I was told the firm believed that family was important. I wouldn't be expected to miss games or tournaments so long as my work got done and the clients were happy. This was more than just the partners trying to sell the firm; it was the truth. I was able to structure my work schedule to be at all my son's events. I'm not sure I would have had that same freedom at a bigger firm, the type of firm you're encouraged to see as a marker of success when you're a law student.

Now, seventeen years after I graduated with my LLB, and fifteen years after starting at Scott Phelps & Mason, I'm still here. It wasn't the path I planned or how I expected to end up when I started law school, but I landed in a place that I fit, where I'm happy to be. I'm glad things didn't go as planned; they went as they needed to and everything worked out.

SEEK MENTORSHIP–
PROFESSIONAL AND PERSONAL

Mentorship is a much-discussed topic today. People talk about the importance of mentorship, and professional organizations host mentorship events and meet-and-greets between senior practitioners and newcomers to the profession. Truthfully, the importance of a good mentorship relationship cannot be understated. This is true from both sides of the equation: you can learn and grow by being mentored and by mentoring someone else.

Throughout my life and my career, I have had the privilege of being mentored by some amazing people. Many of my most influential mentors have been women, although I have had male mentors as well.

Professionally, one of my most important people was Trish Monture. I met Trish the first season our boys played hockey together, back when I was doing my law school readings at the rink. Those days at the rink grew into an irreplaceable friendship. Trish listened to me vent through law school. She encouraged me to do my master's when I did and acted as an independent study advisor to me throughout that process. Trish hooked me up with my first teaching job at the university. She encouraged me to be true to myself while looking for articles and deciding how and where I wanted to practice.

She was also my friend. We watched hockey together for years. Our boys grew up together. We watched football and ate Chinese food. We talked, we laughed, we listened. The relationship I had with Trish was so very important to my professional development. I often think of her when I need guidance or inspiration.

Her journey inspired me to want to make positive social changes through my legal education. Trish was an amazing scholar and teacher. She opened doors for me, and she exposed me to different perspectives and new ideas—things that I hadn't known or contemplated before I knew her. She taught me about her culture and traditions. This encouraged me to appreciate what I had and where I came from, while also being able to empathize with others even if they came from a different background. Trish taught me to value differences.

I have also had the benefit of support and guidance from senior female lawyers throughout my career. The first mentor I matched with at a first-year female mentoring event is still someone I reach out to with questions on occasion. I have also benefitted from general advice and support from senior practitioners. Tips on courtroom etiquette or suggestions on how to deal with a case from experienced members of the bar are invaluable.

Personally, my grandma was the most influential figure in my formative years. She was strong, fierce, and independent. She always spoke her mind and encouraged me to do so as well. She was opinionated, and she did not conform to social ideals or expectations. She baked amazing cookies, but she wasn't a stereotypical grandma. She had served in the navy as an ambulance driver, and she played sports. She taught me that I could do or be anything I put my mind to. She defiantly empowered me to forge my own path and follow my heart, regardless of what society said about how girls should behave. Much of who I am today is the result of my grandma's influence.

I have also had some amazing male mentors. My principal at the court was a male judge. He provided me with unlimited guidance and knowledge. He was thoughtful and caring. He arranged for meaningful placements during my secondments outside of the court during my articles. I still go to him for advice when making career decisions, and he always has insightful wisdom to share.

The partner from the job interview who told me I would never have to miss any of my son's events has been a rock throughout my career. He is always there to listen to my concerns, to bounce ideas off, and to listen to me vent when needed. I know that he always has my back. There have been times when other lawyers have challenged me and I have been able to deal with that knowing he is always on my team and always in my corner.

Athletically, I have been coached by amazing men and women. I have participated in sport my whole life and competed at an elite level as an adult. Coaches, although maybe not technically mentors, provide important life skills. Coaches teach you to thrive in the face of adversity—to challenge yourself to get past the point that you believe you're ready to quit. Good coaches can inspire dedication and commitment. They encourage personal growth and help you develop as a person. Good coaches and mentors can be life-changing influences.

Appreciate your mentors. Tell them you value them, make sure they know how they have affected your life in a positive way.

GIVE BACK TO THE COMMUNITY–
INSPIRE GIRLS

Given how much I have benefitted from the mentorship of amazing women, I feel very strongly about giving back to my community through involvement with young women and girls. To this end, I have coached girls' sports for years. I was also a Girl Guide leader. As I mentioned in the last section, I get as much out of being a coach and a leader as I do out of the relationships wherein I have been mentored.

I have coached dozens, maybe hundreds, of young women in the sport of rugby. I have had the pleasure of watching them grow and mature throughout high school. Some of the girls move on after high school and I run into them randomly years later. I love hearing how they're doing and where their lives have taken them.

Many of the girls I have coached have joined our senior women's team after high school, so I've gotten to follow them as they become adults. I've been to their weddings, met their babies, and watched them succeed professionally. I really value the relationships I have with the young women I have had the opportunity to coach.

Some of the girls I have coached have risen through the ranks of sport to represent Canada internationally in competition. Regardless of where they end up, I am so proud to have had a part in their development, however big or small it may have been.

The girls I deal with through Girl Guides are younger than the girls I coach. It's a different environment, with more variety in the activities we do together. My fellow leaders and I are able to teach the girls about women throughout history, feminism, and female empowerment. We also get to play games, do crafts, perform skits, and sing songs. I love watching the girls playing their favourite games or expressing themselves creatively through crafts, songs, and skits. Watching them gaining confidence and feeling comfortable being themselves is so rewarding.

We also get to go camping, which presents an opportunity to get to know the girls better than I can during weekly meetings. Some girls open up about struggles they are having at school or at home. Once a relationship is established, they can express their hopes and fears. As a leader, I can be a neutral party who just listens without judgment. I believe that for some girls, this is a very needed outlet. I am honoured to be able to be there for the girls.

Professionally, I try and mentor women in the legal profession whenever possible as well. This can be as simple as trying to be there to answer questions when younger women need some guidance. It can be more in depth, in the form of teaching practicum students. I try and make myself available to younger women in the profession whenever I can. I want to return the benefit that I have received from senior practitioners to the young women entering our profession.

One problem I see is that sometimes, young female lawyers feel a need to align themselves with male lawyers. There seems to be a misconception that male lawyers have more clout or are better professional mentors. In reality, people of both genders can be great mentors but only women can guide you in the unique challenges that we, as women, face throughout our legal journey.

Men may be able to understand sexism intellectually. They may know it is not okay when clients call women "honey," "darling," or "dear." They can step up and tell colleagues that sexist jokes aren't funny or that women's ideas are just as important as men's. This is all important, and I appreciate the men who take these steps and assist in the fight for equality in the office, the partnership, or the courtroom.

The reality, though, is that men can never understand these things emotionally. They can empathize, but they will never truly know how disempowering it can be to be talked down to by a client, senior counsel, or a judge. They don't understand how it affects your career to be judged by your clothes or your appearance, because that doesn't happen to them. Certainly not with the frequency it happens to women.

Men are rarely accused of "sleeping their way to the top." They don't understand how demeaning it can be to have your accomplishments dismissed entirely based on your gender. So while men can be great mentors, young women who align themselves exclusively with senior male practitioners lose out on the insight and understanding that is unique to a female mentor.

HAVE AN IDENTITY OUTSIDE THE OFFICE

My final piece of advice is that it is important to have a personal identity outside of your professional identity. You don't want everything to be tied up in your work. Lawyers get pretty caught up in their careers. The law is exciting, and it's very easy to let this profession define who we are.

Don't.

Have something outside of the law. Give yourself an outlet, an escape for when this profession gets to be too much. The law, in addition to being exciting, can be draining. It can suck you dry mentally, emotionally, and sometimes physically. When you eat, sleep, and breathe your work, it takes a toll that you may not see until it's too late. You need an outlet, somewhere else to expend your energies and talents.

My outlet is sport. I've been involved in sport my whole life. As I child, I figure skated. I loved it passionately, and still do. I also played ball growing up. The bar association slow-pitch tournament is one of my favourite events of the year.

As an adult, I found my most-loved sport, rugby. I played rugby for over 20 years. I've travelled the world playing and (mostly) watching rugby. Some of my best friends are people I met through rugby. Some of my most memorable experiences have been on or near a rugby pitch. The rugby community has often been the place I run to when I need to escape from real life.

I've also excelled at football and powerlifting, representing Canada internationally in both sports. In 2010, I had the privilege of being selected for Canada's first-ever national senior women's tackle football team. We finished second at the world championships in Sweden.

After coming back from worlds in 2010, I was part of an amazing group of women who founded the Saskatoon Valkyries. This represented the start of women's tackle football in Saskatchewan. The Valkyries have gone on to win several WWCFL titles and be recognized locally for their achievements. I am extremely proud to have been part of initiating this opportunity for women to participate in a sport that has traditionally been for boys only.

I again represented Canada on the football field at worlds in 2013, again finishing second. I was a member of Team Canada for powerlifting in 2015, competing at the Commonwealth (second-place finish) and North American (third-place finish) competitions.

Wearing the maple leaf on my chest and representing Canada through sport has been one of the greatest honours of my life. Being able to share my passion for sport with younger female athletes through coaching has been right up there too.

FINAL THOUGHTS

You always need some final thoughts to tie everything together, right?

Historically, the legal profession has typically been a male-dominated forum. Thankfully, strong, courageous women throughout history have broken down barriers and paved the way for me and other female lawyers to enter the profession. So much change has happened that it isn't a big deal to be a female lawyer these days.

Nowadays, we hear so much about how women and men are enrolling in law school in equal numbers, so obviously one day they will be represented in the profession in equal numbers.

Unfortunately, that doesn't seem to be panning out. We also hear about how women leave the profession in greater numbers than men or how they leave private practice for alternative legal careers. We still hear about the pay gap between men and women. Why is that? What can we do to address these issues?

Frankly, I'm not sure. I haven't had to face many of these issues. My firm is very balanced compensation-wise, and I haven't had to fight for equal pay in my employment. As a partner, I strive to ensure that our associates are paid the same whether they are male or female. I am fortunate that my male partners agree with me on this point. It just hasn't been an issue at our firm.

I also didn't have to deal with maternity leaves holding my career back, as I made the "wise" choice to have my son when I was still in high school. I'm not sure how a firm can positively address this issue for female lawyers. The reality is, with very few exceptions, women need to take time off to have babies. Biology dictates that. While you are on leave, your files continue on. Hopefully someone smarter than me sees fit to tackle this issue in a meaningful, constructive manner.

Ultimately, I hope that one day, not too far in the future, we can talk about lawyers as a profession without the need to distinguish between separate realities for male and female lawyers.

Jessie Buydens is a partner with Scott Phelps Mason in Saskatoon. She is the mother to an adult son and remains heavily involved in women's sports.

AN UNHAPPY COMPROMISE

JULIA QUIGLEY

2017 JD

My history with the University of Saskatchewan College of Law starts just a few days after I was born in September of 1990. My dad was a law professor, and my mom was in her third year of law when I was born. My mom is not the kind of person to let something as insignificant as a newborn baby hold her back, so after I was born on a Friday afternoon, she was back in class on Monday. My dad had a playpen for my two older sisters and me set up in his office, and my mom would drop me off there between feedings. Those feedings would often happen in the law library, which prompted a complaint to the dean from a male student. The eminently wise dean told the aggrieved man that he should first bring his complaint up with my mom directly, and then come back if the matter wasn't resolved. Well acquainted with my mom and knowledgeable about her feminist leanings, the Dean knew full well that this young man wouldn't dare invite her wrath.

I'm not sure why I decided to go to law school, but probably it seemed like the logical thing to do because of who my parents were. I lived with my parents as I did my undergraduate degree in political studies before I started law school. I distinctly remember seeing my mom coming in the door late after a long day of work, maybe at 7:00 or 8:00 p.m., and asking her, "Another day, another dollar?" She quipped back, "Another day, another 80 cents." My mom's quip that night about the gender pay gap was just one of many ways in which my parents engrained in me an understanding of the impact of gender in work and life.

My mom has other stories of the toxic gender dynamics she experienced in law school in the 1990s. It was a yearly tradition for the men to hire a sex worker to come to the first party of the year. A raffle was held so that one male student would receive oral sex from the woman if their name was drawn. If this wasn't disgusting enough, the lottery was rigged so that the nerdiest guy in the class would have his name drawn. When my mom and her friends caught wind of this tradition, the College of Law was quick to condemn it, and to my knowledge, the raffle wasn't held again.

My dad tells the story of when he was an articling student back in the 1970s and the office had hired a female articling student. At the meeting where the new hire was announced, one of the lawyers said, "Are we going to hire another f-ing woman?" The male articling students approached the director of the office to complain about the comment, who in turn banned articling students from "partner meetings" going forward. To her credit, when the female articling student came on board, she confronted the director to ask if the ban would apply to her as well, and the ban was quickly rescinded.

I graduated from the University of Saskatchewan College of Law class of 2017, completed my articles with Legal Aid in Saskatoon, and have continued my career with Legal Aid as a criminal defence lawyer in La Ronge, Regina, and now Prince Albert. Fortunately, I can say things have improved drastically for women in law school and the profession since my parents started out, and the kind of blatant misogyny and sexism that they saw has evolved into something less visible.

I was fortunate to have grown up in a very privileged household in a general sense—my parents had high incomes from good, stable jobs; my sisters and I were always encouraged to further our education; and we enjoyed our parents' financial and emotional support in doing so. Both my parents are lawyers by trade, with my dad retiring from his career as a professor of law at the U of S a few years ago. My mom worked at Legal Aid for twenty-five years, doing mostly duty counsel, helping clients who had just been arrested get out on bail or get their matters resolved quickly without a trial. My privilege in a general sense has been augmented by what I call my "legal privilege," by virtue of my parents' professional backgrounds. Privilege manifests in many ways, the most obvious being skin colour, social and economic status, and access to educational and job opportunities. There are also more subtle ways that privilege can place a person on a metaphorical elevator to the top, and one that I think I have benefitted from in a very basic way is to have had the possibility of a career in law transformed into something achievable because I have had two loving and exemplary people show me that it was all attainable. My background bears all of these hallmarks of privilege, and I have no doubt that I owe much of my success to these factors entirely outside my own capabilities.

I have had a pretty easy ride in pursuing my career. In a class of about 120 people, few people would have come to law school with the amount of legal privilege that I had. Despite all those benefits

I enjoyed, law school was daunting and arduous, and I can't imagine how difficult it would have been for my Indigenous classmates, particularly the women, who were often single mothers with limited incomes and difficult backgrounds. A friend and colleague of mine, an Indigenous woman, had to leave her First Nation and all her social supports to move to Saskatoon to attend school, and accumulated exorbitant debt, all while raising her two kids. I have watched as she is often treated differently than I am in subtle ways by members of the Bench and the profession, as well as by police. She has been berated for being slightly late to court, where I have escaped the same criticism with a quick apology. Her judgment has been questioned by police officers, judges, and clerks, where mine has not. I have no doubt that she is dismissed and undervalued due to her gender and Indigeneity. She has had to explain herself and her decisions, when I have not in similar situations.

Although my own experience has been vastly different than that of my Indigenous colleague, I have felt the impact of gender in my work. I grew increasingly frustrated in my first year as a lawyer when I saw my fellow male Legal Aid lawyers getting treated in a markedly different way by male (and female) prosecutors, whereas I would sometimes be disrespected and scorned by them for no apparent reason. At times, I detected that these individuals were reacting when they felt their (fragile) egos were being bruised if we were battling it out in court on a contentious matter and things didn't go their way. One prosecutor in particular would regularly lose his temper, mostly at me, and sometimes at my male colleagues. He would usually offer an apology to the men for his behaviour, but he never once did to me, although he treated me far worse.

Another male prosecutor questioned my judgment on a drug trafficking case I had with him, accused me of having a vendetta against the police, and generally treated me with disrespect. My client was ultimately acquitted because of police misconduct in breaching his rights under the *Charter*, by the way. A few years later, the prosecutor and I had another drug case together, and I naively thought our history might be water under the bridge. We were talking on the phone one day when he started yelling at me, and eventually accused my client of manufacturing her version of events to match a previous reported case in which the judge had found the police's actions to be unlawful. My friend and colleague walked in the room while this man was yelling at me, was utterly shocked that he was speaking to me this way, and acknowledged he never would have done the same to him.

I had pointed out this pattern of differential treatment to the same male colleague and cited several instances when I had been derided or disrespected by a Crown, when in the same situation, he got no such treatment. He acknowledged that I was being treated unfairly, and his advice to me was that I had to learn how to "play the game"—that is, to act deferentially, even when I didn't feel like it, make concessions on some things so I could accumulate goodwill for the more important ones, and generally be less adversarial in my approach. The problem, of course, was that the legal system is adversarial in nature, and I was being told to modify my own professional personality so I would be less threatening to the male ego.

Ultimately, I have followed that advice to some extent, although I resent it. I have often felt that I wouldn't have to change my approach if I were a man, because my actions wouldn't provoke the same reaction. That being said, I have recognized that I have obligations to my clients that are sometimes better served by modifying my approach. It's an unhappy compromise that I've had to make with myself. Every lawyer has a different skill set and strategy; some are excellent negotiators and brokers of back-room deals for their clients, where others are more suited to trial work where the judge decides the case at the end of the day. In the end, I've found that the adversarial system works for me. I prefer to fight things out in court than to rely on the stereotypically "feminine" skills of negotiation.

My young women friends have had similar experiences in the profession. One friend was an articling student when she was reviewing some video evidence with her principal in his office. He joked that she should sit on his lap because there weren't enough chairs in the office for her to sit elsewhere. This was a person she respected deeply, and she has chosen to interpret his words through a more generous lens—as a hapless joke by a well-meaning older man—rather than seeing them as illustrative of blatant misogyny toward a young woman in a professional setting. The same friend had a friendly but professional relationship with a deputy sheriff at court that soured when he requested she send him nude pictures of herself one weekend. These experiences of being casually sexualized are commonplace for young women lawyers, and something we often have to downplay to ourselves to minimize our discomfort. It's a necessary form of self-protection that men simply don't have to invoke.

The differential treatment extends beyond the gentle sexualization of young women to include judgment of young lawyers who become mothers. One friend hid her entire pregnancy from all of the judges, lawyers, and court staff where she practices because she didn't want to have to deal with the incessant questions about how long she would be on maternity leave. She felt she had to do so to avoid the subtle judgment she would get because she had decided to only take a couple of months to be at home with her baby before returning to work. She explained that she wanted the focus to be on her work, not on her new role as a mother. She wore clothes to cover her belly and went on a short "vacation" when the baby came, and continues to pump breast milk in her car or in closets at remote court points. She prefers the elaborate ruse over having to answer the endless questions about her pregnancy and baby.

Much of this sexism is nearly invisible, so young women are easily gaslit when we relay these experiences, especially to our male colleagues. It took my closest lawyer friend a long time to finally acknowledge that my getting treated differently wasn't only because of personality, but also had to do with my gender. Most young women lawyers will tell you that they feel dismissed and discounted by judges, other lawyers, or the police, but the examples they give are easily written off because they're seen as overly sensitive, or perhaps as imagining things. The problem, of course, is that most young women will have had these experiences, and the possibility of coincidence doesn't hold water.

It is often said that the Crown is the most powerful person in the room. I agree with that assessment, and my own observation is that discretion provides the ideal environment for unfairness to thrive. While I have felt the impact of this discretion in terms of the gender dynamics in my interactions with the Crown, prosecutorial discretion has often affected my clients in negative ways too. The Supreme Court and Parliament have recognized the danger that discretion can translate to unfairness by mandating that judges consider an Indigenous offender's personal background and the impact of the colonial legacy on that person at sentencing. The duty to consider these Gladue factors arises from the understanding that sentencing is a highly discretionary process, and this discretion has resulted in more and longer custodial sentences being imposed on Indigenous people relative to their non-Indigenous counterparts. More recently, amendments have been made to the

Criminal Code that require those same factors to be applied at the bail stage, in recognition that an Indigenous person's background, including whether they live in poverty, suffer from addictions, or have faced personal and intergenerational trauma, should not dictate whether they are released from custody pending trial. Despite these amendments, the rate of Indigenous people being incarcerated has only increased over the years, particularly here in Saskatchewan, where over 75 percent of inmates are Indigenous.

Having worked for my entire, albeit short, career at Legal Aid, I am of the view that the ideological underpinnings of the tough-on-crime agenda are simply not based in reality. Approximately 90 percent of my clients are Indigenous, and about 100 percent of them are deeply traumatized due to living in poverty, the impact that residential schools have had on their families, intergenerational trauma due to addictions and violence, and the profound systemic and overt racism they have faced in this province. Some of the crimes they have committed are heinous, but the vast majority of crime is fairly minor, and almost all of it is rooted in a person's life circumstances rather than any kind of innate criminality.

While judicial discretion has been guided by these changes to the Criminal Code, prosecutorial discretion remains basically unfettered. It is my own belief that one of the main reasons our jails are still filled with Indigenous people is because the Crown has carried on with the status quo of seeking harsher penalties and prosecuting crimes that are based more in addictions and trauma than in actual criminality. The discretionary decisions to prosecute a person in the first place, hold an accused in custody, and to pursue a harsh sentence upon conviction are all influenced by the tough-on-crime agenda that has been pushed in Canada and Saskatchewan for several decades. The rhetoric from our provincial government in particular in recent years has inflamed fears about rural property crimes and gang-related crimes in urban centres, and implied that enforcement and punishment are the solutions to the problem. Prosecutors are not immune to these influences, and their discretionary decision-making is often guided by these political beliefs.

I knew maybe a handful of Indigenous people before I started practicing law. My legal career has exposed me to the reality most Indigenous people face, when I otherwise would have almost no contact with Indigenous people or communities. I think I have yet to meet an Indigenous person who has not been touched by the legacy of colonialism in some way. Overall, men are involved in the criminal justice system at a rate far higher than women. This is one area where women are actually treated better than men: often, the police and the Crown use their discretion not to prosecute women, and the Crown and judges tend to give women more lenient sentences. One defence lawyer once made the argument to me at a dinner party that women are actually treated better than men in society, and gave the examples of women on the Titanic being given priority for the life boats, and women in the justice system. Aside from those examples, I can't say I agree.

There are still examples of women being disproportionately affected by what I believe is a severely flawed criminal justice system. A friend of mine was representing a woman who was nine months pregnant, and the Crown decided to remand her from North Battleford to Pine Grove in Prince Albert on a minor charge. There was nothing my friend could do to prevent this woman from being transported hours away from her home community in a medically vulnerable state. There was no consideration given by the judge or the Crown to her condition—she was branded as a criminal to the exclusion of all else. I got in a furious spat with a judge one day when my client was being sentenced. She was a hard-core addict who had suffered inconceivable trauma in her life. She had stolen a cellphone from someone, and the Crown was seeking a sentence of six months time served and six months probation, with a condition that she pay $100 in restitution to the victim. I pointed to the fact that she had no income whatsoever, a long history of addictions, and a criminal record that included five convictions for sex-work solicitation offences, starting when she was fifteen years old. I implied that to impose the restitution condition would either result in her being charged for a breach or in her resorting to some kind of illicit behaviour, possibly sex work, to pay the money. The judge ordered the restitution.

These are horrible examples of prosecutorial and judicial indiscretion. But discretionary decision-making has a negative impact throughout the criminal justice process. At the front end, police have an absurd amount of discretion in their investigations and decisions to lay charges. I recently had a client who was riding a newer bike through "the hood" in Prince Albert. For no other reason than that he was a young Indigenous man riding a nice bike, he was stopped by three officers who started questioning him and asked him if they could look in his bag. That search revealed a firearm, so his file landed on my desk. Aside from the blatant racial profiling, I was most offended that the officers in this case didn't even bother to conceal it.

In my university years, I learned a lot about residential schools, the systematic removal of Indigenous people from their lands, underfunding of Indigenous health and education, and the over-incarceration of Indigenous people. Having worked for some years at Legal Aid, I have seen first-hand the inevitable fallout of our colonial history and the ongoing deleterious effects on Indigenous people and communities. I'm currently assigned to the Whitefish circuit court point, which means most of my clients are members of the Big

River First Nation. It is a beautiful community where a majority of people speak Cree and their ceremonial grounds are bustling with people in the summer months, with cultural events being held on a regular basis. The RCMP are detested in this community, mostly because they ticket for just about every traffic infraction that they observe, while most people earn a meagre $255 per month in assistance from the band. I fail to see the point in police exercising their discretion this way. I grow increasingly furious at how our police and courts are complicit in creating more hardship for Indigenous people in this province, whether it's ticketing for traffic infractions or sending them to jail when there are other, better options.

There are some positives to being a woman in this profession and experiencing casual sexism from other actors in the system, which is not to say it is acceptable—it absolutely is not. However, most women coming into the profession come from backgrounds like mine: we are typically upper middle class, white, with educated parents. Few of these women will have a true understanding of the deep inequities that exist in our society, aside from what they may have learned in a textbook in university. For women like me, it's not a bad thing to get incensed about the toxic gender dynamics that still exist in society and the profession, and to start recognizing that there are other, more nefarious dynamics at play, such as the engrained racism toward Indigenous people we see here in Saskatchewan, and how other minorities such as immigrants and members of the LGBTQIA2S+ communities are often dismissed or treated unfairly. To understand unfairness on a personal level, even if to a small degree, will make a person a better advocate when the stakes are much higher.

The saving grace has been the support of colleagues and judges who do not give into the insidious misogyny that some of their counterparts do. I can think of many judges who have gone out of their way to celebrate young women lawyers, I think in part because they recognize the extra barriers we face. I have many friends, male and female, who have helped and validated me when I have faced those particular adversities. Legal Aid is a great community of lawyers and staff who are dedicated to their clients and their colleagues, and who are willing to fight for fairness in and outside the courtroom. It is crucial that young women and Indigenous lawyers are not left to fight alone, and my hope is that we will see a culture shift over time that gets better at recognizing and eradicating misogyny in the profession.

My advice to young women in the legal professional is simple: if you come from privilege, recognize where you came from, and all the benefits that have helped you get where you are. Understand that you will carry the burden of the cumulative effect of the sexual comments you get from other lawyers and judges, the moments when you are dismissed or disparaged for no good reason, and the times you have had to work harder than your male colleagues. The accumulation of those experiences will make a hard job even more frustrating some days, but use those experiences as a window to peer through so you can see the inequalities that your clients face as Indigenous people, those living in poverty, or whatever prejudice or unfairness they may face.

When things are a little bit harder for you than for your less competent male colleagues or opponents, let that frustration fuel you so you can take on the cops, the corporations, or whatever adversary you might be facing.

Julia Quigley is a criminal defence lawyer with Legal Aid Saskatchewan and graduated from the U of S College of Law in 2017.

THE POSTER

KATE BILSON

2000 LLB

Life isn't about waiting for the storm to pass;
it's about learning how to dance in the rain.
—VIVIAN GREENE

Dear Alexander,

Not long after I finished law school, Grandma framed one of my favourite images as a gift. My first sighting of the picture had been years before on a magazine cover, which I carefully removed and hung up in my high school locker. It is still in a box of memorabilia. Somehow, she tracked down a poster-size version. A young dancer, in animated form, is in mid-pose in the middle of a large studio, her teacher leaning against the piano and her classmates sitting on benches around the perimeter of the room. Although small in stature, the dancer emanates grace, confidence, and strength. She conveys that if you are willing to keep your chin up, the world is indeed full of possibilities. Over the last twenty years, the poster has spent most of its time hanging in my various offices, keeping me going on the hard days and reminding me to celebrate the good ones. Its message has varied over time in concert with the ebbs and flows of my career. As I write this letter to you now, the image makes me think of the link between my evolution as a dancer—from the early days of learning the first basic poses to the later days of picking up complex choreography—and my career journey in law. Grandma likely has no idea that the poster is one of my most treasured possessions, an inspiration that has helped bring me to where I am today.

And thus begins the story of a dancing lawyer...

Plié: when a dancer is basically bending at the knees...
Correct use and development of a plié is a basic but
essential movement to a dancer's technique.[1]

No matter the genre, dance classes always begin with a series of pliés, the most basic foundational movement. These bending motions are one of the very first things that dancers learn, be they in a preschool ballet class or an adult beginner jazz class. Pliés are an element necessary for almost every dance movement and provide both the impetus into a movement and the cushion to safely finish. Dance cannot happen without the plié.

The foundation for a legal career is perhaps not so clear, something clearly illustrated in my own law school class. One of the things I most loved about the class of 2000 was the diversity of experience. Notably, for the first time in the law school's long

---

1   "Ballet Dictionary" (2023), online: *American Ballet Theatre* <https://www.abt.org/explore/learn/ballet-dictionary/>.

history, equal numbers of men and women took seats in the library for the dean's address on the first day of term, a fact that was not lost on Dean MacKinnon that day. He pointed out that such gender parity had taken far too long to arrive and that he hoped our class was a positive symbol of what could come in the profession. Teaching, military logistics, information technology, business, non-profit work, theology, liberal arts, science, farming, urban planning, elite athletics, and railway operations were some of the backgrounds that formed our class. That gender balance and diversity were central components of my law school experience, and, in fact, continue to inform my professional interests. It brought a richness to our classes and our relationships with one another over the three years spent together, an early lesson that the legal profession does not and should not run on a single track. Diversity makes things more interesting. As my interactions with my classmates consistently showed, different perspectives teach us to open our minds to other points of view.

In my own case, law was certainly never where I intended to end up—throughout my high school and undergraduate years, I had my heart set on being either a dance therapist or a clinical psychologist. Human behaviour and the intrinsic connection between social conditions, physical experience, and growth outcomes have always held a certain fascination.

In the summer of 1990, after graduating from high school, I went to England where I spent a year studying at the Laban Centre for Movement and Dance (the Laban) in London to complete a certificate program in dance studies. Dance has been a long-standing passion for me, one that found me in a studio regularly between the ages of four and twenty-two, and perhaps obsessively during high school. The studio was where I felt safe, happy, and most like myself, where I could express thoughts and feelings without the stress of having to speak them in words, just like the girl in the picture. At the Laban, I was able to focus on dance in a way that I had not been able to before while exploring up close its renowned dance therapy degree program. Unfortunately, I quickly learned that there was no existing market for dance therapy in Canada. At the time, the cost of living and going to university in the United Kingdom were prohibitive. For all those reasons, I decided to return home to Saskatoon and to instead pursue psychology.

My honours BA program in psychology only heightened my passion for those subjects that had already fascinated me for years. It just all felt right. As Grandma and Grandpa had modelled, I assumed graduate school would be next. I had graduated with high honours in my chosen subject and done well on the GRE exams to support my graduate school applications, but also applied to a variety of law schools as a backup plan. When rejection letters started to come from the graduate schools, I was devastated. My hard work had not paid off in the way I always understood it would, and I didn't understand why. When the acceptance letters from the law schools started to come, they provided little comfort. I honestly didn't know what to do, so chose what was already familiar and decided to stay in Saskatoon and carry on at the University of Saskatchewan—"Grandma's University," as you call it.

Ongoing grief over losing your Grandpa Bilson to cancer a few years earlier, when I was in high school, and the realization that such a loss would likely never be completely resolved, only magnified my sadness. My dad was the centre of our family universe, the person I could talk to when I felt stressed. He always helped me figure things out. Life was immeasurably different without him, and I felt very alone in managing the loss. In addition, I was in a relatively new relationship that was unhealthy and defeating, slowly eroding my confidence, and that provided no support for my decision about what to do next. These elements negatively affected my sense of self-worth and the perceptions I had of myself as a capable person or a person worth spending time with, patterns that would follow me for years to come.

Going into a new degree with no self-confidence set me back from the outset. I spent my whole first year in a state of emotional paralysis and depression, believing that I should not ask my professors for help because as it was her own workplace, that might somehow be embarrassing for Grandma. For the first time in my life, schoolwork was an uphill climb, and I felt completely out of my element. By the end of first year, I was ready to quit.

A significant stroke of luck came with a summer student offer from Sanderson Balicki Popescul (as the firm then was) in Prince Albert. Away from the daily pressures of law school, I rediscovered my aptitude for research and writing and, perhaps more importantly, my ability to ask for help. My mentor, (now Mr. Justice) Marty Popescul, encouraged me and reassured me that being a lawyer was something I could do, something I could even be good at. The positive correlation between effort and outcome was restored. I started to feel better and learned so much. Work was challenging and interesting, the atmosphere was supportive, and the firm's approach to practicing law was exactly the kind of model that I was hoping to find. What still stays with me today is the balance, kindness, and deep humanity that all the lawyers presented. This first glimpse into law firm life showed me that as unexpected as the path was that I now found myself on, it could still be one leading to fulfillment of my innate desire to help others, to be good to my community, and to establish a career rooted in compassion and warmth.

That summer between first and second year helped me find my feet again. Through the remainder of law school, my academic confidence returned, although there were still some moments of paralysis (including on a couple of those dreaded 100 percent final exams—if only I could rewrite Criminal Procedure and Remedies today!). My classmates—truly wonderful people—buoyed me and inspired me to keep going, while new experiences like the Laskin Moot spurred courage to reinvest in myself.

Faltered career dreams, parental loss, a destructive personal relationship, and having to forge an unexpected new path compromised my sense of self and self-worth, but also created a more stable foundation for my life in law. These experiences showed me that each time I fell and picked myself up again, I became stronger, not weaker. More importantly, each time I fell, those innate desires just mentioned were what gave me the impetus to get back into dancing again. Starting from a place of kindness and compassion not just toward others but towards myself as well forged the stability of my pliés. Perhaps that is the wisdom that comes with hindsight. In the moment, challenges could easily appear insurmountable. Today, though, I see that every obstacle through my high school and university years made those critical pliés better able to propel me off the ground and cushion the landing.

Arabesque: a position where the body is supported
on one leg, with the other leg extended directly
behind the body with a straight knee.[2]

Building on the strength and foundation of the plié, another fundamental pose in all dance genres is the arabesque. It requires balance and strength and is clearly woven into grander movements like the grand jeté. The arabesque provides a breath between

---

2   *Ibid.*

movements, linking different poses together and re-establishing the base of balance. The motion is striking in its ability to demonstrate strength, while also offering a window into a dancer's fragility, the space where necessary balance can easily be lost.

A persistent and unfortunate message that wove its way through the law school experience for my generation of lawyers was that true success only happens if you work at a large law firm in a large metropolitan centre. This messaging often incorporated a gender-based subtext that female law students' and lawyers' skills and capabilities were continuously being measured against their potential to do things like start a family. I was asked in a few of my articling interviews about my intentions for the long term—would I stay committed to the firm, was I planning to get married or have children, was I willing to work hard? I found these questions disappointing and confusing, knowing that my male classmates were not being asked the same. In one case, a partner on a panel dismissively asked why I would bother with a dance certificate if I was going to go to law school. The tone underlying the question implied the endeavour was obviously a complete waste of time, although I still maintain that it is one of the most interesting parts of my background. More significant, though, was that these kinds of interviews sadly showed a certain level of naïveté on my part that things were measurably different from what Grandma and her female classmates commonly endured. Echoes of the defeat I experienced in first year surfaced.

The articling interview experience did, however, have the great benefit of confirming that workplace environment was going to be important to me. Ultimately, I had the good fortune of being able to choose between offers from firms that were on my top choices list. Interestingly, the offers came from firms that did not raise the kinds of questions just described, a signal in itself that finding the right fit must work both ways. The choice of which offer to accept felt impossible at the time. Each presented amazing, but different, opportunities. While the articling interview experience threatened to knock me off a relatively fragile balance, having a choice between law firms that positively embraced my background, that were clearly compassionate (those exams mentioned earlier just didn't matter!), and that accepted me for exactly who I was allowed a chance to fully extend one of my legs off the floor, believing that I would still stand. Ultimately, I decided on Woloshyn and Company.

Articling and the first couple of years of my practice were a time for building up my confidence and finding my stride. My principal, (now Honourable Judge) Doug Kovatch, was an exceptional mentor. He demonstrated the same level, reasonable, respectful approach to his work that Marty Popescul illustrated. There was never a question that was too stupid to ask him, nor did he ever convey that I was wasting his time or getting in his way. He took the role of principal to heart and ensured that I was given every opportunity to learn and develop throughout the year. Never once did he question my long-term intentions. Humour wrapped itself around his teaching, a characteristic that let me see that sometimes a good laugh is the best way through a stressful moment. Generosity was also one of his trademarks. Partway through my articling year, a close childhood friend lost her father very suddenly. She called me at work to let me know what had happened and asked if I could come. Without hesitation, Doug said he would drive me from Regina to Saskatoon so that I didn't have to worry about winter driving. I can't imagine how many things he set aside on his ever-stacked to-do list for me, but that moment has stayed with me as an example of exemplary and caring leadership.

An incredible gesture from a close friend also found me back in the dance studio during my articling period for a weekly modern dance class. Getting back to that part of my heart during what is typically a monumental year for lawyers proved a significant element in strengthening my arabesque, both on and off the dance floor. The class literally helped me work on a better balance, one that was imported into my work, and helped me to see that amid all the angst that came with articling, there was still room to be myself. It gave me a place to release the stress of moving into professional life and contributed to building more confidence again. Just as the high school student felt safe, happy, and most like herself in the studio, so did the articling student.

My early years in private practice, following my call to the bar in 2001, were generally enriching, and I found a combination of practice areas that appealed to my long-held desire to help others—the basis of my pliés. Labour and employment law, a largely pro bono immigration practice, and some Indigenous law proved the right mix, allowing me to delve more fully into my ongoing interest in the principles of human rights, equality, the fundamental relationship between work and identity, and individual dignity.

Early 2004 saw me move to a larger law firm for a brief period, where I added other areas of civil litigation work to my practice. My decision to move was primarily driven by the opportunity to work with a senior lawyer whom I had always greatly admired. She was a gifted litigator and an incredible model of how to stay true to yourself in a profession that does not always allow for authenticity. At the time, I believed the change would help my arabesques become more solid, allowing me to move into more complex poses. Shortly after I started, however, the senior lawyer left the firm, which left me feeling very shaken and unsure of my future. While I struggled to learn the new dance that would then be set, in a firm culture that was ultimately very different, my confidence quickly declined and I lapsed into a more depressed state again. Time has shown me, however, that the fit simply wasn't there, which I also now recognize is why I couldn't feel successful in my work during that period. I formed a few good relationships, a couple of which remain strong today, but it is a chapter of my life that I associate only with wavering, with not being able to keep up with the choreography. Notwithstanding how hard that year was, it was a critically important one. The experience illustrated the necessary interconnection between confidence and professional growth— where one suffers, it is difficult for the other to thrive. Those lessons continue to inform the choices I make about my career.

Community work also burgeoned during the early years of my career, providing an additional space for me to grow skills and meaningfully contribute to the greater good. Experience with a variety of organizations, including the Global Gathering Place, an agency for new Canadians and refugees, and the Saskatchewan Action Committee on the Status of Women, reinforced the very real point that much remained to be done to achieve a true appreciation for equity and diversity. Surrounded by the good fortune of mostly positive work environments, as well as strong relationships with men and women in my professional circle, I see those days as instrumental in building awareness of my social responsibility to those around me and cementing the connection with fruitful career development.

The combination of work and community activity helped me find an identity again. Ongoing support from long-time friends and meeting your dad helped more consistent leg extensions evolve. Consciously returning to practice my pliés regularly also provided important reminders that choreography always starts from basic poses. This period was not without hitches. There were still moments of losing my balance and falling out of that arabesque. Observing rifts between partners, moving to a new firm for the wrong reasons a few years into my career, feeling overwhelmed by certain files and not knowing how to raise that with anyone, worrying that I was inadequate based on billable hour records, and experiencing what I now recognize as entirely unreasonable reactions from other lawyers both within and outside my firms all shook me at various points in time.

Pirouette: a classical ballet term meaning "spin" [-i]t describes when a dancer is turning around on one leg with the other off the ground.[3]

The pirouette typically appears in the dance vocabulary once dancers have a good sense of balance and have developed some fundamental strength in their legs. Novice dancers start with a single spin, while professional dancers will often be seen performing triple or quadruple pirouettes as a matter of course within a choreographed combination. The trick to a good pirouette is to spot properly, to find a point to focus on before the turn, and to bring the gaze back around to that point as quickly as possible in the turn. Spotting prevents the dancer from getting dizzy or disoriented and helps maintain balance throughout the turn. Perfecting the pirouette offers a great sense of accomplishment to young dancers and provides a challenge to more mature dancers as they work to add more spins. Regardless of the challenge, though, the pirouette is undeniably fun.

In 2005, your dad and I took a chance and moved to Calgary. He had a great opportunity at a highly regarded law firm, which

---

3   *Ibid.*

was too good to pass up. Saskatoon had always been home, a place that enveloped me in a constant hug, the one where I absolutely wanted to live my life. I had a strong base of friends there and loved being able to see Grandma on a regular basis. As it did for your dad, the change I was uncertain about ultimately gifted me many opportunities in different aspects of life. I have been working on adding spins to my pirouettes, sometimes in the rain, but more often under sunny blue skies.

Just after the move to Calgary, a chance coffee date with one of Grandma's former students led to an almost nine-year adventure as a member of the in-house law department at Canadian Pacific (CP), where I focused primarily on labour and employment law and developed a niche in railway safety regulatory work. CP is an iconic Canadian company, one to which I was attracted because of its role in building the Canada that we know today. The opportunity was an exciting privilege, and I was thrilled about the chance to work in an area of law that felt like a good fit to me. The poster went back up on my office wall too—during those years, it really came to symbolize my growing strength as a lawyer.

The railway industry is heavily male-dominated, a factor that made me nervous at the outset. In my early days at the company, I was working with the employee relations team on equity reporting, and can remember seeing a statistic that only about 20 percent of the workforce was female. Notwithstanding the strong female influences in my career to date and the generally positive support from the male lawyers I had previously worked with, I was not immune to understanding that there was still a wide gender gap in the legal profession and, more broadly, the corporate world.

Some early experiences in my tenure did cause me to wonder what I had signed up for. About six months after I started, an operations manager appeared in my doorway for a meeting. He began the discussion by asking me how long I had been at the company and why I already had an office of my own. These were not friendly questions. My answers did not satisfy him, nor apparently did my legal advice. Later that afternoon, I happened past a senior (male) lawyer's office as he was on a telephone call with the same manager. My colleague waved me into his office and motioned for me to sit down. He carried on with the conversation; it became apparent that the purpose of the manager's call was to question the advice I had provided. The main concern was that as I was a young woman and new to the railway, did I really know what I was talking about? My colleague answered by strongly agreeing with my advice and by letting the manager know that any such future similar behaviour was not acceptable. He asserted that the advice provided by company lawyers, regardless of gender, was reliable, well reasoned, and thoughtful. Throughout my time at CP, this lawyer remained a key advocate for my work, and we worked together on some of my all-time favourite files. He cheered on numerous other elements of my universe, especially my becoming a mother. And he thought my dance background mattered.

Similarly, about a year into my time at the railway, a female colleague and I were acting as caddies for a group of players during the annual corporate golf tournament. One of the players, a senior manager in the eastern operations division, inquired about our backgrounds. When he learned that we were both lawyers, he asked if we had worked our way up to those positions from administrative assistant roles and if we had gone to university at all. His tone and line of questions implied surprise that women could: (a) ever work up to more senior roles and (b) have the capacity to complete university degrees. We were literally speechless. In those kinds of moments, my balance certainly wavered. Thankfully, these two scenarios turned out not to be commonplace.

Ironically, the male-dominated railway industry is where I truly developed those shoot-for-the-stars, four-full-spin pirouettes. A constellation of factors, each highlighted by trust and support, contributed to my growth as a lawyer and brought a renewed level of confidence that I really had not felt since my undergraduate days.

First, the railway was a place of mentorship. After the early experience with the operating manager, I expected that I would be fighting an uphill battle to be taken seriously because I was a woman. The reality was much the opposite. Several senior lawyers in the law department had been with the railway for upwards of two to three decades. Their institutional knowledge was unparalleled and their legal skills were second to none. Above all, this group included some of the most generous and inherently good people I have ever encountered—generous with their time, their willingness to share what they knew, their support and guidance, their senses of humour, and their friendship. Fundamentally, these principal dancers in our law department treated everyone in the department in the same way, regardless of their place in the organizational structure. These remarkable souls actively encouraged me at each turn, allowing me not just to learn new choreography, but to also return daily to those foundational pliés. There was a broad view that we each had a significant role to play and that none of us could not be successful without working together. Gender and stature were not factors. We were all just colleagues.

Early on, I was also matched with a mentor in operations. Like the senior lawyers in my group, he had been with the railway for decades, starting as a guitar-playing conductor in the railway town where he grew up. Again, he was incredibly generous with his time, meeting with me every week and teaching me about all aspects of railway operations. We spent time walking along track together, physically checking train cars, and observing railway traffic controllers in real time. I learned about yard operations by going out to a rail yard and about track maintenance by going out into the field to watch a track crew switching out rail. These lessons were immeasurably valuable in my practice as a labour and employment lawyer. More subtly, the information gained through these experiences granted me more credibility with my business clients—it allowed me to speak in railway language, as well as legalese. This piece alone quickly bridged the age and gender gap that I had earlier worried about.

My work was inherently collaborative. In-house counsel has a bird's eye view into all the functions of an organization. For example, I participated on a committee whose mandate was to review safety sensitive and safety critical job classifications. Representatives from a host of departments—law, labour relations, human resources, safety and regulatory affairs, occupational health and safety, and operations— were involved. Each of us came to the table with a different perspective, collectively important to the task at hand. More critically, though, these kinds of initiatives helped me to build my confidence in a way that I had never been able to in private practice. Understanding how a legal perspective fit in with day-to-day business decisions enhanced my skills in presenting and explaining the legal perspective, but they also provided a window into the complexity of how business processes are built. In that way, I was able to become part of a working team and contextualize my legal work and advice in a more coherent way.

The collaborative nature of my work at the railway also allowed me to spend time on building relationships with my client groups in a wholly different way than in private practice. Not only were the formal work meetings a forum to get to know my clients, but so too were the casual opportunities like running into them in the hallway or elevator banks, participating in corporate social initiatives, and getting involved in things like the company's diversity committee.

Together, the mentorship opportunities and collaboration inherent in my work at CP also created a structure in which my gender did not act as a barrier to professional growth. Instead, learning to speak railway language and to show that I could engage with my clients not just as their legal counsel, but as a regular person, strengthened my voice and then my pirouettes. There were many moments when I was the only woman in the room, a fact that was initially intimidating. It became less so, though, as I found my stride and built my client relationships.

CP provided significant opportunities for personal development. Perhaps the greatest gift from my time there was that the work pushed me. It was incredibly challenging and forced me to develop quickly. Again, I think that in-house counsel often suffers from the external perception that our work is less substantive than the work of private practitioners, that we cannot manage sophisticated legal work, that we are just in place to manage the relationship between our clients and external counsel. These perceptions also tend to further perpetuate the notion that female lawyers tend not to work as hard as male lawyers based on the historical statistics that more in-house counsel are women. Having worked both in private practice and in-house, I can tell you the reality is that in-house counsel work just as hard as lawyers in private practice, but in a very different way.

In fact, some of the most complex work I have done in my career occurred during my tenure at the railway, and was made possible by the factors I have just described. I worked on significant grievances and arbitrations, complex work investigations, human resources policy development and reviews, corporate restructuring initiatives, human rights matters, disability cases and occupational health and safety matters, collective bargaining strategy, pension considerations, and privacy law questions. The work was rich and engaging. The role also appealed to my original interest in human behaviour and dynamics, a wonderful way to bridge my original career aspirations with where I ended up. What I noticed most was that I was truly happy in my role as a lawyer.

Underlying these factors was another critical feature—being released from the world of the billable hour, a point of significant tension for many lawyers. On my first day in-house, I asked one of my administrative colleagues for some timesheets. She gave me a big smile and explained that we didn't have to log our time. In short order, I no longer felt like my worth as a lawyer was tied to a running total of how many billable hours I produced in a day, a week, or a month. This was an aspect of private practice that had always been exhausting and stressful to me, one that caused a continuous pulse of anxiety and literally kept me up at night. Instead, I could primarily focus my energy on the actual substance of my files. This fundamental change immediately made the ability to spot in a pirouette much easier. I maintain that a shift away from obsessing over time has in fact allowed me to become a far better lawyer.

One of the most profound experiences that has shaped my career and my own view of myself as a lawyer came with the opportunity to be part of a multi-disciplinary team (and the sole woman) tasked with representing CP in the federal review of the *Railway Safety Act* (RSA). This project occupied much of my time between 2006 and 2013. It found me travelling across Canada for public consultation hearings; writing submissions on behalf of the railway for the RSA review panel and for Parliamentary and Senate committees; attending hearings in front of the said committees; engaging with stakeholders across the railway industry; and learning voluminous details about railway safety and its impact on the industry, railway employees, the public, and the environment. In addition, I was spending a lot of time with the most senior leaders in the company, all seasoned railway executives, and they were listening to me! The assignment played to my strengths, and I will always believe that some of my very best work occurred here. I saw myself giving it my all, like the dancer in the picture on my office wall.

During this time, the other parts of my work portfolio also remained busy and demanding. Throughout it all, I was genuinely thrilled with my work, pirouetting through the days and feeling a deep sense of place within my workplace. As busy as I was in this period, work was never a burden. The knot in my stomach that had existed in private practice was essentially gone. I could see new growth in myself every week, and felt that my contributions mattered and that my voice was heard. I was interacting with people across the organization, at all levels. The gender lens I worried would be a significant factor when I entered the railway industry proved not to be a big one. Instead, my work was measured on its merits. For the most part, client relationships were rooted in mutual trust and respect. Overarching all these pieces is that I was able to be myself. The intrinsic values of kindness, compassion, and collaboration that I learned from Grandma and Grandpa, and that guide my approach to life, proved compatible with my work at the railway. Even in the grittiest cases, those foundational characteristics were relevant and welcomed.

Unquestionably, my tenure at CP propelled my skills to a significantly different level, but never at the cost of being true to myself. I started to look at the picture on my office wall in a different way. The dancer wasn't faltering out there in the middle of the room anymore—she was demonstrating a more complex form of pirouette to her classmates. I recognized that time spent in the studio focusing first on pliés and then building stronger balance in arabesques and pirouettes would eventually result in exciting choreography. The choreography during the CP chapter of my legal career is something I continue to be immensely proud of—it meant that I was able to truly develop as a lawyer. And yes, as a female lawyer.

At the same time, I wove developmental opportunities into my life. Concurrently with starting at CP, I pursued a part-time LLM program at Osgoode Hall Law School, York University, specializing in labour and employment law. Some of my research focused on the connection between work and identity, and the resultant impact of termination on dignity, allowing me to reach back to my first love of psychology. My leader and colleagues viewed this pursuit as not only beneficial to my personal growth as a lawyer, but to the growth of the department. They supported me without hesitation, and I was able to treat the time as work-related. Not only did this support give me a chance to complete a graduate degree, a long-held goal, but I enriched my legal skills and knowledge for the direct good of my employer. The confidence that I gained from my work environment was central to my ability to work on a graduate degree while I was working full time. The combination of working in a complex legal role and concurrently completing a graduate degree—and finding success in both endeavours— sparked a new confidence.

Lest others question my rose-coloured perspective of the railway, there is no question gender discrepancies still abound in the industry. A telling example of this came on a field trip out to watch the track crews, during which we stopped at the crew's accommodation, where I discovered that the female crew members had no operating lights in their bathroom cars! On more than one occasion, stakeholders raised their voices at me in meetings, noting that I was a "naive young woman" who didn't understand the business. Union officials sat across the table from me at arbitrations, purposely calling me by the wrong name to intimidate me. I filed away these kinds of moments, as well as other, similar observations, to raise when I felt confident that I had the ear of those who could effect the right change. Those relationships with senior leadership that emerged during the RSA initiative certainly contributed to my ability to get those ears. Still, the telling lesson in those moments was that more remains to be done for a better gender balance in the corporate world.

> *Grand Jeté: a classical ballet term meaning "big throw" [-i]t describes a big jump where the dancer throws one leg into the air, pushes off the floor with the other, jumping in the air and landing again on the first leg.[4]*

The grand jeté is one of the most impressive movements in the dance repertoire. It is an inherent showstopper, a demonstration of strength, balance, and focus. The movement incorporates pliés, arabesques, and the turning control of a pirouette. Grand jetés are often used as exclamation marks in choreography to inject a "wow" moment when something major happens in the story, either good or bad.

In January 2014, I began a new adventure when I accepted a legal counsel position at what is now TC Energy (TC). After much reflection at a CP that had recently changed, I determined that I needed to find a new path on my own terms. Like in the initial move to Calgary, I felt a great sense of unknown leaving my railway family, but the strength I gained from my tenure there also confirmed my resolve that it was the right decision at the time. In fact, it has been the best decision.

---

4   *Ibid.*

Close to eight years on, I know that I am in the right workplace. The nature of my employment law work at TC has included many parallels to what I was doing at the railway: workplace investigations, disability matters, corporate restructuring work, pension matters, and privacy issues. While I miss the complexity of work I was doing at the railway—in particular, nothing has ever come close to the RSA assignment —I have been able to delve more fully into privacy law, a burgeoning area ripe with constantly evolving issues and requirements. My work in this area led to the company appointing me chief privacy officer in early 2018 when my predecessor retired, providing a new dual role. In this moment, I could see my grand jetés becoming more defined, more consistent. The pace of work at TC has been similarly intense. My days are full. They are challenging. They are rewarding.

Akin to the railway, the energy industry is a male-dominated one. Interestingly, though, the Canadian group within which I have worked in the legal department is almost entirely female. The group, led by a female vice president, includes the employment law, litigation, corporate secretarial, and finance law wings of the legal department. It is a circle of strong, fiercely talented people who do highly skilled work. What has inspired me the most, though, are the young women within this group, the next generation. They demonstrate a level of resilience, tenacity, and confidence that I don't recall having at the same age, a testament to all the work that has been done by Grandma's generation of female lawyers and others since. I value their spirit and positivity, elements that I draw from, especially in the moments where deadlines converge or things are a bit fraught. These young women give me energy and remind me that life is there to be lived. My closest colleague, ten years my junior, is one of these young women. We work together in a positive, supportive way. Without a doubt, she is one of the funniest people and most capable lawyers I have ever met—we laugh together every day, which always reminds me of those lessons my principal taught me about how humour can help manage stress.

The environment at TC provides the best illustration of how much fun it can be to practice law, something that the law student version of myself would never have been able to imagine. At the same time, it provides a comprehensive model of how an atmosphere of mutual support can bring out the best in a team of people and drive excellence in work product. Our leaders set intense expectations and require a high calibre of work from us, but my own experience has been that they do so in a respectful, measured way that helps us find the way to success. Moreover, they encourage and help seek out developmental opportunities, whether professional or personal. Their tutelage has helped me refine my grand jetés. My faith that I can propel myself higher, turn more tightly in the air, and land safely on one leg has grown considerably at TC. A continued ability to focus on my work in the absence of a timesheet also remains a gift, one that I recognize I ought not take for granted.

Like at CP, I have also found a tremendous arc of support and acceptance from my male leaders, colleagues—one of whom is an extra special gem to both of us—and clients at TC, as well as within the senior leadership circle. Gender lines generally do not cross my mind in the daily course of my work, which is the ideal that Grandma has always wanted for her students and worked to build in the profession. There are certainly differences in how we communicate with each other, but those differences do not create insurmountable obstacles. Instead, those differences have often been enriching, sometimes teaching me to reflect on my own communication patterns, and sometimes providing excellent fodder for working with my human resources clients on policy development and other corporate initiatives.

One of the unique aspects of working as an in-house employ-ment lawyer is the ability to participate directly in policy develop-ment for an organization. In my experience, the crucial distinction between my private practice experience and my in-house career is the intentional formalization of workplace culture in the latter arena through policy and procedure. This formalization offers practical mechanisms, such as mandatory training for all personnel, reporting processes, and structured compliance oversight, that help dim gender-based inequality, as well as other forms of inequality.

To be clear, though, my career has also illustrated that the ideal bubble within which I have been fortunate enough to work does not tell the whole story. Juxtaposed against my own experience are those grim chapters evidenced in the employment, privacy, and workplace investigation files which have crossed my desk, as well as in the work that I have done with the Canadian Bar Association over the years. Reminders that historic equity barriers still very much exist surface in these aspects of my work. For example, legis-lative mechanisms intended to stem the tide of gender inequality, such as statutory requirements for equity reporting in the feder-ally regulated sphere, continue to be a necessity. Framed in such terms, these reminders are discouraging and disheartening—they cast a dark shadow over my own notions of where I believe the gender equality conversation is and should be. They also remind me that I cannot take my bubble for granted. The very nature of my work drives a heightened sense of responsibility to do what I can within my role to encourage the positive efforts being made within my organization to celebrate diversity.

And yet so much work remains to be done. Notwithstanding the hope for the profession hinted at by the young women I described earlier and the environments in which I have been fortunate to practice law, I still hear too many stories about female lawyers who are marginalized in their firms, who are subjected to sexual harassment or other damaging behaviour by those they work with, or who are working to fit into a workplace environment at significant cost to their mental health.

With my role comes the recognition that I am not dancing as a soloist, out there pirouetting and doing grand jetés across the stage alone, but that I am part of a much larger cast with many other dancers. A sense of responsibility and loyalty flow from the notion that the dance production involves all of us together, and that my fellow dancers need me to do my part to remember the choreography, the timing, the places we will each take on the stage. Together is the only way to bring to life the story that needs to be told about gender equity and diversity in the legal profession.

This story would not be complete without acknowledging one of the best rewards that my role at TC brings—flexibility to fully embrace motherhood, the aspect of life that brings me the most joy. The corporate approach explicitly recognizes that we all have lives outside of work and that time must be given to our family, community, self-care activities, and other personally meaningful commitments. My various leaders at TC, men included, themselves live this commitment. Opportunities abound for me to spend time with you just being a mum—there is room to participate in important school activities, purchase additional holiday hours (my "Alexander Days"), adjust my work hours to manage your schedule, work from home when need be, and enjoy extended long weekends in the summer months. You have a fan base in my colleagues, who help celebrate you regularly. This reward fundamentally contributes to positive outcomes in my productivity and quality of work, my ability to manage heavy stretches or converging deadlines, and my sense of commitment to my team. The environment stands in stark contrast to what was hinted at in some of those articling interviews so many years ago. Though not always easy to maintain, the personal balance that comes from this aspect of my working life means everything. It is the central element that allows me to keep doing those grands jetés.

Injury: hurt, damage, or loss sustained.[5]

Injuries are an inevitable aspect of dance. It is an entirely physical medium, one that often pushes a dancer's body to its limits. Torn or sprained muscles and ligaments, stress fractures or other causes of broken bones, and back conditions are not at all uncommon. Although it is not often discussed, the constant pressure to perform and to be perfect in doing so can lead to other kinds of injuries, including mental health issues. The degree of injury will dictate how and if a dancer can resume the art—recovery considerations cannot always be foreseen at the outset. While some dancers choose to follow recommended treatment, others put themselves at further risk by continuing to dance with an untreated injury. In all cases, injuries will cause some degree of pain.

In August 2019, I was forced to address a significant injury following a breast cancer diagnosis. On the eve of the big trip to Italy with our beloved English cousins in July, I found a lump in my left breast. In that moment, I knew that life would never be the same again. It was my secret until we returned home two weeks later and I was able to see our trusted family doctor. His concern and immediate referral for diagnostic testing unleashed the storm clouds that had been building since July.

With the cancer diagnosis confirmed, I stepped into an entirely different world. My balance was completely compromised, and

5   *Merriam-Webster.com Dictionary*, sub verbo "injury".

the string of grand jetés I had been practicing stopped abruptly. I kept trying to find that focal point to right my stance again. Not at all surprisingly, work was incredibly supportive and provided critical help through the corporate benefits program. It occurred to me many times that when one is faced with critical illness, secure employment in a corporate setting is akin to winning the lottery. Not only was there income security, there were formal mechanisms in place to protect my job and the resultant space for me to face gruelling treatment without the burden of worrying about being away for an unknown period.

My leaders' and colleagues' care and action were immediate and unwavering, as were the generous gestures of family, dear friends from all corners of my life, and your school community, things I still cannot think about without becoming emotional. These elements united to help me pivot quickly into a string of necessary and incredibly stressful experiences—bone scans, chemotherapy and some resultant trips to the ER, electrocardiograms, surgery, and radiation, among others. Early on, I made a conscious decision to maintain a positive mindset and keep one foot in front of the other. The space work gave me allowed me to focus on the crisis in front of me and constituted an important pillar in my ability to stay positive. The only choice was to go straight through the eye of the storm. I braced against the driving rain and put my energy into getting through the physical and emotional marathon of cancer treatment, which was made yet more complicated by the onset of a sustained global pandemic.

Cancer does not discriminate. It cuts across gender, age, sexual orientation, ethnicity, religion, socioeconomic status, and other health conditions. The Tom Baker Cancer Centre here in Calgary, along with supporting cancer care organizations where I have spent many hours over the last two years, yields an incredibly diverse group of people. There is a community of connectedness, acceptance, positivity, and care that has been life changing for the better. Those characteristics create an atmosphere that belongs everywhere. It reflects the world in which I want you to grow up and start your own career.

A stark illustration that this ideal community does not yet fully exist in the legal profession occurred in the midst of my four months of chemotherapy, the first and most arduous stage of my treatment odyssey. While I was in sitting in the waiting area to start a session, I met a woman who happened to be a partner at a large multinational law firm. We started chatting about our situations. She mentioned that no one knew about her illness; that she felt she could not share it with her partners at work, especially the men, for fear that it would impact her position; and that she was determined to carry on as normal throughout treatment. My immediate reaction was immense sadness for her. Our experiences could not have been more different. In my case, I had an amazing circle of help, with friends and family beside me every day. The delightful colleague I described earlier was given carte-blanche discretion by our VP to be at my side whenever I needed her. She came and worked remotely from my house on occasion, appeared some days to make me lunch or walk with me, and, of course, continued to make me laugh as often as possible. That conversation in the waiting room only reinforced my view that work environment and culture make a fundamental difference to the gender dialogue in my profession.

The poster is currently hanging in our home gym, where I spend time almost every day building back up my physical strength through exercise and yoga. Mindfulness work, meditation, and counselling buttress my emotional strength. Today, that dancing figure reminds me of how much we have come through together, my little bear, and symbolizes the sheer strength of human spirit.

THE NEXT ACT–
CHOREOGRAPHY IN PROGRESS

This letter has been written in pieces, interrupted along the way by my cancer odyssey. Bouts of extreme fatigue, heavy brain fog, and stretches of managing all the complex and difficult feelings that cropped up have caused further interruptions as I find my way back from a health crisis and try to fit fully back into my roles as a legal professional and corporate colleague, a community volunteer, a wife, a sister, a daughter, a friend and, of course, a mother.

The most important mantra that I learned during this time is to "start where you are and do what you can." It is one that I think about each day, one that has been a guiding principle through treatment and recovery, as well as my graduated return to work, one that I also now use as a leader to encourage my own team members to be kind to themselves. No two days are the same for anyone.

During my absence, my dual role in TC's law department was split up, and the chief privacy officer piece was moved to the corporate compliance group. I have thus returned to a different group from the one I left in 2019. In many ways, though, the change has only solidified my positive perceptions of TC mentioned earlier. My new leadership and colleagues are equally kind and supportive, actively taking interest in my development as a leader and ensuring that I can keep some balance. Now as a people leader myself, I can more intentionally set the choreography for the new dance ahead and help my group members practice their own suite of dance poses. As we practice together, I will be better able to assess what impact the recent injury has truly had on my own poses. In the meantime, the perspective I have gained through cancer and the fact that who I am is still warmly welcomed at work means I can start from an inherently stronger position.

Moreover, a concrete benefit of these strange pandemic days is that I am also returning to a workplace that is focusing more explicitly on mental health and diversity. TC's Mental Health Champions program aims to create a more supportive, inclusive, and welcoming environment for everyone, regardless of background. The program also works to open an active dialogue at all levels of the company on how to effect positive change and strategize ways to ensure everyone feels valued. By all accounts, it is already making a difference. Psychological safety and inclusion moments are becoming commonplace at the start of meetings. More time is spent on team-building. These activities can't help but take us in the right direction.

Other changes that are appearing on the horizon include the introduction of equity, diversity, and inclusion as an external measure of corporate success and maturity. The current focus on environmental, social, and governance measures (ESGs) necessarily requires companies like CP and TC to consider how they manage issues relating to gender, race, sexual orientation and identity, disability, and other points of inclusion in a substantive, formalized way. I am so encouraged to see these kinds of measures taking hold, in part because they allow companies to impose similar expectations on service providers such as law firms. Ideally, these kinds of developments will eventually force similar change across the whole legal profession, along with the work that we are starting to see from law societies across the country, many of which are looking at inclusion, equity, and diversity, as well as mental health, in more detail than ever before. In the meantime, I continue to learn from my work those indicators of what remains to be done.

I am buoyed by the fact that some of my classmates and contemporaries are now themselves being appointed to the Bench and elected as Benchers, leading law firms, companies, and non-profit organizations, and caring for their communities. It was a true privilege to be part of the class of 2000. The diversity, wealth of knowledge, kindness and compassion, and humour displayed by my classmates has informed my own career and continues to inspire me. A special circle of exceptional women from the legal community in Saskatchewan, including Grandma, have profoundly influenced how I approach work and my own commitment to improving the profession. Those bonds remain entrenched. The group of young female lawyers at TC signal positive change for all the reasons I talked about, as do your stepbrother and his partner, a yet more recent generation of lawyers. A special uncle in Winnipeg, also a lay Bencher, undoubtedly brings his openness and determination to create a more accepting world to his work. And then there are your stepdad and my beloved brother, as well as your dad and his brother. They are lawyers, leaders who believe in treating everyone well, all so kind and wise. Because of these people, I choose to believe that the future of the legal world looks brighter than ever.

Stepping out of my career and being forced to focus on self-care for an extended period has been a valuable chapter. I have learned to celebrate the positive in each day. The experience has shown me the possibility of living a joyful life amid crisis. It has provided a time of quiet contemplation to observe that looking after myself is the best way to look after everyone else in my life, including you, but that self-care also deserves more focus, especially in the legal profession. Not least of all, it has allowed me to reflect on the village of family and friends around me, many of whom have now been part of my life for decades. This village is what makes me feel truly successful.

Working on this project in the same time period has also illuminated how fortunate I am to have landed on my professional path. As a law student and young lawyer, I didn't always make decisions about my education and career for the right reasons. Hindsight says that I wish I had expressed my gratitude more clearly for the opportunities and investments of time that some senior practitioners gave me, and had stood up for myself more solidly in those moments of being treated unreasonably by others. I wish that I had made more decisions based on what I truly wanted, what I believed was right for me. Those thoughts stay with me, not only as a marker of what I want to change in my own behaviour, but also as a point of comparison for my own leadership approach. By the same token, I am proud of that law student and young lawyer who struggled so much with her confidence and sense of self-worth. She has worked so hard to build an approach to her work that aligns with who she is as a person, and has clearly learned how to dance in the rain.

My hope for your generation is that gender influences will continue to become less evident, less in need of conscious change. The good news is that when I hear you talk about school, about the people in your class, about where you want to go, I already feel encouraged that gender does not assume a role in your central perceptions of how the world should work. You do not seem to live in a world where boys so clearly do one thing and girls something different. You speak of everyone in your class as an equal. You do not see limits for the future based on gender and gender identity. You embrace diversity, believing that curiosity and acceptance of differences are means for positive change in our world, that learning from each other's experiences and perspectives makes our community richer. Not only that, but you are already leading positive change through your own individual efforts to bring other kids around the world together to talk about these very issues. I cherish your insights every day—your spirit and efforts show that the gender barriers Grandma had to overcome and the formal need for legislated inclusion, equity, and diversity mechanisms under which my generation has grown up might someday just become remnants of the past.

Where the next act takes me remains a work in progress. I visualize a new kind of dance, perhaps something in the modern lyrical vein rather than a traditional ballet production. Whatever it turns out to be, it will tell the story of a happy and fulfilling albeit unexpected career, where I have grown to feel valued and respected. One of your compositions will be the music.

Given the opportunity, I would ask the artist to add a couple of things to the poster. First, I would ask her to dot some male figures around the room—they would represent my very first mentor from summer student days and my articling principal; your dad, stepdad, uncles, and stepbrother; the men in my law school class, especially those from my close circle; my railway and energy families; and some other close friends. Finally, there is an empty chair next to the piano in the picture. I would ask the artist to draw you there, perhaps a little larger than the other characters, with your sunshiny smile. Thank you for always lighting the way and for strengthening my hope every day that we can all come to see that diversity makes the world go around.

All the love in the world,
Mummy

POSTSCRIPT

In June 2022, the contributors to this anthology joined each other for a workshop at Grandma's (beautiful) University. We shared our professional experiences, learned about storytelling (you would have loved, loved, loved the story bundle!), and gave each other glimpses of our respective hopes and dreams for the profession.

It was a powerful, humbling, and joyful experience, which came at a perfect time, as I had been feeling disengaged in my work for the last little while. I entered the workshop questioning whether my contribution to this anthology is valuable at all given the relatively positive bubble that has been my career. I worried that other contributors would think my story was not worth telling, because it perhaps doesn't evidence the same breadth of challenges or frankly harrowing experiences others have faced. What I learned in the workshop, however, is that all stories are worthy of being told, including those that illustrate hope. As we reimagine what utopia might look like for the legal profession—ideally, it is one that embraces diversity and showers acceptance, support, compassion, and flexible thinking—my wish is that my own career story will thread the possibility of hope for a professional environment where every member, regardless of background, client base, or identity, can be a valuable part of the dance troupe.

Kate Bilson, BA (Hons.), LLB, LLM, is Chief Privacy Officer and Manager, Privacy Office for TC Energy. She lives in Calgary with her husband, Glen, and her son, Alexander, where she still loves to dance.

DRESS *for* *the* WEATHER

KATH STARKS

2019 JD

I feel a bit out of place in this collection of early-career and late-career women lawyers. First, file me under "pre-career." I am still a student. My legal experience is limited to law school, summers as a research assistant, and now clerking at the Court of Appeal for Saskatchewan. Second, while I am happy to claim a place in a collection of women's writing, I can't say that I have an established record of success at being a woman either, as a gender non-conforming woman, a queer person, and a butch lesbian. In these circumstances, all I can offer are some preliminary observations on gender and my career in law, and only from my particular vantage point.

Writing about gender poses the challenge of putting an embodied experience on the page. To contextualize my reflections, I think it is helpful to explain a bit about how I look and how I am perceived. I am white, five feet nine inches, slim, with short hair and glasses.

I mostly wear "men's clothing"—at work, a suit and tie. I do not know what most people think of me when they see me, but it is apparent that sometimes I am read as a woman and sometimes as a man. Most of the time, people seem to immediately and firmly land on one side or the other without any direction from me. They confidently assert their conclusion into our interaction: "What can I get for you ladies?"; "Excuse me, ma'am"; "Sir, this is the lady's room!"; and even, "Katherine, nice to meet you. That's an unusual name for a man."

These experiences can range from funny or awkward, to grating and exhausting, to frightening. They are also routine experiences that I have learned to expect and manage. I understand how I look, and it is deliberate. As much as I experience my gender as innate to my identity, I also choose to be myself, to dress and carry myself in a way that is genuine. Being myself *on purpose* is a great feeling, which I owe to the queer and trans people who came before me and my own queer community, which nurtured my self-acceptance and confidence. I also occupy a position of privilege as a white, middle class, masculine, non-disabled person, for whom being gender non-conforming is usually safe.

So this is the self that I bring to my career in law. My path to law school was, I think, fairly typical: a humanities education, some time in the workforce, then back to school to study law. I love reading and writing, and first completed a BA and MA in English. Shortly after I finished my MA, my girlfriend and I moved to Toronto. I had a haphazard collection of work experience—childcare at summer camp and the YMCA, farm labour, driving a school bus in my hometown. The only guideline for attire that I had encountered in my working life to that point was "dress for the weather."

I blanketed west Toronto with resumés and ended up with a job interview for an administrative assistant position at a condominium developer. I had no idea what to wear, but I intuited that

I could not wear the ratty sneakers I had worn every day in grad school. I went to a nice shoe store, hoping to get expert advice. I told the salesperson where I was interviewing, and she said, "Oh, you'll need pumps, a low heel for sure." By that time, I dressed and looked much as I do now—a masculine person, but someone the salesperson recognized as a woman and to whom she therefore prescribed women's professional shoes. It was like being told I would need to attach a different head to my body for the interview.

Pumps were impossible, and given the uncompromising standard described by the salesperson, the interview seemed impossible too. But the rent in Toronto was even more impossible, so my girlfriend put me in a pair of plain black Chelsea boots and sent me to the interview. I arrived at the Etobicoke office and found myself interviewing with the broker of record, who was indeed in a low heel, and her long-time assistant, who happened to be a lesbian and was *not* in a low heel. They hired me. I was put at the front desk of a glass-walled sales office in the Queen West neighbourhood, where I suspect my appearance may have been seen as an asset to the brand, or at least not a liability.

I spent two years in administrative support in real estate offices. At the same time, I began volunteering as a one-on-one tutor for adult newcomer English language learners. Though ostensibly English instruction, work with my first student actually consisted of supporting her goal of opening a massage therapy clinic. We wrote emails to her landlord together and I helped her interpret city regulations to prepare for a health inspection. I found myself applying the research and communication skills I had built studying English to assisting in real-world problem solving, and I found it rewarding. At work, I glimpsed the work of lawyers, playing an essential role for individuals and organizations undertaking transactions. I started to formulate a goal of working as a lawyer to help individuals navigate the administrative systems that stood between them and their aspirations. In transitioning back to school, I benefitted from support from my bosses, women who encouraged me to pursue my goals.

Some of my first-year classmates were twenty-two years old when we started law school. They were smart and capable and were more than equal to the task, but for me, entering law school any earlier in my life would have been a mistake. From the first day of law school, students are confronted with the imperative to look and act "professional." Like the idea of "fit" as a job qualification, this seemingly innocuous expectation can have exclusionary force. I think I was more able to navigate this context because I had already established my sense of self as a queer person. I am glad that by the time I started law school, I had at least figured out what kind of suit and shoes I wanted to wear.

Studying to be a lawyer means seeking entry into a profession that remains resistant to inclusion. Constance Backhouse traces how the "concept of 'professionalism' has been inextricably linked historically to masculinity, whiteness, class privilege, and Protestantism" through Canadian history.[1] She begins with the establishment of entrance examinations by the Law Society of Upper Canada in the 1820s. The examinations sought to limit admission to individuals with demonstrated "proofs of a liberal education," with the practical effect of excluding all but the male children of well-off Anglo-Canadian families. The diary of Patrick MacGregor, a Scottish immigrant who gained admission in 1834, provides an account of preparation and completion of the entrance examinations:

---

1   Constance Backhouse, "Gender and Race in the Construction of 'Legal Professionalism': Historical Perspectives" (2003) 2–3.

Went over six books of Euclid. Read Paley's *Moral Philosophy* twice-over, and read the revised Algebra, Tyler's *Elements of General History*, Goldsmith's *Greece and Rome* (abridged), Revised Geography and Astronomy, Cicero's *Select Orations*, and some of Virgil...On the 19th of April 1834, in the morning, after being furnished with money and a new suit of clothes by my uncle, I set out for the City of Toronto, Capital of Upper Canada (formerly Little York) to be examined by the Benchers of the Law Society. [...] Presented my Petition and fee of £10 to the Secretary. [...] After delaying some time, till there was a quorum, we were examined. I was called in, and Baldwin gave me the 7th chapter of Cicero's speech on the Manilian Law to translate. [...] We were afterwards called in to read our translations. Knowing their prejudices, I imitated the English style, as well as I could and succeeded.

Backhouse observes how MacGregor's position—receiving a classical education at school, taking a further three months to study, and, "[e]qually important" to making the requisite impression on the Benchers, wearing a new suit on the day of the exam—enabled him to succeed in the "formidable task" of gaining admission.[2]

Against the barriers deliberately erected by the profession, trailblazing individuals sought admission, sometimes successfully. These included Delos Rogest Davis, a Black lawyer admitted to the bar in 1885; Andrew Paull, an Indigenous man denied admission in 1922;[3] and Norman Lickers, an Indigenous man admitted to the bar in 1938.[4] The history of Indigenous exclusion from the profession is intertwined with the broader history of colonialism. Paull

---

2   *Ibid* at 2–4.
3   *Ibid* at 2–11.
4   *Ibid* at 2–12.

was denied admission in part because he lacked sufficient instruction in Latin, but also because membership was contingent on the member's right to vote in the province of admission, a right denied to Paull as an Indigenous person in BC until 1949. At the time of Lickers's admission, provisions of the *Indian Act* that stripped individuals of Indian status upon admission to the bar were still in force.[5]

With respect to gender, in 1897, Clara Brett Martin became the first woman admitted to the bar in Canada. One might add to this list of trailblazers Judge Kael McKenzie, a Métis man who became the first openly transgender judge appointed in Canada in 2015.[6] Saskatchewan has yet to see an openly transgender person appointed to the Bench; the first openly gay members of our Bench, Justice Krista L. Zerr and Justice Graeme Mitchell, were both appointed in 2018.

The stories of members of excluded communities making inroads into the profession is the story of their remarkable successes, and also the story of their contradictions and the limits of those successes. Backhouse observes that as a "well-to-do, white Torontonian of Anglican-Irish heritage, with a degree from Trinity College, Martin fit the contemporary image of the legal professional in every respect but gender."[7] This consistency extended to her sharing in and advancing the profession's prejudices, as her anti-Semitism has since been documented.[8] As Brenda Cossman and Marlee Kline write, "Whatever Clara Brett Martin accomplished…and whomever's interests she has since been interpreted

---

5   Indian Act, 1876, s.c. 1876, c.18, s.86(1).
6   Laura Beeston, "Canada appoints its first transgender judge", *The Globe and Mail* (18 December 2015), online: < https://www.theglobeandmail.com/news/national/canadas-first-transgender-judge-named/article27876501/ >.
7   Backhouse, *supra* at 2–7.
8   *Ibid.*

as advancing, her successes must be recognized as being limited as to the range of women to which they must have been meant to apply."[9] Furthermore, the stories of these trailblazers are also the story of a profession resistant to inclusion, which forcefully maintains its traditional boundaries.

For the most part, I have not encountered the hard edges of those boundaries in my own experience. I approach the profession in a position not unlike Martin—as a white, middle-class person with professional parents and a humanities education, it's fair to say that I "fit the contemporary image of the legal professional in every respect but gender." At the same time, I have found that my difference registers more acutely in legal professional spaces than in many other areas of my life.

As I now transition from law school into the profession itself, I am unsure how my gender will bear on my career. The closest I've come to practice is a term as a clinical law student at Community Legal Assistance Services for Saskatoon Inner City (CLASSIC).

It was immediately apparent to me as a clinical student that the formal language of many legal contexts remains highly gendered. One's status as a man or a woman no longer demarcates the boundary of legal personhood in Canada, but it certainly continues to define the terms of address in court. This is "Mr." and "Ms." territory; Saskatchewan's Court of Queen's Bench and Court of Appeal still require counsel to address the Bench as "my Lady" or "my Lord."[10] I must say, very respectfully, that the closest comparator to court in this regard is a public restroom. Everyone demands

---

9   Brenda Cossman & Marlee Kline, "'And If Not Now, When?': Feminism and Anti-Semitism Beyond Clara Brett Martin" (1992) 5:2 Can J W&L 298 at 309.

10   After this contribution was written, both the Saskatchewan Court of King's Bench and the Saskatchewan Court of Appeal amended this practice. Gender-neutral address is now preferred by both courts.

that you explain whether you are a man or a woman before you can do your business.

As clinical law students, we were forever appearing at docket court seeking adjournments on summary criminal matters. In an interaction as brief and efficient as that, do you correct the judge if they use the wrong gendered honorific in addressing you? I feel there is no perfect option. Legal ethics class jumps to mind: "When acting as an advocate, a lawyer must not knowingly attempt to deceive a tribunal[.]"[11] Is there some duty to set the record straight? An immediate correction guards against the possibility of belated disclosure and worse problems. But if I can just get the adjournment as Mr. Starks and get off my feet, why risk embarrassing the judge?

I ran into a delicate situation as a clinical law student representing a client at a small claims case management conference. It was held in a small, full room, with two lawyers present for the party opposite, and two judges—in addition to the presiding judge, a second judge, newly appointed to the court, attended the proceeding as an observer. Despite my name being on the record, the observing judge took me to be a man, and used he/him pronouns with reference to me. The presiding judge recognized that this might not be quite right, and I witnessed her search for a gender-neutral term of address for me, I think seeking to be respectful of me but also avoid embarrassing the observing judge. She landed momentarily on "counsel" before correcting herself that I was a clinical student, not a lawyer. It fell to me to sort it out, and the goal of completing my articles took on an added dimension—I am working toward the privilege of access, not just to the profession, but also to that gender-neutral term of address.

---

11   The Law Society of Saskatchewan, *Code of Professional Conduct* (2012), 5.1-2(e) & (g).

Another experience of accounting for my gender before a decision-maker arose when, after working extensively on a refugee file at the legal clinic, the lawyer in charge brought me along to the hearing. The panel member and language interpreter were video conferencing in from two different locations, making it a three-way, split-screen conference call. In fairness to the panel member, I am sure it was hard to see or hear me. At the outset, the lawyer explained my presence and sought leave for me to attend the hearing. The panel member had no concerns about my attendance per se, but some concerns about my name and gender: "The name is what? Katherine? I'm sorry, Mr. Starks or Ms. Starks?" This exchange felt different, more vulnerable, because the questions and confusion were directed at my supervising lawyer, rather than directly at me. While managing situations like this is routine for me, I am never certain how another person will react to them.

In these earliest stages of my career, as I cope with the challenges of learning new skills and navigating unfamiliar environments, I have found that other legal professionals' reactions to my gender expression is simply another challenge to manage. Again and again, I encounter the unspoken expectations that everyone is a man or a woman and must be readily identifiable as such at a glance. My life is evidence that gender is more complicated than that. I so appreciate efforts such as the use of gender-inclusive language, and sharing and asking pronouns during introductions as a matter of routine. These small changes make my life markedly easier, and the implied recognition that folks like me exist in law nudges us toward a more inclusive profession.

While I am unsure about what challenges face me in the future, I believe that my gender and my experiences as a queer person are a strength that has served me so far in my legal career and will continue to do so.

My gender has helped me learn how worldviews shape reality. Once, when I registered to vote, an official commented that my name, Katherine, was unusual for a man. She had my ID and registration—both marked female—and she'd heard my voice. Yet she could ignore the evidence in order to fit me into her worldview. Thanks to experiences like this, when something seems incongruous to me, I ask: What can't I see here? What possibilities have I not yet imagined?

My gender has shaped and nuanced my own worldview. For example, my understanding of sexism and discrimination is informed by experiences that flow from my gender. I've met men who, taking me to be a young man, buy me a beer and offer fatherly career advice. When people see me as a woman, I find I am taken less seriously. This extends to violence—like most women, I have been verbally and physically harassed. I have learned from my experiences on both sides of this gendered divide.

Finally, I am so privileged to be part of queer communities, which have challenged and nurtured me and enriched my life in every way.

I sometimes encounter people who are angry that I don't fit into their view of the world. I always had trouble in public washrooms, and now I have occasional troubles in court, too. Navigating these difficulties has made me a more confident person. I have learned to advocate for myself, a skill that I hope will serve me in learning to advocate for others as a lawyer. My gender is a strength. I look forward to my career in law with confidence and excitement.

Kath Starks is a civil litigator in the federal public service. She previously clerked at the Court of Appeal for Saskatchewan and for Chief Justice Wagner at the Supreme Court of Canada. Kath grew up in Prince Albert, Saskatchewan, and now lives in Edmonton, Alberta, with her family.

WHY DO YOU DO ANYTHING *when* YOU'RE TWENTY?

MERRILEE RASMUSSEN, KC

1973 LLB

Dear Lena,

There are many questions I wish I had asked my grandparents when they were still here to answer them, but I never thought of asking until it was too late. I am writing now to answer some of the questions I think you will be wondering about, even though you haven't yet asked, and I suspect you will wish you had asked me after I'm gone. As your grandmother, I am particularly concerned about your future as a woman in society. I think that I have generally been underestimated in my career—not just because I am female but also because I am short and because, until my hair turned white, I looked much younger than my age. And actually, being underestimated by others can often be an advantage.

My paternal grandfather came to Canada—and specifically Saskatchewan—from Denmark in 1914. When he was in his eighties, I asked him why he had come here, and he said, "Why do you do anything when you're twenty?" I had just turned twenty when I started law school. Why did I do that? That's a good question. My parents were working-class folks. There were no lawyers in our circle of friends and relatives. I think the only lawyer's name I would have recognized at that time was Morris Shumiatcher, who was well known in Regina. I do remember I thought the study of law would be interesting. And it was, and continues to be. But it never occurred to me in 1970 that I would actually *be* a lawyer.

It's shocking to think that was fifty years ago. When I started law school, the tuition was $550 per year. My family was comfortable, but didn't have a lot of extra money, and I had two younger brothers still living at home. I thought, "If I can get a student loan to cover the fees, I'll go." The loan I eventually did get was for $570 and so I went. That's how serendipitous these things are.

The law school in Saskatoon was quite different from my undergraduate university experience in Regina. It was much more staid and more conservative; professors addressed students by their last names. In Regina, I had good friends whose last names I didn't even know. We had sit-ins over something on a regular basis. And of course, women's lib was a big deal.

In my family and in school, I never thought that I was in any sense second class because I was a girl. I'm sure no one ever actually said these specific words out loud, but I was certainly indoctrinated with the thought that I was a Rasmussen, and I could do anything. My mother had always worked outside the home, and it never occurred to me that I would not. Of course I would go to university, get a good job and be successful. Whatever that meant.

Nor do I recall any overt sexism while I was in law school, although I think there were only six women in a first-year class of 113. I just remember one time in a property law class that there was a reference to a woman being a prostitute because she wore red shoes. I have absolutely no other recollection of the case or why that would have come up in relation to property law, but I had red shoes on that day, and I felt very uncomfortable. The comment wasn't directed at me; it was just a coincidence that I was wearing those shoes.

Law school was the first time that I ever felt there was a possibility that I might fail. I had always done well in school, but there was a lot of pressure and a lot of competition in law school. One of the professors was known to say to all his first-year classes, "Look to your left, look to your right. One of you won't be here next year." There were no computers and no Internet, and research had to be done with actual books. Some students actually cut pages out of case reports so that other students wouldn't be able to read them.

We had to do a moot court in first year. I think that's still a requirement. It's a pretend submission to a court, with one of the faculty members acting as the judge. They videotaped them, which was a very new thing in 1971, and it was like a movie set with big, bright lights and big cameras. I had those photo-sensitive lenses in my John Lennon–type wire-rim glasses (also a new thing then), so that when I went out into the sun the lenses would darken and I wouldn't need to have sunglasses. Of course, under the lights my lenses turned dark, and I was embarrassed when I saw the videotape. But I only had one pair of glasses. That was the whole point. I was also embarrassed by the legal gowns we had to wear for this appearance in "court," because of course, since I am only five feet tall, they were all way too long.

At this time, my mother, who was a nurse, was the director of nursing at a nursing home in Regina. The administrator of the home was an old friend of Dean Roger Carter's. So I got the third-hand report from the dean, who apparently said, "Once I got over her height and those glasses, she wasn't bad." I was greatly relieved by that message and managed not to be one of the three who didn't make it past first-year law.

In 1972, toward the end of my second year of law school, I became pregnant with your aunt Zena. I wasn't sure how that would go over, so I talked to one of the professors, who had become a friend. He spoke to the dean who said of course this was not a problem and to remind me that if I needed to have a deferral on medical grounds that would be available. Zena was born in December 1972. The graduation picture of me in the law school was taken about twenty-four hours before she was born! Dean Carter sent me a huge bouquet of pink carnations. I didn't understand that then, or now, to be in any way undermining of me as a woman, but to be a sincere expression of congratulations. I certainly appreciated it.

Dean Carter continued to be an important early influence. In the summer of 1972, I did research for him when he was chair of a committee established by the attorney general of Saskatchewan, then Roy Romanow, to make recommendations for a legal aid system for the province. I know the current legal aid system has many flaws, but legal aid is at least now available as a matter of right rather than as a matter of charity.

Dean Carter also hired me to be a student tutor in the first Summer Program of Legal Studies for Native Persons in 1973. The objective of the Summer Program was to provide a bridge over the cultural divide that made it extremely difficult for Indigenous persons to get into law school and to graduate. Legally, 1973 is also an important year because this was the year in which the Supreme Court of Canada issued its decision in the Calder case, essentially holding that Indigenous Peoples in Canada have rights. I was first exposed to these issues in the Summer Program, and they ultimately came to dominate my career in many different ways. But it's also important that anything I know about Aboriginal law in Canada I learned myself; it was not a topic in law school in the 1970s.

I don't know if it is still the practice for the dean to have a sherry party at the Bessborough Hotel in Saskatoon for the graduating class, but it was in 1973. My grandfather, who was at the time the Danish vice-consul in Saskatchewan, came dressed in the tux that he wore when he was presented to the King of Denmark. I was embarrassed by that too, because it was after all the seventies, but I look back on that with great pride because of the importance he placed on each of these events. Charm bracelets were very fashionable then, and he gave me a charm bracelet with a "key to success" as a graduating present. I have it in a box somewhere. I should give it to you.

My first job out of law school was in research. I was a legal researcher for a special committee of the Saskatchewan Legislature investigating highway traffic and safety. My office was in the Legislative Building. At that time, the entire Attorney General's Department (as it was then known; the more pretentious "Department of Justice" label came later) had offices in the building, and everyone went for coffee at the same time. I would sit at the long table and mostly listen to the conversation, which was usually about law. One of the debates around the table in about 1974 centred on a situation involving one of my former female law school classmates. Her husband had sold a piece of land, and she had had to complete the homestead consent. She had signed it with her name, and the land titles system had rejected it because, they said, her legal name was her husband's name. She argued that a woman taking her husband's name was a social convention, not a legal requirement. The debate around the coffee table among the law-yers in the Attorney General's Department (I'm pretty sure they were all men) on this point was rather heated. *The Change of Name Act* was later amended to make it clear that a woman may take her husband's name or not; she gets to choose.

I articled after completing the research project. I know that many women had a difficult time with articling and private prac-tice in general. I was asked questions like how I would cope with a family and a career, when I had already demonstrated how I would do that, since by this time Zena was three years old. I'm sure my male colleagues were never asked this question. I had another lawyer tell me that if I articled with him, he wouldn't be able to have coffee with me because he and his wife had an understand-ing about that sort of "conduct." I thought, "No problem, because I won't work for you."

I articled for Garrett Wilson, and although he had a (deserved) reputation as a difficult individual, for whatever reason he and I hit it off. He had many interesting stories about the law and I learned a lot from him. He was a sole practitioner at the time and president of the Liberal Party in Saskatchewan. I started articling with him in April 1975, and there was a provincial election in June. As a result, he was gone a lot of the time, and I guess I was more or less babysitting his practice. I remember I was reading through the statutes that I was going to be tested on in the bar admission exams and I came across a provision in *The Legal Profession Act* that said "the Benchers may make rules for the admission of women." The Benchers are like the board of directors for the law society. I was shocked and disgusted, and I wrote a letter to the attorney general (still Roy Romanow) to say this provision should be removed. It was. *The Legal Profession Act* was amended in the following ses-sion of the Legislature to repeal this section. I realize now that it was probably there because of the legal view prior to the famous *Persons* case in 1928 that women were not "persons" under statutes. However, it was rather an anachronism by 1976.

I spent almost fifteen years after I articled as legislative counsel for the Saskatchewan Legislature, drafting legislation. Since there are really very few persons doing this work in each Canadian jurisdiction, drafters from all jurisdictions meet once a year to exchange information and experience, and to develop model legislation for all jurisdictions to enact, with the objective of making the law uniform across the country. When I first went to this conference in 1978, there were only two women in the room: me and the other drafter from Saskatchewan. A few years later there were more women present, and I made a remark about this to the then legislative counsel in British Columbia. He made a comment to the effect that it was a bad thing for more women to be engaged in drafting legislation because it would lead to lower salaries. I was annoyed at that comment, but in retrospect my annoyance was because he was stating a fact, not an opinion.

While I was legislative counsel, I also provided administrative support to the Statute Revision Committee. This was a committee of lawyers that was convened every ten years or so to revise the legislation of the province by incorporating the amendments that had been made each year into the statutes that had been amended, correcting any obvious errors and updating all the references. The statutes were then reprinted in one big collection. Before computers, this was a daunting task. Paper copies of everything had to be literally clipped and pasted, and corrections hand-written onto the paper paste-up. Then it all had to be printed. In 1978, the revised statutes consisted of more than 10,000 pages.

I would get several calls a day from the foreman at the Saskatchewan Government Printing Company, which was printing the revision, with questions. The men who had worked at the printing plant for years spotted errors. One for example was a statute that referred to the "Court House in North Battleford." The guys knew that the courthouse was actually in Battleford, and the foreman called to get authorization for the change.

But what appeared to be an error wasn't always. There was a reference in *The Vehicles Act* to turning "seasonably" to the left. The printer called to say this looked like an error and should have said "reasonably." I said to let me check. I then discovered that the statute had always said "seasonably" from the time it was first enacted more than fifty years previously and had continued to use this word in several previous revisions. I finally looked the word up in the dictionary and discovered that one of its meanings was "at an opportune time." It wasn't an error; it was an example of words changing their primary meaning over time. I told the printer to leave it as it was. The use of the word disappeared when the Act was revised in 1983.

When an error to be corrected was not an obvious one, such as a misspelling of the word "Saskatchewan," we would tell the printer to print it incorrectly and then we would add the correction to be made to the next *Statute Law Amendment Act*. We did this because the law isn't what the drafter (or the printer) thinks is correct, but what the Legislature has enacted. Then once the Legislature enacted the amendment, we would have the printer print the correction in the loose-leaf version of the statutes. At one point I had a conversation with the Queen's Printer in which I said I thought that the guys at the printing plant thought those "dizzy broads" in the Legislative Counsel's Office didn't know what they were doing. We were talking on the phone, and there was a long pause. Then he said, "You may have a point there."

I left the Saskatchewan Legislature during the Devine administration in 1988, not because of gender discrimination but because that government did not understand what it meant to have a professional opinion. Not to put too fine a point on it, they were equal-opportunity bullies. If you didn't agree with their political position, you were the enemy.

I entered private practice when I was in my late thirties and after fifteen years as a practicing member of the legal profession, although I had only darkened a courtroom once or twice as an articling student. I joined a partnership with Garret Wilson, the lawyer I had articled with and with whom I had maintained a connection, and we practiced together for another fifteen years. I used to (still do) go the office wearing jeans and one day, fairly early on in our partnership, he came in and sat down and said, "Do we have a dress code here?" He was clearly referring to the fact that I was wearing jeans, but when I did not have to go to court or a meeting, why not? I said, "Well, I don't know about you, but I always feel very uncomfortable wearing pantyhose." His face turned beet red. He didn't say a word, and he got up and left my office. Dress codes were never mentioned again.

I had the opportunity to do some fantastic work during this time. I went back to university full time for a year and then completed a master's degree in political science. My thesis advisor was Dr. Howard Leeson, who has become a very close friend. He was also your mother's thesis advisor when she completed her master's degree twenty or so years later. Howard had been deputy minister of intergovernmental affairs in the Blakeney government in Saskatchewan, and in 1991, when the NDP were returned to government under Roy Romanow, he came back from the university to act as the premier's constitutional advisor during the intergovernmental negotiations that led to the Charlottetown Accord.

I have a very clear memory of meeting with Howard one Friday afternoon in the cafeteria in the Legislative Building, when he explained to me how the negotiation process was going to work and asked me if I wanted to be a member of this constitutional "SWAT team." Of course I said yes, and he told me who else would be involved. There were only six of us initially, and the others were all male. He also told me that there would be a number of different working groups established, so negotiations would be ongoing in each of the primary subject areas at the same time. One of those working groups was to deal with the issue of Aboriginal self-government. I said, "Well, you don't have any Indigenous people on the team but I'm the only woman so you should put me on the Aboriginal working group." And he did.

I was in my first meeting in Toronto the following Tuesday, and during the next six months I think I logged about 30,000 miles of travel by plane back and forth to Ottawa and other locations where meetings of ministers were held. I felt guilty about being away from home all the time. Your mother would have been about eight years old at the time. I—rather pretentiously, I admit—told her I had to be away because we were working on "saving the country." When I had to go away again, your mother said, "Didn't you do that last week?"

It was a fabulous personal experience for me to be involved in those negotiations. Bob Mitchell was the responsible minister. He had been the minister responsible for amendments to the *Human Rights Code* in 1993 to add "sexual orientation" to the list of prohibited grounds of discrimination, which had been a very controversial change. He was a committed feminist, and his only instructions to me during the constitutional negotiations were, "Don't let anyone get to the left of you."

I was joined very soon after starting by Professor Donna Greschner, who was then at the University of Saskatchewan College of Law. Donna was from Goodsoil, Saskatchewan, originally, and had been a Rhodes scholar. There were only the two of us on the Saskatchewan team in the Aboriginal Working Group. The rules were that there could only be two persons at the table in each working group, but large jurisdictions like Canada and Ontario had two different persons depending on the specific issue being discussed. We were at the table the entire time, for every issue. It was gruelling, although important and personally rewarding. I also acted as the Saskatchewan representative on the drafting team that prepared the legal text of the Charlottetown Accord. The Accord was not supported across Canada in the referendum held in October 1992, but there was a "yes" vote in the riding where I lived. My joke at the time it was because I had to talk to everyone I ran into at the grocery store about it.

I continued on after that as a constitutional advisor for a couple of years with the Department of Intergovernmental Affairs, where Howard Leeson was appointed as deputy minister. I also began work on a master's degree in law, exploring the fiduciary relationship between the provincial Crown and First Nations. Donna Greschner was my thesis advisor for this one. She had a poster on her office door with a quote from Dame Rebecca West that said, "I myself have never been able to find out precisely what feminism is: I only know that people call me a feminist whenever I express sentiments that differentiate me from a doormat."

My experience in the Charlottetown negotiations led to other work in the field of Aboriginal law. Bob Mitchell was retained by the FSIN (now the Federation of Sovereign Indigenous Nations) to negotiate a province-wide, treaty-based self-government agreement by which Canada and Saskatchewan would recognize Indigenous jurisdiction over the seventy-four First Nations in Saskatchewan. We worked hard on this project for three or four years. I volunteered to "hold the pen," as they say, in the preparation of the rolling draft of the agreement in principle. This was a strategic decision; acting for the FSIN, we felt that it was important to be the one writing down the words, even though they were still all negotiated. My drafting experience was recognized by all parties, and we proceeded in this manner. During all of this process I felt more conspicuous for being "white" than being female. It may be that being female actually helped to make me more acceptable to the First Nations who employed me. We did manage to arrive at an agreement in principle that was initialled by the negotiators for all three parties, but it was never implemented. I think too many elections intervened, both federally and provincially and with the First Nations.

It was at about this same time that I started searching for work in the new territory of Nunavut. A new jurisdiction doesn't get created in a country very often, and I thought it would be interesting to work in this new territory and perhaps have some sort of influence on the development of legal systems there. I was familiar with the concept of Nunavut as a public government for the Inuit from my negotiations in the Charlottetown process. The Inuit representatives in those negotiations had always been very impressive to me. They were prepared and rational. They didn't just speak to hear themselves talk. This was not to say they were without passion. At one point, when the Charlottetown discussions finally got to the touchy subject of money, one of the Inuit representatives finally said, in a tone that I would describe as controlled anger, "You're going to spend the money. The question is, are you going to spend it on education or jails?"

I responded to an advertisement from the Government of Nunavut inviting applications from lawyers to be vetted and added to an "eligible list" if they were found to be acceptable. My name was thus added to a list of lawyers who could be hired to do work for the government or its agencies. I had kind of forgotten about that until I received a phone call from the lawyer in the Nunavut Department of Justice in charge of these things, who asked me if I would be interested in doing some work for the Nunavut Liquor Licensing Board. I confess that if I had been asked to list the agencies that I would like to do work for I wouldn't even have thought of this one, but administrative law is administrative law, regardless of the particular tribunal involved. So, of course, I said yes. That was in 2003. The Board is now the Liquor and Cannabis Board, and I continue to act for it, together with your aunt Zena.

I became a full practicing member of the Law Society of Nunavut in 2004, and more recently have been engaged to act for the Labour Standards Board and the Public Guardian. The work for the Public Guardian has given me a greater understanding of the North and the situation of the Inuit. Unlike in southern jurisdictions, the Nunavut Public Guardian handles all guardianship applications, even those where a private guardian is to be appointed. In preparing the documents, dealing with the people, and appearing in court in Nunavut, I have had a close-up view of the very difficult conditions under which many Inuit live. It makes me realize that any issues I have experienced in my life as a professional in southern Canada, even issues connected to my gender, are really in the category of "first-world problems."

But it's not just the far North where life is difficult for Indigenous persons. I was appointed as an adjudicator of residential school claims in 2006 and over the next ten years I heard from about 500 claimants about the serious sexual and physical abuse they endured while being forced to attend residential schools set up by the Government of Canada to "civilize the Indians." Many of the claimants I heard from had long histories of run-ins with the law, some of them quite serious. One of the first hearings I held involved the claim of an individual who was then in his sixties. He was a big guy and had all the jailhouse tattoos on his arms and hands. He was not a person you would want to run into in a dark alley. He was in tears while he told me about being sexually abused as a six-year-old child in residential school. Another claimant, who was obviously very intelligent although he lacked formal education because of the abuse at residential school, said to me, "You took me away from my family. They may not have been perfect, but they were my family." It amazes me that non-Indigenous institutions and officials apparently continue to think that they know best when all of the evidence is overwhelmingly to the contrary. I don't understand why we can't let Indigenous people make their own decisions; they can hardly do worse than we have.

In between these large projects, I did all kinds of other legal work. Private practice is hard on people because it is demanding work, often with impossible deadlines. Many firms require lawyers to record 1,800 or more hours of billable time in a year. That's about five hours every single day of the year, including weekends and holidays. Since women are the ones who give birth and are typically the primary caregivers of children, it is especially difficult for women to juggle the unrealistic demands of private practice. I spent a brief period of time with a medium-sized firm and found it to be a lot of pressure that I wasn't able to do anything about. I left to be on my own, because I thought even if I didn't make much money, at least I'd be sane. That was in the fall of 2005.

At this point in time, your aunt Zena was at Cambridge completing a master's degree in law, having completed an undergraduate degree in Saskatoon and prior to that, a degree in linguistics in Regina. We kind of stumbled along together, I in Regina, she in Saskatoon, not formally working together but helping each other out a little. My brother, your uncle Colin, had also completed a law degree at the same time as Zena. He had spent twenty years doing cancer research and when he ended up at the U of S College of Medicine, he told me he had always been interested in the law. I said, "Well, the law college is just across the road from your lab!" It's something of a long story, but he ended up in southern California, a member of the Law Society of Saskatchewan and the California State Bar, working in a law firm there, when one day he got fed up with the commute and said we should establish our own law firm. So, in March 2008, that's what he and Zena and I did.

The advantage of this type of "family law firm" is that we have each other's backs. While of course we want to be properly compensated for the work we each do, it's also of less importance that one of us might receive "more." And all of these ups and downs have a tendency to work out over time.

Now, at one point, when your mother was about ten years old, a friend of mine asked her if she was going to be lawyer too, when she grew up. She said, "No, you have to work too hard." But in 2010 or so, she changed her mind and decided she would also go to law school. She had worked with me providing administrative support, first part time and then, as I became busier and busier, full time. She continued to provide that support while she was in law school. She graduated in 2015 in the same class as your dad, and they both became lawyers in the family firm the following year. I don't think many other private firms allow you to bring your newborn to the office or leave at 4:00 p.m. to pick up kids from daycare. In these respects, I think gender is immaterial. In fact, I suspect it may be more difficult for men to ask for these kinds of accommodations because, I believe, there is still a general idea that this is women's responsibility. In many respects, I think it is easier for us to help each other out with work and also looking after kids or doing other things that aren't "work" because we are family.

I guess I have been isolated from much of the gender-based discrimination that many women experience, in part because of my education, in part because of my early upbringing that taught me I can do anything I want, and in part because I can be oblivious.

I hope that your mother and your aunt have found their gender to be even less of an issue as they make their way through life and their legal careers. And I hope that it will be a non-issue for you.

As I look back, I can see that there has been a great deal of improvement in the situation for women, at least in Canada and Saskatchewan, in the last fifty years, even if things are still not perfect.

Merrilee Rasmussen, KC, BA (Hons.), LLB, MA, LLM, continues to practice law with her daughters in Saskatchewan and Nunavut. She lives in Regina, Montevideo, and Kelowna, depending on the weather.

THINK (MUCH) BIGGER

THE HONOURABLE
MICHELE H. HOLLINS
1992 LLB

W hat advice would I give to my younger self?

"Trust your instincts"? "Be more open minded"? "Wear that bikini!" :).

This sounded like such an easy assignment, but it has challenged me considerably.

First of all, I have to reach pretty far back in the memory vault to connect with my younger self. She feels like someone I knew very well at one time, but with whom I have lost touch. I feel a great deal of affection for her, but some guilt that I haven't thought about her in so many years. I have bought into the premise so thoroughly that I wonder for a moment what she is like now.

Let me begin with a brief description of this young woman, the hypothetical beneficiary of my advice. She is about twenty-nine years old and has just completed law school. She is a bit older than most of her classmates, having had some years in the workforce before law school. She has completed a court clerkship and is moving away from her family in Saskatchewan to begin her articles with the Calgary office of a large national law firm.

Certainly, the defining feature of her life at that moment is that she is single parenting two five-year-old twin girls. These girls were fourteen-month-old infants at the beginning of law school. This young woman has already survived the dissolution of her marriage during law school and graduated with good marks. She can fairly be described as ambitious and ready to embrace challenge, but she also realizes that she really has no idea of what will be required to complete her articles, secure future employment, and "succeed at law," whatever that means.

With her reckless mixture of confidence and naïveté, she sets out to do the best job she can of whatever is put in front of her. The little ones have a good but not idyllic childhood, involving *way* too much McDonald's and "play with these markers" time. However, they all survive the ups and downs of these early years of her career. She learns, makes friends, and begins to build a practice.

All in all, she does pretty well. I don't need to rescue her from any unseen cliff edge, nor do I have any wish to chastise her for many but minor failings in judgment. But now, with the almost thirty years of life between her and me, I do think I have something important to tell her, and it is this:

Think bigger!

The Internet tells me that Michelangelo once said, "The greater danger for most of us lies not in setting our aim too high and falling short but in setting our aim too low, and achieving our mark."

I have achieved some things in my life, and I'm proud of them. I don't minimize those achievements, even as I acknowledge that all of them were largely the product of the involvement of others or of my considerable privilege, including financial stability and supportive parents. However, I now believe that my approach to life was, at least early on, too short-sighted.

I had married and had children in my early twenties, so post-graduation, I was focused on building my career, not on finding or nurturing another romantic relationship. I followed these steps:

1. Get job
2. Do job
3. Keep job

This is not a bad or blameworthy approach to life. I could have done a lot worse than go to school, get a job, and keep that job. And I did not just do the minimum of these things. I think I can fairly say that my personality is such that whatever task is set in front of me is the next challenge, and I immediately resolve to conquer it, whatever that requires. Those are good or at least valuable qualities in a busy young lawyer. Further, I must acknowledge here that I genuinely enjoyed my work, which sadly sets me apart from many lawyers who work very hard at something they don't enjoy.

Basically, I always made a very good employee, but my dedication to the everyday tasks of work and family left me no time for imagination, for really big thinking. I am beginning to realize that everyone should have that time, or more accurately, should create that time.

I want also to be clear that I am not overly critical of my younger self in this regard. I have loved my life in the law. I believe that I generally made good career choices, and I am proud of the work that I have done and all the clients, and now litigants, that I have been able to work for during my career. I just wish that I had been more directed and more aspirational in my thinking.

My dad was diagnosed with terminal prostate cancer in his early seventies. For a month or so while he was in the hospice, we had time every morning to visit—one of the most precious experiences of my life. Although he talked mostly about how grateful he was to have lived the life he had, there were a few occasions when he spoke more wistfully about feeling that he had not done everything he believed he could have done, that he wasn't finished. It was a general expression, not an enumerated list, but I remember realizing that I too might evaluate my own life in that way eventually. Someday, I will also likely ask myself, "Did I do what I wanted to do?"

Life is both shorter and longer than we think.

When we are young, time is measured in relatively small increments and so stretches out to great lengths in front of us. That temporal elasticity allows us, as young adults, to focus on a longer list of tasks with which we have limited experience. I have always been a list-maker. When I was in my early years of practice and the girls were getting older and busier (i.e., eight to twelve years), I took to writing, in colour-coded ink on our calendar, every single thing that needed to get done every day. At some point, one of my then adolescent girls admonished me that I should not write "take a bath" on the calendar for their friends to see, as though that were only an occasional event at our house.

But that was the very granular nature of my life at that time. Prioritizing tasks was itself almost a full-time job. For many years, my typical day ended with putting the kids to bed and going back to work on my computer. I was working from home long before it was fashionable or, worse, a public health necessity.

All of this to say that it is hardly surprising that I did not allocate time to daydreaming about what I really wanted to do with my life. I was definitely masterclass level at identifying what I wanted or needed to accomplish in the next twenty-four hours or the next week. I occasionally even thought about career goals for up to the next year (e.g., I want to have 20 percent of my practice be my own work, I want to prepare and conduct my own examination for discovery). What I did not do was the next-level thinking about any bigger picture.

> *Most people overestimate what they can do in one year*
> *and underestimate what they can do in ten years.*
> **—BILL GATES**

This statement is so simple that I resent it took a billionaire computer genius to say it, but it is so descriptive of me that it rings in my ears constantly since I read it. I still make lists all the time but they are inevitably "to do" items for the next week or so. I congratulate myself every time I actually book that eye appointment or organize my tax receipts.

Just as I have made an excellent employee but a bad entrepreneur, I am good at goal-setting but not at dreaming. I have now done a bit of reading about the difference between the two, which I think I intuitively knew but have never studied. Goals are shorter-term objectives, measurable and achievable on a fixed or at least knowable timeline. They are meant to be the actual steps to get us from A to B.

But what *is* B? Where is B? What about H or Q or Y?

Thinking big is thinking fancifully, imaginatively, selfishly. Before proceeding to worry about whether something is realistic, there is great value in simply musing about what might be ideal or even really good. Why? Because without some dreaming, we are more likely to simply keep moving forward, accomplishing the tasks set before us, which are most often dictated by someone else. We may miss the opportunity to identify a different or additional direction toward something else that might bring greater happiness and fulfillment to our lives.

For example, you could start with:

What activities, professional or otherwise, make you happy? When do you feel proud? When do you feel at peace?

With whom do you wish you could spend more time? Who makes you happy?

If you could reach any position or level within your current profession, what would that be?

If you could design your perfect job, without regard to security, income, advancement potential, or status, what would it be?

If you were not working within the legal profession, what non-legal work would make you happiest?

If you could live anywhere in the world, where would that be?

If you could travel without limits, where would you go? With whom? How often?

These are not just fun over-the-dinner-table games, these are real conversations we should be having with ourselves.

I have stumbled into a few of these almost by accident. For example, I was reading an article many years ago about happiness and the author posed this question: "What is the one thing in your life, that if you could change it right now, would result in the most positive impact?" or words to that effect. In my mind, I immediately answered, "My kitchen!" I have always loved to cook (which is different than being a good cook) and for years, I had hobbled around a tiny kitchen with dysfunctional cabinets and often-failing appliances. I resolved to renovate my kitchen. Although it took a while and was not free, I loved my "new" kitchen every moment of every day I lived in that house. I cannot overstate how that renovation improved my experience of living there.

Now the kitchen example may actually be closer to a goal than a dream, but I did think of another example. Somewhere early in my career, I remember saying to myself that I wanted to stop renting accommodation and be living in our own house with a yard by the time the girls were ten years old. I forgot all about this until well after we moved into our first home that I owned in Calgary, the very month that the girls turned ten. Coincidence? Probably. But just think about what might happen if I actually put my mind to dreaming. What other far-flung adventures might eventually come to pass?!

In addition to exhorting my younger self to think bigger, I would give her these guidelines and caveats, in the form of a list, naturally:

THINK MUCH BIGGER!

Nothing is too outlandish. Dreams are not inhibited by reality, finances, or time. They may be possible or they may be impossible. Achieving them is not actually the point—simply giving voice to your deepest, wildest desires is the point. I sincerely believe that there is power in allowing yourself to want big things, even if the value is primarily about affirming the fact that you're worthy of the grandest measures of happiness and fulfillment.

This task was not expressly gendered—i.e., the advice to our younger selves was not mandated to speak to the fact that our younger selves were women.[1] However—and this is strictly anecdotal—I do think that generally, dreaming big and selfishly is not

---

[1]   And in fact, I actually do not know the gender identities of my fellow authors, then or now, so mean no offence in referring here to young women.

something that comes as naturally to women as to men. There is plenty of empirical evidence that women tend to underestimate their own value and chances of success or advancement. This is not a criticism of that type of expansive thinking in men at all, but rather a wish that we all shared that proclivity.

We have likely all participated in institutional or organizational "blue sky" meetings, in which facilitators have encouraged us to describe the ideal structure, direction, or goals of the organization. It is no surprise that those facilitators have to continually remind us that true "blue sky" thinking is not advanced by all the Debbie Downers, who can only interject "but we tried that already" or "there is no budget for that."[2] Debbies are focused on making sure the objective can be achieved. Eventually that must be discussed, but it is expressly not the point of a dream.

By allowing yourself, or forcing yourself, to think big-picture about your life, you will likely discover passions, talents, directions, and unspoken wishes that you did not know you had. Even if you don't ever become an astronaut, realizing that you love all things space may inform more rewarding pastimes. And, at the current pace of development of private space travel, who knows??

BE DISCIPLINED

It may sound counterintuitive to say that we should be disciplined dreamers but, at least for my own part, I do not tend to think expansively or creatively when left to my own devices. My thoughts will inevitably drift only as far as whether or not it is garbage day or what to wear to work.

---

2   Apologies to all "Debbies," and a confession that I have absolutely made these kind of comments—verbatim—myself.

I have to actually force myself to think in this bigger way while still having some light in the distance on which to focus. For example, maybe on tomorrow morning's walk, I will try to focus on big thoughts about my non-work time. What do I love to do? Where do I love to be? This may ultimately be related to dreams about travel or to ideas for hobbies or volunteerism, but the first step is to set aside time for the exercise of dreaming, of visualizing, of articulating.

All writing that I could find, whether on goal-setting or dreaming, made the point that we must actually set aside time for these activities. In the "olden days," all kinds of self-care measures were often disparaged or characterized as inconsistent with ambition. Thankfully, that is changing. So, if you can make time—as you should—for exercise, meditation, yoga retreats, and therapy, you can make time for some dreaming. If you do not, you may miss out on personal or professional directions that are perfect for you, if not now, then someday.

SAY IT OUT LOUD

When I taught an advocacy course years ago, we encouraged (okay, we forced) the participants to do a drill on objections that involved them physically standing up and loudly saying "Objection!" The exercise could have simply required them to raise their hands when they felt an objectionable question had been asked, or even to list the objections in writing and review them at the end of the mock testimony. But none of that would have accomplished the real goal of the exercise, which was to get people more physically comfortable with interrupting another speaker.

I have done a fair bit of public speaking over the years and I have learned, slowly and painfully, that it was a non-negotiable part of preparation to read the speech out loud beforehand, even if I have written it myself. Inevitably, there is something that has not come out as tight or as funny as it sounded in my head.

Dreaming is not generally thought of as an "out loud" endeavour. Certainly, the pure musing stage of dreaming takes place internally for me. But the "I want to go to space" expression of that musing should absolutely be said out loud. Don't worry that it sounds crazy. Everyone who has achieved a really big dream sounded crazy when they first articulated it. Further, if the accepted purpose of big thinking is not to necessarily achieve that idea but to allow yourself to admit that you want big things, then tell yourself what you want!

...TO YOURSELF

Yes, you should articulate your big thoughts, but I would suggest doing so to yourself. Not that you cannot share them, particularly with your close people whose lives may be affected if you decide to pursue one or more of your big thoughts. But, at least initially, knowing that these are private mental adventures will reduce any inhibitions in your thoughts. Who cares what your colleagues think of your dream of publishing a novel? They don't need to know until and unless you convert your dream into a goal and they buy your book.

I'll break my own rule and tell you that one of my dreams is to throw out the first pitch at a Major League Baseball game. Totally weird and exceedingly unlikely to happen. But who cares? It's fun to think about, and maybe it will eventually tell me something about myself that will translate into something concrete.

I think most of us have an unfortunate tendency to treat others' dreams as goals, immediately springing into an analysis of how (un)realistic they are, how long they will take, how much they will cost, etc. Don't subject yourself to that. And please don't write me to explain why I will never get to throw the first pitch for an MLB game.

BE NICE TO YOUR DREAMING SELF

Recognize that you won't get all (or perhaps any) of these things. Forgive yourself everything that happens in Dream World. The purpose of thinking bigger is not to set yourself up for failure and chastise yourself when you don't get whatever fantastical thing you allowed yourself to want (cue the story of my disappointment when as a five- or six-year-old, following a sermon on the power of prayer, I prayed for a basket of puppies and woke up to no such basket).

You are allowed to want big, illogical things for yourself. You don't owe anyone an explanation of that. Unlike goals, which are finite and conquerable, your dreams are more like a flashlight that may illuminate different directions or doorways you might otherwise have missed completely. You don't need to explore all of them. You may, but there is no commitment to any particular path. It is like being on that virtual air gliding ride at Disneyland—you can see everything below, but there is no actual risk of crashing.

Also recognize that your dreams will change over time. I, for example, am now quite happy with one dog (maybe two), but a basket of puppies sounds like a nightmare. Your dreams *should* change. I think my younger self missed out on a lot of this type of big thinking, but even if she had spent more time like that, her dreams then would not be my dreams now. I won't share any more of them here, but I feel with certainty that the drivers of my happiness and fulfillment have continually evolved over my lifetime.

It is never too late to think big. In fact, I see this as particularly important even later in life. For example, although the idea of being a bird watcher does not sit well with me just yet, I have discovered that I do indeed love watching birds and, in fact, wildlife of all sorts. So, perhaps I need to actually consider some research into things that may evolve into hobbies eventually.

In all things—career, family, friendships, volunteer time, personal activities/hobbies—you should try to spend as much time as possible doing what you want to do, or at least moving in that direction. So ask yourself:

What do you want?

If you get silence the first time (as I have several times), don't give up. Ask again:

What do you want?

> *The idea is there locked inside. All you have*
> *to do is remove the excess stone.*
> —MICHELANGELO (reportedly)

Take care, younger self. I love you very much.

Michele H. Hollins was in private practice for twenty-five years before her appointment to King's Bench in Alberta in 2017. She is enjoying watching her twin daughters live their amazing lives and is delighting in her grandchildren.

TO *the* GENTLEMAN'S CREDIT, HE WAS MORTIFIED

NICOLE SARAUER

2009 JD

Dear Graduating Class of 2040,

It feels strange to write a letter to those I have not met, whose concept of Canadian life and law may be very different from my own.

Although many things may change in the next twenty years, the practice of law is in many ways inherently resistant to transformation. As such, there is a good chance that the profession will not be significantly different when you enter practice. There is something mildly comforting in that knowledge, but something sad as well.

I love the practice of law. I have never regretted obtaining my law degree or entering the legal profession. Through legal practice, I have learned an immense amount about law, and about life more generally. One of my favourite aspects of legal practice is advocating for the client. I love courtroom advocacy.

My law degree has opened many doors in my career. It continues to do so. I'm sure I would not be an elected Member of the Saskatchewan Legislative Assembly if my education and career had taken a different turn. Many of the skills I acquired in law were easily transferable into politics.

With that said, the legal profession is not perfect. There are times when advocating within the system is frustrating beyond measure, where one feels like a cog in an overly complicated machine rather than an advocate for justice.

The work of a lawyer can be stressful. Some have said that the practice of law is like a pie-eating contest, with the only reward being more pie. Given the pressure inherent in the role, it is not uncommon for young lawyers to quickly feel like they've had their fill.

Furthermore, despite the great strides made by female graduates (I believe the University of Saskatchewan College of Law is currently at gender parity), the number of women in practice beyond their five-year call is significantly lower than that of their male counterparts. This disparity is particularly pronounced in private practice.

A friend recently made the following observation on social media, after noting two prominent female lawyers were litigating one of the most public and contentious matters in Saskatchewan's recent history:

> I think the stats show a roughly 50/50 split of male/female lawyers leaving law school, but far fewer women than men become courtroom advocates, and even fewer do so in private practice.

Her observation gave me pause, and has been sitting with me for a while. The basic fact is that significant gender disparity remains in the legal profession, particularly in the courtroom. Ignoring this reality would do a disservice to our profession.

The dynamics that perpetuate this reality can be complex. They are often reflective of broader societal issues. But without addressing these issues, young women will likely never truly feel like they belong in our profession.

As a young lawyer, I remember multiple clients mistaking me for a legal assistant, on the assumption that a young woman couldn't be their lawyer. Of course, my male colleagues did not have the same experience. I remember feeling overlooked for mentorship opportunities, while male colleagues were invited for drinks or golf with senior male lawyers.

I am not alone among my female colleagues in having had these experiences.

I am not in private practice. I often wonder how much of that has to do with some of the experiences I had as a young woman in the profession. Unfortunately, my current profession is no better in terms of gender disparity. Many young women do not view politics as a desirable or viable career path, and as a result, this profession is not even close to gender parity.

The world of politics is similar to that of law: the speed of change can be glacial. Older gentlemen make up a disproportionate number of those at the top. This has consequences for how people think of politics, and politicians. I remember many comments concerning my marital status, and how I would balance being an MLA with raising children (I was single at the time and had no plans for children), being made on doorsteps during my first campaign. My male counterparts did not, and do not, face similar questions.

A few years ago, I was in our caucus office at the Legislature, chatting with colleagues in our reception area. A gentleman came through the door, a high-level bureaucrat who had worked in the public service for decades. I greeted him as my colleagues were leaving, and he was kind in his hello to me. I had not had the opportunity to meet him until that moment, although I had been elected for two years at that time. He gave me a smile and asked whether I would be joining himself and another MLA for a meeting, adding, "as an intern, it would be a good experience for you." To the gentleman's credit, he was mortified after I pointed out that I was an MLA.

This exchange happened just a few weeks before I became interim leader of my party and the leader of Saskatchewan's opposition.

When we close our eyes and think of a politician or lawyer, the face of a woman under thirty-five does not reflexively come to mind. This creates an extra hurdle of credibility for female professionals to overcome in taking their seat at the table with their peers. It is even more difficult for women of colour or women with disabilities.

This is evident in how I was treated by the media and public when I announced my recent pregnancy. My husband and I were ecstatic and wanted to make a personal announcement on social media to friends and family. I did not think anyone would much care about me and my future child, but I was wrong. Much to my surprise, my pregnancy announcement made it into the papers and onto the evening news, as did the birth of our daughter and a number of other milestones.

Why?

I think it's because a pregnant MLA is a very rare thing in this province. This is not to say MLAs with young families do not exist. I have several male colleagues, on both sides of the aisle, who balance young families and politics with grace. However, I am only the second MLA to have given birth since Saskatchewan became a province. That says a lot about how much we must grow as a province when it comes to the diversity of our elected representatives.

Although most of the responses to my pregnancy were positive, I faced many questions about how I was going to balance my responsibilities to constituents with caring for my baby. Again, these are questions my male colleagues are not asked when they have young families.

When my daughter was fourteen weeks old, I had to bring her into the Legislative Chamber to burp her. I had just finished feeding her and Question Period was about to begin. My colleagues from both parties were generally very supportive. This was not the first time a baby had been inside a Canadian legislative chamber, but it was a first in Saskatchewan. As such, media made note of it. Again, most responses were encouraging, but the negative ones highlighted some of the issues faced by young women considering a career in politics:

> Seen your dilemma on your child coming to work...I totally *disagree* with this 100%...you want her with you quit your job or better yet hire childcare with your government paycheck.

As mentioned, my child was fourteen weeks old. You will likely appreciate that it is somewhat difficult to arrange childcare for a babe that young.

There is a group of female lawyers in Regina I enjoy spending time with. We often get together at CBA events. We are around the same year of call. Some are still in private practice, some work in government. Some have been partner in law firm for a few years, or are close to making partner. Many of us juggle busy lives as professionals and parents to young children. In many ways we feel professionally old: somewhat tired, somewhat jaded, but more assertive and confident than we were at the beginning of our careers.

We often share stories of our experiences in our workplaces. The pressure to excel and meet billable targets. The frustration when someone is overlooked in favour of a male counterpart. The difficulty in balancing practice with family and active volunteer and social lives.

We know we are in a much better position than those women who came before us. We owe them a great deal.

Our predecessors, who had to fight to be taken seriously in law school—to prove they belonged there.

Our predecessors, who had to push past and break through harassment in the workplace, and fight to become partners at their firms or senior leaders in their workplaces.

Our predecessors, who were turned away at the doors of certain establishments within this province because of their gender, when male clients and colleagues were ushered in without comment.

Our predecessors, who thrived in spite of these challenges to become senior partners and judges, businesswomen and politicians.

Our predecessors, who, in turn, became our role models.

We know there is still progress to be made. Discussing the need for such progress does not minimize the accomplishments of those who came before. But it should push us all to do better, and to be better.

I want the same thing for the legal profession and the public service. I want the idea of women, especially young women, in leadership roles to be so ubiquitous that it is no longer noteworthy. I want women in politics to be able to give birth without making the news. I want women in legal practice to not have to worry about whether taking six months off to care for a newborn will jeopardize their careers. I want male lawyers and politicians who want to take time with family to be treated with understanding and respect for the many different roles we all have in this life.

In short, I want female lawyers, especially young female lawyers, to be able to fully take their place at the table. Our profession needs this. Our society needs this.

It's been ten years since I graduated from the University of Saskatchewan College of Law. There have been significant positive developments in those ten years. But we have much more work to do. I look forward to helping with that work in the next twenty years. Hopefully you'll be able to join me after you graduate in 2040.

Nicole Sarauer has been the NDP MLA for Regina Douglas Park since 2016. She has served as interim leader, deputy leader, and house leader, as well as critic for many files, including justice, corrections and policing, and labour. She lives in Regina with her husband and two young children.

LEADING *the* WAY

A CALL *to the* NEXT GENERATION *of* INDIGENOUS WOMEN

***

SENATOR YVONNE BOYER

1996 LLB

I was asked to speak to the students at the Indigenous Bar Conference (IBA) in 2019, and parts of the speech are repro-duced here. It is important to go back in time and remem-ber where I was when I was a law student and a member of the Indigenous Bar Association. I want to share with you (the students; the future) some of the things that I learned along the way.

I graduated with an LLB in 1996 and finished my articles in 1997. Law was my second career. What I wanted to hear most back then was the solid truth of what I was getting into. But today I want to recount my observations about opportunities, risks, and the disappointments I overcame as I ventured through my career and life. Sometimes we face harsh realities before finding the places wherein we thrive. On harried days, when you wake up asking "Why am I here?" and forget why you are doing what you are doing—I hope the following words will serve as a guide. I hope that I can plant a seed today so that the journey in front of you may be a little clearer. As I share my journey, I hope you can learn from my challenges as you confront yours.

My name is Yvonne Marie Boyer. I am the granddaughter of Mary Rosalie LaRocque and Louis Amable Boyer of the Red River, specifically the Pembina area. My ancestry is Cree and Chippewa from the Northern United States, Southern Manitoba, and Southern Saskatchewan. My mother is Irish—her family are all Irish immigrants. I am Metis and have been raised in a Metis household. As custom goes, I was raised by my Auntie Lucy. I am a lawyer and was previously a nurse. I am a mother and a grandmother and an auntie. My lifelong and professional work is grounded in, and focused on, the intersection between health and the law and, in particular, the myriad issues in Indigenous health.

My grandmother was born in 1881, and my father was the youngest of thirteen children. He had sisters twenty years older than him, and he was very loved by all of these very wonderful and powerful women/sisters/mothers and aunties. The aunt I lived with is my father's sister, Lucille Bernadette Boyer. My bedtime stories were stories of the tuberculosis sanatorium where my aunt spent ten years of her life. It was at Fort San in the Qu'Appelle Valley in Saskatchewan. Those were the days before antibiotics, when the only treatment for tuberculosis was bedrest and cold air. Bundled in big iron beds with heated bricks put at their feet, the patients were wheeled out to the porch and left to sleep. My aunt's body was immobilized and completely in a cast for five years. She spoke of the constant hacking and coughing, and often of her friends and the children who were dying. In stories, my auntie brought to life the grim realities for a tiny little Chippewa/Metis girl in a tuberculosis sanatorium. Despite her decade of near-death struggles, she courageously kept upbeat and gave me three important life lessons.

The first is that health care for brown children is different than for white children. The second is that there are some very mean people that hurt others because of their race, especially when there is no family watching close by. My aunt saw her family once in those ten years. The last lesson she taught was that there are predators in the hospital systems and that monsters do walk the halls. My auntie was institutionalized from 1925 to 1935. She was never able to bear children, although I do not know if she was sterilized, as her records were destroyed.

I had many aunts and uncles. My aunties and grandmother were healers and health care providers—they cared for each other and others. It was expected that I go into nursing when I graduated from high school, and that is what I did. What I saw in the 1980s mirrored my aunt's descriptions of the realities of the 1920s and 1930s. There was racism, discrimination, intentional meanness, and sexual abuses, and I did meet a few of the monsters she spoke about. I worked in small fifty-bed hospitals and as the years went by, I got angrier and angrier with what I was seeing. The institutionalized racism, the candid comments made to me—because the racists thought I was like them as they spoke of my sisters, my aunties and my brothers—about how those Indian women should be sterilized to prevent them from breeding. Those words still haunt me.

Fed up with what I was seeing and hearing, I began complaining. Then it dawned on me. I had the option to be complacent and let these abuses continue, i.e., keep complaining, or to respond to the call and do something about it. So I started taking university night classes. I was a single mom, and I went back to school to become a lawyer with a focus on remedying the injustices within the health field. I really believed that if I had a good set of tools, I might go about fixing some of these issues. I had my fourth baby during my first year of law school. I managed that gruelling schedule because I was completely insane, driven and on fire to stop the atrocities that I witnessed. There was no stopping me. And that is what I did—I got started and couldn't stop. From the very beginning, I have been vocal about the racism and substandard care for Indigenous people in the health care system.

My introduction to the Indigenous Bar Association came in the summer of 1991. Let me set the scene for you. I had arrived in Saskatoon from Nova Scotia, where I was temporarily living (as the Metis ancestral pull goes, I was quite nomadic); I had three little kids aged five, seven, and eight; three little suitcases; a borrowed car; and a temporary apartment with a few pieces of furniture. I was accepted into the Native Law Program (Summer Program) and was awarded a small scholarship from the federal government for this purpose. When they awarded me the scholarship over the phone, they told me that I barely qualified and I was the tenth and last on their list. That phone call stays with me, and I am forever grateful that I was on their list at all. They took a chance—and I took a chance. Without it, I would not be writing these words for you today.

The day before the Summer Program started, I discovered I was pregnant. The news came as a shock. I had no source of income, no home, a borrowed car, and what now—four kids!!! I was in turmoil, to say the least.

In tears, biting my nails while deciding what to do next, I looked around and I saw a beautiful and confident woman—with her skirts flying—her hair flying—pushing a stroller. She had about three kids tagging along behind her and other students like me talking to her on the run. This is where I thought, "I think I should speak to her."

Well, this was Trish Monture and she turned out to be my angel. She was a teacher in the program that year. I caught up with her, she handed me a Kleenex, and I started talking—babbling more precisely. After listening with a calm focus, she very kindly said, or was it gently yelled, "*Of course you can do it*." Anyone who knows Trish will hear her *booming* those words out. She calmly explained to me the beauty of being able to go home from being inundated with white man's law and its Eurocentric assumptions, and the advantages I had in getting love from my little herd of children. I wiped my eyes, blew my nose, shook myself, and said, "She is right—I can do it." This was a huge turning point in my life, because I probably would have quit.

This is the first principle I wish to impart. When you think your life couldn't be more messed up, don't quit. Seek out that person that can give you the words you need to carry on—don't carry the weight alone. Listen to your heart and find wise counsel. Someone is waiting for you; you just have to find them.

As I worked through the Summer Program, I met my legal family. There were many people there I have stayed in touch with over the years, and that family has its roots in the Summer Program at the University of Saskatchewan and through my First Nations, Metis, and Inuit sisters and brothers at the Indigenous Bar Association.

This next point is important.

While in the Summer Program, we had a talk and visit from Don Worme. I will never ever forget that visit. I saw Don standing by the door of the classroom; he had his braids and was trying his very best, and succeeding, to look dashing! Don spoke to our class. He was warm and kind and he was so encouraging. Don brought us the Indigenous Bar Association—he is the one who told us all about it and the importance it would play in our lives. He was right—it did, because all the people we met became our legal family. Today I am still friends with many of those people, whom I consider my sisters and my brothers. I watched Don's career over the years with awe—he has done so much good and left so many positive imprints. Second principle: Find your role models and treasure your new legal family, like all families, no matter what. These are the people that you can call in twenty-five years when you are stuck on a problem and need an extra brain.

The next principle is: Get out of your comfort zone; take a risk. Sometimes you just have to leave the career comfort zone.

I graduated from law school and had a job I liked as director of justice for the Saskatoon Tribal Council. It was a good job, but I knew I would not want to stay forever. One day, I glanced at the office noticeboard. Someone had put up a job posting for the Aboriginal Healing Foundation in Ottawa—they needed a director of programs. The Aboriginal Healing Foundation was a new trust fund that was to provide funding for residential school survivors to create healing programs to address the physical and sexual abuse they had experienced. At this time, I had a law degree and a good job. I asked myself, "Is it utterly ridiculous to think about moving to Ottawa?"

I wavered, then I thought, "What the heck, what do I have to lose by submitting my curriculum vitae (cv)? Besides, if I was ever offered the position, I could always say no." I prepared an application and sent it in at the last minute. Guess what happened: I got a call, followed by sets of interviews, and then I was offered the job. I was confronted with a life-changing choice and another big risk to assess. What if I hated the big city, what if I hated my new life—what if, what if, what if. The other option was comfort and complacency—I now had a husband with a job to share my life with, my kids were settled, there was food on the table, there was security, and I liked my job. Moving to Ottawa with three kids in high school and one in grade two was one of the biggest decisions I ever made and one of the biggest risks I took.

I took a deep breath and jumped on an unknown path. It turned out to be the best decision I ever made. Within two weeks I had moved to Ottawa, with one husband, four kids, two dogs, and four cats. As crazy as it sounds, it was a fabulous adventure. It brought opportunities for me and my children that I never would have seen had I stayed in my safe position at the tribal council.

My advice is that when possible or faced with them, take those risks—don't dismiss them because you are afraid of the unknown. It's okay to be afraid. Forge ahead and consider those apparent off-the-wall opportunities carefully. It is better to take a chance and know what you missed rather than never even know what could have been.

The next principle is that it is all about rejection. Rejection happens and leads you on pathways you did not know existed!

The faster you appreciate that it's okay to be rejected, the happier you'll be. I have been rejected more times than I can count. I have applied for jobs and absolutely believed I was the perfect candidate. I have carefully prepared my cv and cover letter and spent hours agonizing over just the right language. I have made sure I hit all the key points they were looking for and then sent it away—knowing in my heart, beyond a shadow of a doubt, that I would have that job!

And I haven't even been shortlisted.

I've been crushed.

And then there have been times when I did make it to the interview, for the best job I could ever have hoped for. I've known I was on my game. I've been prepared. I've bought a new suit. I've been well rested. I've done a mock interview. I've researched the background of the interview panel. My presentation has been polished. Oh, I've known I was a shoe in—there wasn't any way I could *not* get the job. The interview has been perfect. I have anticipated the questions the panel has asked me. We've made eye contact; I've made new friends. I've felt great!

I've gone home, sure I was going to get the offer. I've even gone so far as to plan my first day and contemplated how I would change the world with this new job.

Then the call has come. I didn't get the job.

I've politely thanked them, hung up, and sat in a sea of bewilderment—what went wrong???

It was one of those times that my son sent me flowers, with a note that said, "Mom—you always said when one door shuts, another opens."

My son was wise.

Life's challenges will define the person you will become.

For every professional rejection, many other doors will open. I have licked my wounds, shed those tears, but slowly picked myself up and forged ahead. I have tried to keep confidence in myself while reaching for that next level whether it was through senior management opportunities, as a Canadian human rights commissioner, or as a member of the Canadian Senate. I have struggled to retain that confidence in myself and the "go for it" attitude that my aunt Lucy imparted even when it has been really, really hard. Sometimes it has been a challenge, but it has been critical for me, as it is for you, to seek out what your heart calls for to have a successful career and a positive life. I have relied on my family, my friends, and my Elders to guide me. Remember, no one succeeds alone. Whether it's asking for help, finding role models, taking chances or moving locations for your career, applying for different positions, or advancing your lifelong learning, lean on your family, friends, Elders, and other Indigenous Bar family members. Be true to yourself, have confidence in your abilities, and follow your dreams. Don't be afraid to push the envelope—take some professional chances and reach for that next challenge.

Accept that challenge and take that risk. Send your cv in for the most obscure and far-reaching points that your heart points you to. I remember seeing a job posting for a Canadian human rights commissioner. I nearly didn't apply for it, but once again, at the last minute, I thought, "What the heck." The deadline was midnight; at 11:45 p.m., I faxed my cv with no cover letter other than "here is my cv." I told myself, in that familiar, wicked self-doubting tone, "People like you never get those jobs," and over the next weeks I didn't think any more of it. Until one day I got the call—yes, people like me do get those jobs, and people like you get those jobs too...when you apply. Not long after I was appointed as a Canadian human rights commissioner, I had a case to decide—and what case do you suppose that was? In February of 2007, the First Nations Child and Family Caring Society and the Assembly of First Nations filed a complaint alleging that the Department of Indian and Northern Affairs provision of First Nations child and family services was flawed, inequitable, and thus discriminatory under the *Canadian Human Rights Act*. It took about a year to move the complaint through the investigation processes, and then it was time to decide whether or not to dismiss, send to conciliation, or send to the Human Rights Tribunal. The case came to me in 2008. The deputy chief commissioner, David Langtry, and I looked at each other and said, "This is a no-brainer"—and off it went to the Tribunal.

Serendipity? I don't think so—I think it was Creator's plan and I was blessed to be able send the case from the commission to the

Tribunal. There is always a bigger plan. Little did we know at the time what a struggle it would be for the next years to come.

The next principle is: you have to be your biggest advocate. Don't wait for someone to find you—get out and do it. You're more powerful and creative than you might at first think. Take that risk.

There is another point I would like to conclude with, and it seems so inane to talk about it when it seems so obvious for me, and that is my gender. I recall seeing a cartoon of a racetrack. At the starting line, dressed in suits, were three women and three men ready to get through law school. In front of the women, however, were children, dirty laundry and meals, and other obstacles. There were no obstacles before the men. They could clearly see the finish line. When I look back, I don't recall any man I met in law school who was a father. To be fair, there must have been, but I do not remember meeting men who were single parents of multiple children or who had the miraculous ability to give birth, bring a newborn to law school, and breastfeed the baby in class. But besides those obvious facts, there is something else about being First Nations, Metis, or Inuit and making it through. Without a doubt, gender and culture are so intertwined they cannot be separated—as an Indigenous woman it is impossible.

I was not an anomaly among my Indigenous peers. It was normal to have an extreme amount of pressure outside of school work and career building. Many of my peers had extended families to care for, and others, entire families to care for, because of the definition of family is different in Indigenous cultures. Foster brothers and sisters, custom adopted sisters and brothers, half-siblings, step aunts, step uncles, stepmothers, stepfathers—all are the western concepts of family, whereas an Indigenous viewpoint calls them all sisters and brothers and aunties and uncles and grandmothers and grandfathers. I did not meet one Indigenous peer who was not struggling to pay the bills and handle the outside pressures. We were all the same, so culture played an important role, and because of who I am as a woman—yes gender was critical. I was the centre of the home and household—my main studying time was when it was quiet at 4:00 a.m. Giving birth to a child in my first year of law school and nursing the baby quietly in the back row as I studied the basic famous tort case of the worm in the ginger beer and criminal law components of *mens rea* and *actus reas*—yes, gender played a huge role, and it pushed my multitasking abilities to the brink of exhaustion...and near extinction.

I wouldn't suggest any of you reading this do it the way I did it. But remember, if I can do it, you can do it. Remember, you are the next generation of advocates, judges, senators, members of Parliament, and human rights commissioners; you are our next prime ministers and world leaders. Take those chances and believe you can do it—because that is who we are as Indigenous people and as women. We have that great advantage of our ancestral power and spirits—no one can stop us, and we can, and we are, changing the world.

Senator Yvonne Boyer was appointed to the Senate of Canada in March 2018. She is the first Indigenous Senator appointed from Ontario. She received her LLB in 1996, a Master of Laws in 2003, and a Doctor of Laws in 2011.

DEAR MOM

YVONNE PETERS
1988 LLB

A note to the reader: I have chosen to tell my story by writing letters to my mother. My mother died in 2016, and while I believe she was proud of my work, she and I didn't or couldn't talk about the personal reasons that motivated my work and passion. For my part, I think I wanted to protect her from having to hear about my personal struggles, some of which stemmed from choices she had to make about my life. This project offers me an ideal opportunity to imagine what I could have said to her and to try to collect the threads that eventually led me to law school.

LETTER #1: AND SUDDENLY
I WAS A LAW STUDENT

Dear Mom,

Remember when I told you I was going to law school? I recall that you were supportive but a little confused. I was happily married and had a job I loved, which provided reasonable reimbursement. My husband and I were well on our way to developing rewarding careers, building a comfortable life, and making plans for a secure future—all a mother could want for her daughter. So why disrupt this fortunate and sensible lifestyle? To be honest, I'm still not sure I can articulate the precise reasons. Going to law school was not on my bucket list. It just seemed like the next logical step in my life's journey.

I didn't decide to go to law school until I was thirty-three years old, which earned me the grand distinction of being accepted as a mature student. Even as I took my first steps into the University of Saskatchewan College of Law, I questioned my decision to risk the progress I had made in building a good life for myself.

As you know from many dinner discussions, throughout most of my life I have cared deeply and passionately about living in a world that cares about and respects the humanity and rights of all people. I suppose this stems from my own personal experience with discrimination and prejudice as a woman who has been blind since childhood. I remember thinking as a young woman that I could either ignore and explain away these negative experiences or I could stand up and take on these challenges. The feistiness and determination I inherited from you, Mom, compelled me to choose the latter.

My own personal struggles opened my eyes to the countless ways in which we devalue, marginalize, and harm some people because they are different from the so-called mainstream. This realization gave me no choice. I needed to do my part to push for greater recognition of human rights. So, in the letters that follow, I try to trace the events and influences of my life that eventually led me to be sitting in my first University of Saskatchewan College of Law class in September 1985.

I think you found my decision to go to law school even more puzzling when I declared that I did not want to become "some high-powered lawyer." I simply wanted to know how laws were made and how I could use this knowledge to advance the issues of concern to me. So not only was I older than many of the students, I also had very different career goals from them. Generally, this difference didn't bother me, but I must confess that there were occasions when I allowed the dominant law school expectation to overwhelm me and cause me to wonder if I too should be striving for that prestigious law firm position. But this was the late 1980s, and the courts were just beginning to interpret the meaning of Section 15 (the equality guarantee) of the *Canadian Charter of Rights and Freedoms*, and I wanted to be a part of that process. Thus, my doubts about what it meant to be a real lawyer never took serious hold.

The fact that I finished law school and was admitted to the Manitoba Bar kind of surprised me. First, I simply couldn't envision getting to the finish line. I'd always thought that one day some university official would suddenly realize that I'd been accepted into law school by mistake, and thus I would be shown the exit door. And second, in addition to the normal student pressures, I had to figure out how to get the infamous amount of law school print materials transcribed into a format that would be accessible for me as a blind student. In the 1980s, universities took little responsibility for removing barriers to post-secondary education for students with disabilities. I tried applying to the Saskatchewan government for help to offset the cost of my accessibility needs, but I was more or less told that if I was crazy enough to go to law school, I was on my own.

Fortunately, the College of Law faculty was very supportive, and did what they could to accommodate my access needs. And more importantly, one of your younger daughters, my sister Debbie, took on the task of reading onto cassette tape just about every page of print material I required to get through law school.

As an aside, I sometimes wonder how much easier it would be to go to law school today, with the tremendous expansion of computer technology and the subsequent increase in access to print material for blind people. Nevertheless, that was then, and with the support of my sister and many others who helped along the way, I made it through.

You were there to celebrate with me when it was all over and done. I still remember the flowers you gave me and our wish that Dad was still with us to join in the celebration.

LETTER #2: RESIDENTIAL SCHOOL—
YOUR ONLY CHOICE FOR ME

Dear Mom,

When I was six years old, you and dad put me on a train bound for a school for the blind in Brantford, Ontario. You told me how gut-wrenching this was for you and how you worried every day about how I was doing. Back in the 1950s, local schools would not accept children with disabilities. The view was that such children would be better served in special schools. The closest school for me was two days and two nights away by train from my home city of Saskatoon. You did not want to send me away, but felt strongly about ensuring that I received a good education, so really you felt you had no choice in the matter.

I am the oldest of five children. I recall you telling me that when I was born everyone remarked on my beautiful blue eyes. Little did they know that this beauty was an indication of acute infantile glaucoma, a rare condition which eventually destroyed my optic nerves, causing total blindness by the age of five. With a houseful of small children, you and Dad had no time to coddle me, and you encouraged me to be independent and learn to take care of myself, skills that became the cornerstone of my life.

On the train to my new school, I sat motionless, clutching my Nancy Lee doll. I could feel the rhythm and rumble of the wheels and wondered where I was going. I was confused, frightened, and lonely. I remember you talking about me going away to school. I was excited because I had just finished kindergarten and I was looking forward to going to school with my friends in Saskatoon. But you explained that because I was blind, I couldn't go to the same school as my friends.

I knew I was kind of different from my friends, but it didn't seem to be much of a problem. I ran around and played like all the other kids, so I couldn't understand why the nearby school wouldn't let me attend. But as I sat on that train, I began to realize that I must be different, because here I was on my way to a special school hundreds of miles from my family and the life I knew. How hard it must have been for you to put me on that train.

There were many other blind children on the train, including some kind senior girls who took me under their wing and looked after me. Upon arriving at the school, I was introduced to the realities of institutional life. This began almost immediately when I stood in line getting ready to go for lunch. I was still clinging to my doll when it was snatched from me by a gruff-sounding house-mother who said that dolls weren't allowed in the dining room. That was the last time I ever saw my beloved doll.

Learning how to follow all the rules and schedules of the school was hard, and that first year I was sick a lot. Still, I enjoyed being in grade one and getting to know new friends. The housemothers were strict and had little time for affection or emotional support, so I resorted to the skills you had taught me and tried to be as independent and self-reliant as possible. Ironically, in my second year, this independence resulted in me being moved to the senior residence, a year earlier than my peers and where there was even less staff support and time for nurturing.

The school was situated in the city of Brantford, Ontario, but the institutional world it housed was securely isolated by a very high chain link fence. Contact with the outside community was rare, and even when we were hauled off to church, we sat in pews apart from the rest of the congregation.

Numerous times, I stood at the fence yearning for someone to stop and talk to me; yearning to be with my family doing normal everyday activities like shopping, watching TV, and eating my mom's good cooking; and yearning for freedom from inflexible schedules and rigorous rules that required acquiescence and conformity. Why, I wondered, did the experts think it was best to rip blind children away from their families and place them in institutions? What was wrong with me that I couldn't go to school with my friends and siblings? These yearnings and questions opened my eyes to the reality that being different often meant being excluded from a so-called "normal" life. This realization had a profound and lasting impact on my worldview.

Added to my newfound awareness was the difference gender made. I learned that the senior boys were given much greater privileges than the senior girls in that they could choose when to go to bed on weekends, had more opportunities to leave the school grounds unescorted, and had more freedom regarding where they could hang out on the school grounds. We girls were regarded as morally weak and in need of control and protection, and so our privileges were few. I remember at one point I was caught with a boy in a place where I shouldn't have been. The boy got a good talking to by the principal about the need to focus on his studies so he could get a good job. I, on the other hand was castigated by the vice principal for having loose morals and a weak character, which meant I probably wouldn't amount to much in life.

I spent eleven years at that school, and as you had hoped, I did receive a good and well-rounded education. However, strict residential life did not agree with me, and I frequently found myself in trouble for failing to conform with institutional expectations. Recent public revelations regarding forms of abuse suffered by children in residential schools are stories that resonates deeply with my own experience. I was miserable, but one day I just decided that the school would not crush me and that I would survive and succeed in life.

Despite being hundreds of miles away, you sensed that as I approached the end of my eleventh year, I was in trouble. My physical and mental health was deteriorating. No one at the school seemed to notice, but you relied on a mother's intuition and informed the school that I would be leaving that year and finally attending my local neighbourhood school. Remember how the principal told you that I wasn't very smart and that I likely wouldn't survive being integrated into a regular school? Thank you for not being intimidated by him and for sticking to your plan. It was probably one of the best decisions you made.

LETTER #3: DISCOVERING MY ACTIVIST SELF

Dear Mom,

You never saw my blindness as a limitation. You encouraged me to be independent and always supported me when I wanted to try new things. I recall you telling me that when it was discovered that your oldest child was blind, one of the ladies in your church suggested that you were being punished for past sins. You said that you told her that in fact you had been chosen to be a mother to a blind child because you were special. And so you raised me in the same way you raised all your children: with praise, encouragement, correction when needed, and love.

Even though no one in our extended family had ever attended university, you believed that this was the right choice for me. Although I have little to say that is good about attending the Ontario School for the Blind, its emphasis on obtaining a university education, regardless of gender, had an enormous impact on my life. Thus, following graduation from high school, I entered the university world and, with some effort, obtained a BA with a major in psychology.

Armed with my degree, I began looking for a job, though I had no clue what I could do with this education. Job opportunities were scarce, but even more surprising to me was the reaction I got from employers regarding my blindness. Their worry and fear about how I would find my way to the washroom, attend meetings, and generally manage in an employment environment meant that we spent most of our time talking about how I functioned as a blind person, and not about the job and my qualifications.

I was completely unprepared for such reactions. I was young and naive, and assumed that I could just convince employers that I was capable. However, I quickly learned that prejudice and stereotypes have strong and deep roots.

My luck turned when I applied for a position with a community aid centre run by an American draft dodger. He was progressive and open-minded and said he would give me a chance. I'm not sure I was the best employee, but I liked the job and I learned about the community and the daily struggles and disadvantages experienced by certain people in our society. As I gained more experience in my job, I decided that what I really wanted to do with my life was to become a social worker. And so in 1976 I went back to university to get my BSW.

Most of the classes I took were aimed towards a career in counselling. However, toward the end of my studies, I came across an instructor who taught classes such as Income Insecurity and Social Work as Social Policy. This is when I came face to face with the concept of systemic discrimination and the impact it had on certain groups in our society. All the counselling in the world wasn't going to help people who experienced disadvantage because of circumstances beyond their control such as poverty, race, disability, and gender. Suddenly, my ambition to be a counsellor seemed inadequate.

My life's work and passion were cemented by one of my final class assignments. I don't recall the exact focus of this assignment, but it caused me to come across the *Saskatchewan Human Rights Code*. I had no idea that such a document, let alone the concept of legislated rights protection, existed. As I reviewed the *Code*, I thought about my own experiences and the discrimination I had encountered with prospective employers regarding my blindness. Alas, I couldn't find anything in the *Code* that would support my right not to be discriminated against. This realization ignited a fire in me, and I knew that something had to change.

Up to that point, I had been very much an individualist, believing that I could overcome any barriers or discrimination on my own. But changing human rights legislation seemed far beyond my personal capabilities. I had heard that there was a local group of persons with disabilities that worked to promote disability rights. I had been encouraged by my employer to attend these meetings, but I resisted, believing that I didn't need such a group. Besides, I was steadfastly committed to "fitting in," and being seen with a bunch of people with different disabilities might taint my efforts and confirm my difference. However, my incredulity that my human rights weren't protected by the law quickly helped me to drop this self-righteous view, and I attended a meeting and never looked back.

Exchanging stories and experiences with like-minded people was exhilarating and empowering. Not only was I no longer alone with my struggles, but my colleagues were knowledgeable and experienced about what we needed to do to bring about change. And thus, I became a disability rights activist.

Being an activist took up a good chunk of my time. My passion and enthusiasm landed me leadership positions at the local, provincial, and national levels. I learned how to analyze issues, lobby politicians, speak to the media, make public presentations, and prepare written briefs.

I am pleased to say that shortly after I joined the Saskatchewan disability rights movement, the *Saskatchewan Human Rights Code* was amended to include mental and physical disability. I like to believe that our actions played some role in bringing about this change. Interestingly, I would go on to have a much more involved relationship with the human rights commission which would have a profound influence on my decision to enter law school.

LETTER #4: FILING A COMPLAINT
AND GETTING A JOB

Dear Mom,

I think there were times when you thought I was just going too far with this disability rights stuff. I think this was especially true when I found myself at the centre of a legal battle about whether I should be allowed to enter a hospital with my guide dog.

I was one of the first blind persons in Saskatoon to use a guide dog. As a result, I spent a good deal of time educating businesses and service providers about the right of a blind person to access public spaces accompanied by their guide dog. Mostly this worked, but when I went to visit my father-in-law in the hospital, my access rights became quite controversial. The hospital objected to the presence of my guide dog. It argued that it should have the authority to restrict the access rights of guide dog handlers. Of course I disagreed, took the matter to the Saskatchewan Human Rights Commission, and filed a complaint against the hospital. After several years and three hearings, the matter was eventually decided in my favour by the Saskatchewan Court of Appeal.

While the matter was being decided, the public weighed in with its views. Some people were in my corner and would stop me in the street and tell me so. Others thought I was self-centred and belligerent and did not hesitate to tell me, sometimes in very aggressive ways, that they thought I was taking the rights thing too far. I don't like public attention, so I found this time to be a challenge. You didn't say much to me about my public rights crusade. I have no doubt that you supported me, but I suspect you found the public debate difficult and uncomfortable. I remember when we went to Dad's favourite restaurant and the manager very sternly told me that my dog was not welcome. You were shocked and I was so hurt that you had to witness this encounter. You didn't say much, but I suspect you wished that my life didn't have to be so controversial.

But you taught me well, and I refused to allow these negative experiences to alter my choices in life. To be at peace with myself, I had to stand my ground and claim my human rights even if this was not well understood by the public.

Amazingly, in 1980, a few years after I filed my complaint with the Saskatchewan Human Rights Commission, the Commission offered me a job as a human rights officer. In those days, passion and activism were regarded as worthy qualities. While employed by the Commission I began learning about the power of the law and its capacity to promote social change. I also learned about the significance of Canada's Constitution and the Pierre Trudeau proposal to enshrine a charter of rights and freedoms into the Constitution. I remember with great fondness the many discussions we employees had with Shelagh Day, the then executive director of the Commission, and Ken Norman, the then chief human rights commissioner, on the value of such a charter and what it might accomplish. I think you could say that these discussions, together with my activist activities which I describe in my next letter, began to sow some early seeds about going to law school.

LETTER #5: A PROTEST AND A WEDDING

Dear Mom,

Can you ever forgive me for missing my sister's wedding back in November of 1980? I certainly planned to be there but at the last minute, the disability rights group I belonged to decided to hold a protest on Parliament Hill to demonstrate our frustration with the government's failure to include disability in the proposed *Canadian Charter of Rights and Freedoms*. None of our strategies had moved the Pierre Trudeau government to rethink its position, so we decided to express our concerns in a public protest on Parliament Hill. It would be the first time that people with disabilities engaged in such action, and I wanted to be a part of it. Still, I do feel badly about being absent from such an important family event. I hope that the following explanation provides some background on why this protest was so important to me and why I put politics over family.

I am honoured and privileged to have had a number of opportunities to participate, along with other disability rights activists, in many important and historical actions leading to the further-ance of disability rights. Of particular significance is the work we undertook to secure protection from discrimination on the ground of disability in Section 15 (the guarantee of equality) of the *Canadian Charter of Rights and Freedoms*.

During the 1970s, Pierre Elliot Trudeau, the then prime min-ister of Canada, began talking about patriating the *British North America Act* and entrenching a charter of rights in the Constitution. In 1980, the Trudeau government issued a document outlining its plans to bring home Canada's Constitution and the contents of a proposed charter. The document contained a narrowly worded non-discrimination clause that made no mention of disability rights.

In the early 80s, the recognition of human rights for persons with disabilities was a very new concept and thus persons with disabilities firmly believed that inclusion in the *Charter* was essen-tial to the ongoing and meaningful recognition of our rights. We therefore took immediate action to express our concern regarding the omission of our rights. The government responded by letter with this observation:

> Since an entrenched Charter is by its very nature a generalized document which does not lend itself to detailed qualifications and limitations, it was ultimately decided to limit the grounds of non-discrimination to those few which have long been rec-ognized and which do not require substantial qualification. Unfortunately, such is not yet the case with respect to those who suffer physical handicaps and consequently provision has not been made in the Charter for this ground.

This response seemed to imply that there was a two-tiered system of rights in Canada. We argued that such a system was tantamount to rejecting the fundamental humanity of Canadians with disabilities.

The non-discrimination clause underwent several drafts, eventually becoming the guarantee of equality, but each time a new draft was issued, disability was conspicuously absent. So this was no time to back down. We had to stand strong and make our voices heard. It seemed like our final opportunity to get elected representatives to take our demands seriously. This is why I had to make the hard choice of taking my protest to the doors of Parliament and missing my sister's wedding.

The good news is that the government relented, and at the eleventh hour, it backed down and included mental and physical disability in Section 15 of the *Canadian Charter of Rights and Freedoms*, a Constitutional document and the supreme law of Canada. This was a monumental victory for persons with disabilities, and has served as the foundation for many Supreme Court rulings further articulating the rights of persons with disabilities in the areas of healthcare, education, transportation, access to services and employment. I am honoured and privileged to have played a role in many of these cases either as counsel of record or as a legal advisor.

LETTER #6: BECOMING A "REAL" LAWYER

Dear Mom,

I probably didn't tell you how hard those early days of law school were for me. It wasn't because of the required voluminous amounts of reading, or the deciphering of convoluted and obscure judgments. It was the change I had to make in my style of thinking.

I was used to being regarded as a leader and someone with some human rights expertise. None of this really mattered once

I entered law school. The main goal of legal education is to teach students how to think like a lawyer—that is, how to assess a set of facts and apply an objective legal reasoning analysis.

As an activist, I was used to taking a position and supporting it with arguments that were often based on personal opinion, political views, or in some cases, emotional sentiment. Law school taught me another form of reasoning. I eventually figured out that this really wasn't too difficult. Assemble the facts, apply the relevant law, and make a determination.

Learning how to apply a more rigorous objective analysis to issues is probably the most significant benefit I obtained from law school. It has proven to be a valuable asset for my passionate, subjective self.

So in many ways I enjoyed law school, but it also had its challenges. Certainly, some of the challenges were connected to the barriers I encountered as a blind student, but a good many of these challenges were caused by the attitudes of some of my fellow students. On the very first day, in my very first class, one of my classmates remarked to anyone who cared to listen that you either have to be a cripple or an Indian to get noticed by the law school. I promptly told him that my guide dog, which was under the table and out of view, would bite his leg off if he continued with that kind of talk.

Even more disappointing were the sexist attitudes of some of the students. I regularly encountered sexist attitudes in the classroom and in law-related extracurricular activities such as the first-year banquet. Many of my fellow female students also noticed and objected to such behaviour, but were reluctant to speak up for fear of career repercussions. I was shocked and saddened to learn that women students still felt that silence and acceptance was necessary if they wanted to succeed as lawyers. Equally frustrating was the way in which sexist behaviour was allowed to flourish unabated in a law school. Interestingly, some years after graduating I ran into some of those female students, who confessed that they wished they'd taken a stronger stand against the sexism that was prevalent during our time at law school.

Law school also challenged my confidence. At times, it was difficult to figure out how a student like me, with no real ambition to practice typical law, fit into the law school. When I shared my goals to continue working in human rights, some of my classmates referred to this work as "soft" law. In other words, not real law. Was I cheating myself by not wanting to be a typical lawyer? Nevertheless, I persevered with my goals and got what I needed from my legal education: a much better understanding of how law was made and how to think more analytically and critically about legal issues.

In 1989, I completed my articles and bar admission requirements and was granted the right to practice law in Manitoba. By some remarkable miracle, I got my dream job shortly after being called to the bar. The *Charter* guarantee of equality had only been in effect for just over five years. The *Charter* was the hottest new legal flavour on the block, and it was attracting intense interest and scrutiny by lawyers, judges, and civil society alike. Equality-seekers in particular were eager to persuade the courts that Section 15 required a broad and substantive interpretation. With this in mind, a number of test cases were being prepared to advance this analysis to the court.

Among these equality-seekers was a brand-new organization dedicated to pursuing disability rights test cases under Section 15 of the *Charter*. I was hired to act as both the executive director and litigation director of this organization. During my time in this position, I was involved in a variety of cases dealing with issues such as the right to vote, the right to due process when found not criminally responsible, employment rights, accessibility rights, and immigration rights. It was exciting and inspiring work. It was also very affirming to witness the transition of disability rights from political demands to judicial recognition.

I loved this work but after a time, I found that I no longer wanted to confine my practice exclusively to disability rights. As a woman, I cared about women's rights and how they intersected with disability rights and other equality interests. I therefore decided to leave my dream job and set up my own practice in the hopes of engaging in broader equality rights work.

I established a comfortable practice, taking on a few litigation clients, but mostly assisting governments, the private sector, and community organizations with policy and legislative matters that raised questions about rights. Then, one day, I was sitting at my dining room table when another dream opportunity came my way.

A woman from Manitoba Health called and asked if I would be interested in heading up the Legislative Committee of the Midwifery Implementation Council. I was taken aback, as I had no experience with midwifery. She said they were looking for a feminist, and she had heard me speak. She liked the way I talked about equality rights and women's reproductive choices. Of course this piqued my interest, but the fee the government was offering was not very attractive, and I worried that it was just trying to find somebody cheap to do its work. She persisted, and after doing some of my own research, I discovered that establishing regulated midwifery was a growing trend in women's healthcare. Moreover, it was a trend that essentially promoted the right of women to choose a less medical and more woman-centred form of maternity care and birthing options. Clearly, this was an important equality rights issue for women, and I was hooked despite the remuneration. This began my eighteen-year career love affair with midwifery.

My first task was to draft the *Midwifery Act.* While I could muddle through the rules and practices governing legislative drafting, I had no substantive experience with the practice of midwifery. And so the drafting process became a collaboration with midwives, educators, and other women's health experts to ensure that all bases were covered. I provided my collaborators with a basic tutorial in legislative drafting, learning myself as we went along. We ended up with approximately twenty-one drafts before we were finally satisfied. It was gruelling, but ever so rewarding, to craft a law designed jointly by lawyers and midwifery experts that had the potential to improve maternity care for women. Our efforts resulted in regulated midwifery being implemented in Manitoba on June 12, 2000.

Midwifery was now a passion for me, so when Manitoba Health asked if I'd assist in rolling out regulated midwifery to the regional health authorities, I gladly accepted. While the authorities were interested, they were also nervous about a health profession they knew little about. The first request of just about every health authority was to have the option to put off home births until midwifery was better understood and fully integrated into the health-care system. As this was a contentious issue that could take years to implement, Manitoba Health wisely decided to push forward with home birth, providing authorities with the information and support they needed to reduce anxiety. Again, it was very rewarding to assist the various health authorities to learn about the benefits of midwifery and to observe how they eventually embraced it as a regular component of their healthcare services.

My next midwifery venture introduced me to the long-standing practice of Indigenous midwifery. At one time, this had been a flourishing practice in Indigenous communities, but threats of lawsuits and time in prison issued by law enforcement officials significantly limited its availability. As a result, most women were forced to leave their homes and families several weeks before giving birth and travel to large urban centres, where they were often surrounded by strangers who did not understand their culture or language. My job was to learn about Indigenous midwifery and develop recommendations as to how this practice could be re-established as a part of regulated midwifery.

I am eternally grateful to the many women, Elders, and communities who shared their knowledge, wisdom, and experience on how Indigenous midwifery could be resurrected. With the collaborative efforts of Indigenous midwives, educators, and Elders we were able to develop comprehensive recommendations on the types of programs and services that could assist in restoring an important cultural practice. While some progress has been made in this regard, dominant mainstream systems take time to change, and I fear that there is still much work to do on this project.

My final midwifery venture gave me the opportunity to take on the role of project coordinator in the development of a freestanding birth centre. It is the first of its kind in western Canada. Its purpose is to provide a home-like facility where women with normal pregnancies can give birth surrounded by family and friends. The Birth Centre celebrated its opening in 2011.

As I mentioned earlier, I began thinking about law school when I worked at the Saskatchewan Human Rights Commission. In 2001 I returned to Commission work as a member of the Board of Commissioners of the Manitoba Human Rights Commission. In 2013, I was appointed as chair of this board and served in this capacity for four years. It was gratifying and important work. When my appointment expired, I decided my career had come full circle, and it was time to retire as a practicing lawyer.

LETTER #7: WAS LAW SCHOOL WORTH IT?

Dear Mom,

According to my bank account, my legal career has not made me rich. However, leaving my good-paying job for law school was probably one of the best career decisions I made. It opened the door for me to create a legal career that has been rich in opportunity and experience and has rewarded me with enormous personal satisfaction.

Of course, I did not accomplish this all by myself. Thank you, Mom, for insisting that I learn to be a strong and independent woman. Thank you also for insisting that I get a good basic education, even though the emotional cost was high for both of us.

I have been blessed to have many mentors in my life who believed in me, helped me hone my career skills, and who gave me a chance to follow my dreams. But law school would not have been possible without the support of my husband of forty-five years. He covered the bills while I was in school, provided me with a glass of wine just when I needed it, and gave me that extra push I needed to keep going.

I sincerely hope that my letters are not regarded as some kind of disability inspiration story: "Woman conquers law school despite blindness." Many women have to cope with life challenges. Mine just happened to be my blindness. My reason for writing these letters is to encourage women, particularly women with disabilities, to go to law school and, if desired, pursue legal careers that may not accord with the prevailing notion of what it means to be a lawyer.

ADDENDUM: THOUGHTS OF GRATITUDE
TO MY YOUNGER SELF

A week after I submitted my letter to the editors in March 2020, COVID became a reality in Canada. Public gatherings were severely restricted and we were advised to stay in our homes. Such restrictions put this letter-writing project on hold, and so I had a good two years to think about my letter. I am not comfortable in looking back and reflecting on past life experiences and events. I prefer to keep moving towards the future. However, with most of my public activities on hold, and as I began my journey into my seventh decade, I took time to ponder my life and the choices I have made.

COVID revealed just how fragile and insecure our human rights are in Canada. This was particularly noticeable for those who are socially and economically disadvantaged, such as the majority of people with disabilities. Despite lots of grand talk by governments about ensuring inclusive accessibility for all, many COVID policies simply ignored or forgot about persons with disabilities. Simple examples included doors granting accessible entrance being locked; visual markings on floors to ensure physical distancing being of no help to blind persons; masks, while essential, making it difficult for Deaf persons to communicate with hearing persons; and much-needed home care being reduced or provided sporadically, making it difficult for some disabled persons to maintain their independence. While I cannot comment with any authority, I suspect that other disadvantaged groups encountered similar experiences of erasure and exclusion.

At first I was discouraged and even a little frightened at how quickly certain groups in society could be pushed aside in a time of crisis. But as we learned how to cope with COVID, I realized that respecting human rights during a pandemic was yet another challenge to be conquered. This got me thinking about my younger self and the experiences and privilege I've had in promoting the benefits of a world that honours and abides by the inherent rights that we all have as humans.

My dear younger self, sometimes I cringe at how self assured and emphatic you were about what was right and what was wrong with the world. You had little patience with those who disagreed with you and I fear that you may not have always fully understood all sides of an issue. But I am so grateful for your unwavering activism and your desire to be a better human rights advocate. It was this burning ambition that ignited the crazy idea of going to law school.

I know that at times your reasons for going to law school felt foolish and insignificant, particularly when professors and fellow students talked about life as a "real" lawyer in the "real" practice of law. I know there were moments when you wondered if you too should aim for the oak desk and prestigious law firm. Thank you for staying true to your goals. You were lucky to have many in the community, even including some professors, who supported your ambition and dreams.

While you have not acquired a lavish bank account, your stubbornness and resilience in making it through law school provided the foundation you needed to enjoy a legal career rich with exciting opportunities to express your passion for human rights. While I am still a little uncomfortable with past self-reflection, I am grateful and indeed pleased with my legal career. Thank you, younger self, for not giving into those who questioned your decision to go to law school.

Yvonne Peters is retired, but continues to be involved in several community groups focused on social justice. She lives in Winnipeg with her husband and two dogs, and enjoys learning to play the flute and belonging to clubs dedicated to breeding and racing horses.

AFTERWORD

Dear reader,

Thank you for picking up this book and for your interest in our project. When our editorial team first embarked on the project, we never could have imagined where it would take us. We have had hours (now years!) of discussion about the strengths and limitations of the book—literally from cover to cover—and reflection on our own positions in the legal profession and society at large.

When we dreamt up this project in 2019, we described it as follows: "Our project aims to help foster leadership, mentorship, and networking among female lawyers through this compilation of letters, a related workshop, and other next steps resulting from the anthology and workshop that both celebrate success and inspire ongoing action."

The women who have contributed their letters to this anthology have remarkably interesting stories to tell about the paths they have followed, and their letters are illuminating and inspiring. Our hope was that collective dialogue at the workshop would then harness the insights—challenges, triumphs, opportunities—illustrated in the letters to envision action and change. The letters and workshop indeed demonstrated to us, and we hope to you, the reader, the power of individual and collective reflection to lead to action and change.[1]

Having read these individual accounts, we invite you to reflect on what the letters collectively say, and what your hopes are for gender equality in the future practice of law—on both the individual level and on the professional one, over the short and long term.

We asked this same question of our participants at the workshop. The participants were asked to imagine a utopian future in which none of the challenges they identified in their letters existed, and to identify their hopes for the future practice of law.[2] The ensuing discussion covered a wide range of topics, including a hope of a future practice of law that focuses on authenticity in the workplace that supports intersectionality; not having to fit the mold of "being more like a man" in order to be successful in the profession; the practice evolving to be more open to different approaches in advocacy, for lawyers to feel like they are an effective advocate in different ways; and encouraging not just mentorship, but sponsorship and celebrating champions of women in the workplace.

Themes of access to justice arose as participants reflected on the interconnectedness between a diverse legal profession and

---

1 "Reflective practice" was the theoretical underpinning for our invitation to contributors to write a letter and to collectively participate in the workshop. The benefit of collective reflection that builds capacity for generative dialogue and action has been a topic in recent literature. See e.g. Michele Leering, "Conceptualizing Reflective Practice for Legal Professionals," *Journal of Law and Social Policy* 23 (2014): 83–106.

2 The questions that were asked at the workshop are based on the adaptive and transformative stances presented in *Transformative Scenario Planning* by Adam Kahane. This same approach was employed by participants at the March 2019 meeting of the Dean's Forum on Access to Justice and Dispute Resolution (the Dean's Forum) at the University of Saskatchewan College of Law when the topic of diversity and inclusion in the legal profession was addressed.

providing services to a diverse client base.[3] Participants imagined a utopia that would provide full legal services for utopians based on ability to pay. The public sector would be well funded and serviced. Participants imagined that a legal profession in utopia provides careers for the diverse interests of all lawyers focused on wellness, family, personal success, and success and service to clients. The legal profession in utopia provides a holistic approach to solving problems to the extent possible, providing clients with avenues to heal.

Once participants identified their hopes and established what a possible future could look like, we asked what this utopian scenario says about what we can—and what we must—do. Participants spoke of ideas in the short and long term, such as the role legal education could continue to play both at the law school and through professional development requirements in improving diversity and inclusivity, teaching topics such as allyship, establishing a National Task Force on Gender Equality, and having more gatherings of women in law in social settings in order to build community. Participants expressed great interest in continuing to consider and reflect on these questions and enact change.

Our hope is that readers are as inspired by the letters in this

---

3   Susan Robertson, *A Study of Gender and the Legal Profession: A Report to the Law Society of Saskatchewan 1990-1991*, (Saskatoon, SK: The Canadian Bar Association Saskatchewan Branch, and the College of Law, University of Saskatchewan, 1992); Beth Bilson, Susan Robertson & Elizabeth Quinlan, *Women and the Legal Profession in Saskatchewan: National and Historical Comparisons: A Report to the Law Society of Saskatchewan, Canadian Bar Association, Saskatchewan Branch and The Law Foundation of Saskatchewan* (University of Saskatchewan, October 2013), available upon request from the Law Society of Saskatchewan Library; Zoe Johansen-Hill, Larissa Meredith-Flister & Coleman Owen, "Diversity and Inclusion in the Legal Profession" (delivered at The Seventh Annual Dean's Forum on Access to Justice and Dispute Resolution, College of Law, University of Saskatchewan, 13 March 2019) [unpublished].

book as we are and feel encouraged to also consider where we go from here and be part of the change. How will you claim your seat at the table, create a seat at the table for the women coming behind you, or build an entirely new table altogether?

—Beth, Leah, and Brea

ACKNOWLEDGEMENTS

Thank you to...

- the participants in this book
- Maria Campbell for leading participants through a writing exercise the morning of the workshop
- our project sponsors and supporters, the Law Society of Saskatchewan, the Canadian Bar Association Saskatchewan Chapter, Jacqueline Ferraton from Paulson & Ferraton, McDougall Gauley LLP, Nychuk & Company Barristers and Solicitors, OWZW Lawyers LLP, Peszko & Watson Barristers and Solicitors, and W Law LLP
- The Right Honourable Beverley McLachlin, for writing the foreword for this book
- CREATE Justice,[1] for support coordinating the project

---

1   CREATE Justice, the centre for research, evaluation, and action towards equal justice at the University of Saskatchewan College of Law, is a hub and catalyst for introducing and implementing design methods to solve complex access to justice challenges. A variety of design approaches have been piloted through the Dean's Forum and then further considered and advanced at CREATE Justice's lab. Transformative scenario planning, which participants were invited to experiment with during the workshop, is an example of a design method that has been tested through CREATE Justice initiatives.

- the University of Saskatchewan College of Law, for logistical support organizing the project and for hosting a welcoming reception before the workshop, and for publishing support through the College of Law Endowment Fund
- Alyssa McIntyre, Crown Counsel, Ministry of Justice, and Kelsey Leik, College of Law student, for support during the workshop
- Taryn McLachlan, student researcher for the project, from the Social Innovation Lab, University of Saskatchewan
- Hannah Jorgenson, College of Law student, for support during the editorial process

Beth Bilson, KC, BA, MA, LLB, PhD, has enjoyed a career of teaching, writing, deaning, arbitrating, and community engagement that began at the University of Saskatchewan in 1979, and she has never run out of interesting things to do.

Leah Howie, B.Eng, B.Sc, LLB, LLM, lives in beautiful Saskatoon. Leah spends her work days thinking about ways to improve the law in her work in the area of law reform, and learning from law students in her role as a sessional lecturer and moot coach at the University of Saskatchewan College of Law. She is a mother of two amazing daughters who are constant sources of inspiration and encouragement. Leah loves reading, spending time with friends and family, taking her dog Nellie for walks, and being by the river or in the forest.

Brea Lowenberger, BA, JD, LLM, is a lifelong learner and collaborator who hopes to leave the individuals and communities she interacts with a bit better than she found them. She is passionate about teaching and improving access to justice in her roles as director of CREATE Justice and sessional lecturer for the College of Law. When she isn't working, she enjoys adventures with family and friends, travelling, being active, reading, and creating music and art.